MW00423796

LUKE

LUKE

A Commentary for Bible Students

KEN HEER

Copyright © 2007 by Wesleyan Publishing House
Published by Wesleyan Publishing House
Indianapolis, Indiana 46250
Printed in the United States of America

ISBN: 978-0-89827-343-4

WESLEYAN BIBLE COMMENTARY SERIES

GENERAL PUBLISHER
Donald D. Cady

EXECUTIVE EDITOR
David W. Holdren, D.D., S.T.D.

EDITORIAL ADVISORY COMMITTEE

Joseph D. Allison, M.Div.
Coordinator of Communications and
Publishing
Church of God Ministries

Ray E. Barnwell
Illinois District Superintendent
The Wesleyan Church

Barry L. Callen, M.Div., M.Th., D.Rel., Ed. D.
University Professor of Christian Studies
Emeritus, Anderson University
Special Assistant to General Director, Church
of God Ministries

Ray Easley, M.Div., Ed.D.
Vice President of Academic Affairs
Wesley Biblical Seminary

Maj. Dorothy Hitzka
National Consultant for Christian Education
The Salvation Army

Arthur Kelly
Coordinator of Christian Education and
Congregational Life
Church of God Ministries

Stephen J. Lennox, Ph.D.
Dean of the Chapel; Professor of Bible
Indiana Wesleyan University

Bonnie J. Perry
Director
Beacon Hill Press of Kansas City

Dan Tipton, D.Min.
General Superintendent (retired)
Churches of Christ in Christian Union

John Van Valin
Free Methodist Pastor
Indianapolis, Indiana

EDITORS
Lawrence W. Wilson, M.Div.
Managing Editor

Stephen J. Lennox, Ph.D.
Theological Editor

Darlene Teague, M.Div.
Senior Editor

CONTENTS

EXECUTIVE EDITOR'S PREFACE

L ife change. That, we believe, is the goal of God's written revelation. God has given His written Word so that we might know Him and become like Him—holy, as He is holy.

Life change is also the goal of this book, a volume in the Wesleyan Bible Commentary Series. This series has been created with the primary aim of promoting life change in believers by applying God's authoritative truth in relevant, practical ways. This commentary will impact Bible students with fresh insight into God's unchanging Word. Read it with your Bible in hand.

A second purpose of this series is to assist laypersons and pastors in their teaching ministries. Anyone called to assist others in Christian growth and service will appreciate the practical nature of these commentaries. Writers were selected based on their ability to soundly interpret God's Word and apply that unchanging truth in fresh, practical ways. Each biblical book is explained paragraph by paragraph, giving the reader both the big picture and sufficient detail to understand the meaning of significant words and phrases. Their results of scholarly research are presented in enough detail to clarify, for example, the meaning of important Greek or Hebrew words, but not in such a way that readers are overwhelmed. This series will be an invaluable tool for preaching, lesson preparation, and personal or group Bible study.

The third aim of this series is to present a Wesleyan-Arminian interpretation of Scripture in a clear and compelling fashion. Toward that end, the series has been developed with the cooperative effort of scholars, pastors, and church leaders in the Wesleyan, Nazarene, Free Methodist, Salvation Army, Church of God (Anderson), Churches of Christ in Christian Union, Brethren in Christ, and United Methodist denominations. These volumes present reliable interpretation of biblical texts in the tradition of John Wesley, Adam Clarke, and other renowned interpreters.

Throughout the production of this series, authors and editors have approached each Bible passage with this question in mind: How will my life change when I fully understand and apply this scripture?

Let that question be foremost in your mind also, as God speaks again through His Word.

DAVID W. HOLDREN

AUTHOR'S PREFACE

God has allowed me to partner with Him in ministering to the spiritual needs of people for over forty-five years. I have had opportunity to implement programs and improve facilities at several churches, but the real satisfaction of ministry has come from watching lives transformed when people encounter the reality of Jesus and the transforming power of His truth. I am grateful that I have been witness to the unfolding stories of grace among the people I have served.

Writing this commentary was an exhausting project. Luke's record of the life and ministry of Jesus occupies twenty-four chapters. Each time I went back to the computer, the Gospel never got smaller, but rather appeared to *grow*. Luke seemed to always find another story to tell. This has been true throughout the history of the Church, and it will not stop until Jesus returns. When the light turns on in a person's life and he or she responds to the offer of redemption through Christ, another story is begun. The energy and enthusiasm for completing the task of writing this commentary came each time the Holy Spirit turned the light on a truth from Luke's record that had the power to transform another life and to begin a new story of grace. That possibility is energizing.

My story is exciting to no one but me. I met Jesus early in my life and grew up with the conviction that I was called to Christian ministry. My life has been enriched by many people along the way. My father and mother pastored and parented in ways that caused me to love God and His Church. The Lord blessed me with a wonderful partner in life and ministry, Nancy, without whose support I would not be effective. Some of God's most wonderful people populated the churches I pastored. I have benefited from people who became mentors to me, such as Leo Cox and Lee Haines. God has spoken to me through many friends in the faith, and He knows their names.

Whatever I am, and am yet becoming, is the product of grace and the influence of godly people. To these many people I dedicate this humble attempt of offering comments on the Gospel of Luke. We are a part of each other's story.

KEN HEER

INTRODUCTION TO LUKE

The Sistine chapel in Rome was completed in 1483 after more than a decade of construction. It was designed to follow the dimensions of Solomon's Temple, and its columns, arches, and walls decorated with frescos and tapestries made it a magnificent structure indeed. As grand as it was, however, it is hard to think of the Sistine Chapel without the paintings of the master artist Michelangelo adorning its ceiling. The addition of Michelangelo's masterpiece enhanced the glory of that already impressive structure in such a way that one cannot now imagine one without the other. Likewise, the portrait of the person and ministry of Jesus that emerges in the gospels of Matthew and Mark is grand, but it is hard to imagine a picture of Christ that does not include the Gospel of Luke, which may well be considered the crown jewel of the Gospels. Barclay calls it "the loveliest book in the world."[1]

Luke's Gospel is one of the three Synoptic Gospels, along with Mark and Matthew. Synoptic means "seeing the whole together at a glance." The three gospels present a common story and relate substantially the same incidents in the life of Christ.[2] However, Luke provides us with insights into the life and ministry of Jesus that complement and complete the picture given by the other writers. If Luke's contribution were absent, the portrait would be incomplete. Our appreciation for the Son of God who became the Son of Man and our understanding of the salvation He brings is enriched by the unique record provided us by Luke.

In content and sequence, Luke generally follows that of the Gospel of Mark. However, Luke adds a significant amount of information not included in Mark, or in Matthew for that matter. Specifically, Luke devotes about ten chapters (Luke 9:51–18:14) to the ministry of Jesus in Perea (on the east side of the Jordan River) and Judea, which Mark covers in an abbreviated form in Chapter 10 of his Gospel. Much of the material provided by Luke is unique, not found elsewhere in the New Testament. Without these chapters we would have no record of some of the most popular parables of Jesus, including those of the Prodigal Son, the Good Samaritan, the Rich Man and Lazarus, and the Unjust Judge.[3] Only Luke gives us detail about the births of Jesus and John the Baptist.

Each of the Synoptic Gospels was written for a different audience and portrays Jesus through titles and activities appropriate to that audience. Matthew presents Jesus to the Jewish audience as the Messiah-King; Mark presents Jesus to the Roman Christian audience as the Servant-Savior; and Luke presents Him to the Gentile Greek audience as the God-Man, specifically the Son of Man.

AUTHORSHIP

The author of this Gospel is not identified in the book, but the early church maintained that Luke was the author of both this book and Acts. Origen was the foremost biblical scholar of the early church, and he indicated that Luke was the author when he wrote near the beginning of the third century, "And the third, according to Luke, the gospel commended by Paul, which was written for the converts from the Gentiles."[4]

Luke was the only New Testament writer who was not a Jew. The Apostle Paul spoke of him as "Our dear friend Luke, the doctor" (Col. 4:14), identifying Luke as a physician. Along with Mark, Luke was a companion worker with Paul (Acts 16:10–11; 20:5; 21:1; Philem. 1:24; 2 Tim. 4:11). Comparing the introduction to Luke (Luke 1:1–4) with that of Acts (Acts 1:1–3) leads to the conclusion that both were written by the same author, with Acts intended to carry on an historic overview of the life of Christ and the continuing work of the Holy Spirit in the early church. Acts picks up where Luke ends.

Luke writes with the disciplined detail of a historian. Yet he is interested in something more than the preservation of historical details. Luke is transmitting essential truth about Jesus and what it means to be one of His followers. This author carefully crafts his record like an apologist who prepares to answer critics and those who would question the authenticity of the claims of Jesus. He is the custodian of salvation history, and he fills that role as if he were trained as a theologian.

As a Gentile, Luke writes with a view of the world that was larger than the Jewish world that is the setting for his work. He dates events by references to Roman rulers and relates some events to those of the greater society and world.[5] He was a non-Jew who wrote to non-Jews, assuring them of being included in God's redemptive plan.

Luke's association with Paul is supported by what are known as the "We" passages in Acts (Acts 16:10–17; 20:5–16; 21:1–18; 27–28). The use of the first person pronoun indicates the writer was a participant in the events described.

AUDIENCE

The Gospel of Luke is addressed to Theophilus (Luke 1:3), as was the Book of Acts (Acts 1:1). The identity of Theophilus cannot be determined with certainty. Some scholars believe him to be a new convert and place him in Antioch, though this claim cannot be made with certainty. Luke addressed Theophilus as "most excellent," the same expression Paul used in addressing Felix and Festus (Acts 24:3; 26:5).[6] William Barclay notes that "most excellent" was a normal form of address for a high official in the Roman government.[7] If this is true, it would appear that Theophilus was a Roman official who possibly held the rank of governor.

The name Theophilus means "friend of God,"[8] or "lover of God."[9] Given the meaning of that name and the fact that Theophilus has not been definitively identified, some suggest that he was not a historical but a fictitious person and that the book is intended for lovers of God everywhere. That would certainly fit God's plan for the use of this writing, but given the fact that Theophilus carries the title given to specific persons, he was most likely a real person.

Beyond the one intended recipient, it would seem that the book was intended for Gentile lovers of God who would benefit from learning the carefully documented facts about Jesus' life and ministry. Of all of the Gospel writers, only Luke makes mention of the Roman emperors who would be familiar to the Gentile Greeks and Romans who would read the record. Undoubtedly, Luke would not have been able to imagine the audience God ultimately intended for this work. Theophilus was not the only new convert who would need to be certain of the things they had been taught. Lovers of God of all ages were included as the Spirit of God moved on the mind and spirit of Luke to write his gospel. We were God's intended recipients of this book.

DATE OF WRITING

This Gospel was most likely written while Luke was in Caesarea during Paul's imprisonment there (Acts 27:1), which would place its writing sometime between A.D. 58 and the early 60s, sometime before the writing of Acts, which took place about A.D. 63.[10]

In approximately A.D. 65, Paul wrote 1 Timothy, in which he quotes the "Scripture" as saying, "The laborer is worthy of his hire" (1 Tim. 5:18). These words are found nowhere else in the Bible except Matthew 10:10 and Luke 10:7. This would indicate that one or both of these books were already in circulation by that time. Since Paul was an evangelist to the Gentiles, it is quite possible that it was Luke's writing to which he referred.[11]

PURPOSE

Luke states that he wrote this account so that Theophilus "might know the certainty of those things" wherein he had been instructed (Luke 1:3). Luke was motivated to provide this new convert with historical information and documented teaching that would assure him of the validity of what he had heard about Christ and contribute to his maturity in the faith. Christianity is based on facts, not fanciful speculation or conjured up myths. Christians should never be afraid of facts. Luke provided Theophilus and the future Christian community with facts upon which faith can be based.

Luke declares that he had personally investigated the accounts others had drawn up "of the things that have been fulfilled among us, just as they were handed down to us by those who from the first were eyewitnesses and servants of the word" (Luke 1:1–2). His purpose is to authenticate and document what had been said and seen regarding Jesus. He sought out eyewitnesses—those who were custodians of the stories they had heard and the events they had witnessed. Luke most likely spent time with Mary, the mother of Jesus, which yielded the insights into the birth and childhood years of Jesus known only to His mother.

God used Luke to provide a perspective on the person of Christ that complements that given by Matthew, Mark and John. God had a purpose in choosing the specific human instruments that He did to be conveyers of His truth. The Spirit of God moved through their unique natures and backgrounds to inspire the writing of the Scriptures that would deliver God's Word without omission of anything needed for salvation and spiritual growth. Luke fulfilled God's purpose in presenting the message that salvation is available to everyone, not just Jews.

MAJOR THEMES

The Gospel of Luke contains material found nowhere else, and it addresses themes with a passion not found in the other Gospels.

The Incarnation is an essential element of the salvation story as told by Luke. The nativity narratives of the first two chapters are found nowhere else. Luke most clearly depicts the unique nature of Christ as the God-Man—both fully God and fully man. Only God can provide for our salvation through the perfect sacrifice of the sinless Christ. Yet it was Man who was condemned to die for his sins. Only Jesus, in His divinity, could make our justification and redemption possible, and only He, in His humanity, could pay the penalty and serve as our eternal high priest who understands our weaknesses and who sits in the presence of the Father making intercession for us. Luke is careful to retain an emphasis on the divinity of Christ while very extensively demonstrating His humanity. Jesus was the God-Man, hence Luke's dominate title for Jesus was the Son of Man.

Perhaps because of his sensitivity as a physician, Luke documents the great compassion of the Lord for the poor, sick, sinners, and women and children—those who are often disenfranchised and marginalized in life. Luke's gospel has been called "the gospel of the underdog."[12]

Luke speaks often of the spiritual world that surrounds us. Angels have a prominent place in the book, as well as demons. Luke stresses the role of the Holy Spirit in both the ministry of Jesus and the lives of His followers.

Luke emphasizes prayer. Jesus is recorded as retreating often to a quiet place to pray. Jesus taught His disciples to pray and taught about prayer in His parables.

The Kingdom of God and its values plays a prominent role in this Gospel. Jesus was not on a recruitment mission to see how many people He could get to follow Him into the Kingdom. There were requirements to be met and costs to be considered. Luke emphasizes the costliness of discipleship.

Luke 15, which records parables about lost things, is key to understanding the human condition in that it reveals what it means to be lost and what it takes to be found. Some people, like sheep, wander away from God. Some people, like coins, get lost among the clutter of life due to carelessness. And some people, like wayward sons, rebel and run as far from God as possible. Some others, like eldest sons, remain close to God yet substitute orthodoxy for real relationship with the Father; they are lost just the same. Luke stresses that Jesus is Savior of all people. His mission was to "seek and to save what was lost" (Luke 19:10), and lost people may be found among Gentiles as well as among Jews—indeed, everywhere. Jesus was concerned for people of all ethnic and racial groups. He associated with common people, sinners, publicans and prostitutes (Luke 5:30–32; 7:34; 15:1). From the opening verses about the Incarnation, Luke unfolds a salvation history that would take Jesus through becoming the sin offering on Calvary to His ascension into heaven. Luke was convinced "there is no other name under heaven given to men by which we must be saved" (Acts 4:12).

ENDNOTES

1. William Barclay, *The Gospel of Luke*. (Philadelphia: Westminster Press, 1956), p. 13.

2. Gary Larsson, *The New Ungers Bible HandBook*. (Chicago: Moody Press, 1966), p. 399.

3. William L. Lane, *High-Lights of the Bible*. (Ventura, Cal.: Regal Books, 1980), p. 32.

4. Gary Larsson, *The New Ungers Bible HandBook*. (Chicago: Moody Press, 1966), p. 399.

5. Walter A. Elwell, Editor. Baker's Evangelical Dictionary of Biblical Theology, (Grand Rapids, Mich.: Baker Book House, 1996). (Elwell, Walter A. "Entry for 'Luke-Acts, Theology of'". http://www.biblestudytools.net/Dictionaries/ BakerEvangelicalDictionary/bed.cgi?number=T450, 1997).

6. J.C. Ryle, *Ryle's Expository Thoughts on the Gospels, Volume Two, Luke*. (Grand Rapids, Mich.: Baker Book House, 1977), p. 7.

7. William Barclay, *The Gospel of Luke* (Philadelphia: Westminster Press, 1956), p. 13.

8. Roswell D. Hitchcock. "Entry for 'Theophilus'". "An Interpreting Dictionary of Scripture Proper Names". <http://www.biblestudytools.net/Dictionaries/ HitckcocksBibleNames/hbn.cgi?number=T2440>. (New York, N.Y., 1869).

9. M.G. Easton, *Illustrated Bible Dictionary*, (Third Edition. Nashville: Thomas Nelson, 1897).

10. Ralph Earle, *The Wesleyan Bible Commentary: The Gospel According to St. Luke*. (Grand Rapids, Mich.: Eerdmans Publishing Co., 1964), pp. 206–7.

11. Henry H. Halley, *Bible Handbook* (Chicago, Ill., 1958), p. 431.

12. William Barclay, *The Gospel of Luke* (Philadelphia: Westminster Press, 1956), p. 17.

OUTLINE OF LUKE

I. From Bethlehem to Nazareth (1:1–2:52)

  A. Introduction—Written with You in Mind (1:1–4)

  B. You Are Going to Have a Baby (1:5–80)

    1. Birth Announcement of John the Baptist (1:5–23)

    2. Birth Announcement of Jesus (1:26–38)

    3. Mary and Elizabeth Meet (1:39–56)

    4. Birth of John the Baptist (1:57–80)

  C. He Became Flesh and Dwelled among Us (2:1–51)

    1. Birth of Jesus (2:1–20)

    2. The Presentation of Jesus (2:21–40)

    3. The Growth of Child Jesus (2:39–52)

II. Ministry in Galilee (3:1–9:50)

  A. The Kingdom of Heaven Is at Hand (3:1–38)

    1. The Ministry of John the Baptist (3:1–20)

    2. The Baptism and Genealogy of Jesus (3:21–38)

  B. Full of the Spirit (4:1–44)

    1. The Temptation of Jesus (4:1–13)

    2. The Announcement of His Mission (4:14–21)

    3. Rejected at Home (4:22–30)

    4. The Authority of Jesus (4:31–41)

    5. Focused on the Kingdom (4:42–44)

  C. Willing and Able (5:1–6:16)

    1. Jesus Calls Disciples to Follow Him (5:1–11)

    2. Jesus Touches the Untouchable (5:12–16)

    3. Jesus Forgives Sin (5:17–26)

    4. Jesus Calls Levi: Willing to Receive Sinners (5:27–32)

    5. New Wineskins: Willing to Break with Tradition (5:33–39)

    6. Jesus Confronts the Law: Willing to Break Sabbath Regulations (6:1–11)

    7. Jesus Chooses the Twelve: Willing to Keep in Touch (6:12–16)

D. Who Will Be Saved (13:1–35)
1. Repentance and a Fig Tree (13:1–9)
2. Healing on the Sabbath (13:10–17)
3. Parables about the Kingdom (13:18–30)
4. Jesus Weeps for Jerusalem (13:31–35)
E. Considering the Invitation (14:1–34)
1. Kingdom Etiquette (14:1–14)
2. Invitation to the Great Banquet (14:15–24)
3. Estimating the Cost (14:25–34)
F. The Lost Is Found (15:1–32)
1. Recognizing a Sinner When You See One (15:1–2)
2. A Sinner by Nature (15:3–7)
3. A Sinner by Neglect (15:8–10)
4. A Sinner by Choice (15:11–24)
5. A Sinner by Lifeless Orthodoxy (15:25–32)
G. The Problem of Riches (16:1–31)
1. Money and the Kingdom (16:1–18)
2. Two Destinations (16:19–31)
H. Watch Yourself (17:1–37)
1. Forgiveness and Faith (17:1–10)
2. Watch Your Gratitude (17:11–19)
3. The Day of the Lord (17:20–37)
I. Seizing the Moment (18:1–19:27)
1. Prayer to which God Responds (18:1–14)
2. Entering the Kingdom of God (18:15–30)
3. Jesus Predicts His Death (18:31–34)
4. Blind Man Healed (18:35–43)
5. Zacchaeus: Small Man, Big Opportunity (19:1–10)
6. Parable of Ten Minas (19:11–27)

IV. In Jerusalem (19:28–24:53)
A. Home Again (19:28–21:4)
1. Jesus Rides into Jerusalem (19:28–48)
2. Questions of Authority, Taxes, and the Resurrection (20:1–47)
3. The Widow's Offering (21:1–4)

Part One

From Bethlehem to Nazareth

LUKE 1:1–2:52

WRITTEN WITH YOU IN MIND

Luke 1:1–4

No one should want to live a life of uncertainty that is based on myth, falsehoods, half-truths, or legends with no foundation in fact. Luke didn't, and neither did he want that for his dear friend Theophilus. So armed with a divine subpoena, Luke set out to collect evidence and interview witnesses about the life, ministry, and meaning of Jesus Christ so that sincere seekers of all ages could build their lives on unquestionable truth.

The Gospel of Luke provides a thorough account of the life and ministry of Jesus Christ, giving details about the birth and early years of Jesus that are not provided in the other Gospels. Most of the events and teachings of Jesus recorded in 9:51–18:35 are exclusive to Luke.

From the earliest days of the Church, authorship of this book was attributed to Luke, and there is no prevailing reason to consider otherwise. Luke also authored the book of Acts, completing the record that stops rather abruptly at the end of his Gospel. The writer only momentarily laid aside his pen at the end of the Gospel to pick it up again to continue the historical accounts of the Spirit of Christ who was alive and active in the emerging Church.

Luke was a Gentile convert who became a close friend, companion, and fellow worker with the apostle Paul (Col. 4:14; 2 Tim. 4:11; Philem. 1:24), Mark, Aristarchus, and Demas. Luke was a Greek doctor, which explains his emphasis on the needy and sick as well as the compassionate healing ministry of Jesus. He has the distinction of being the only Gentile writer in the New Testament, thus his emphasis on the ministry of Jesus to all people. He was educated in the sciences, which explains his passion for detail and documentation.

A number of themes become evident as you read this Gospel. Prominence is given to the healing ministry of Jesus, prayer, women, angels, demons, the Holy Spirit, and Jesus' compassion for the poor.

As you read, prepare to come face-to-face with Jesus. Luke will guide you through the birth, life, and death of Jesus in a way that will compel you to make personal decisions about your relationship with God through His Son. He will place convincing evidence before you concerning the humanity and divinity of the Christ that will demand a verdict.

READING EYEWITNESS ACCOUNTS

The Gospel of Luke has been **handed down to us by those who from the first were eyewitnesses** (Luke 1:2). The life and ministry of Jesus Christ is not a myth contrived by some novelist. The record of the words He spoke is not made up or manipulated by overzealous adherents. People who listened to His teaching and witnessed His ministry wrote down what they observed, and we can confidently read those accounts and accept their accuracy.

Luke did not come to his writing as an uninformed outsider. As a companion of Paul, he would have had direct access to the disciples as he interviewed these eyewitnesses to get the perspective of each of them. He also witnessed the Holy Spirit breathe life and fire into the early church. He maintained objectivity, while at the same time personally experiencing the transforming gift of grace from God through Christ.

Many people, affected by the ministry of Jesus, had **undertaken to draw up an account** (1:1) of what they had seen and experienced. It was important to them, not only because of its personal impact on them, but because what God had proclaimed centuries before was **fulfilled among** them. What they witnessed, as God redeemed the world, was life transforming, world changing, and history making.

When Jesus spoke, He spoke the word of God, and those who heard and recorded His words handled them carefully and reverently as **servants**

of the word (1:2). From the first verses of the Holy Scripture, God demonstrated himself to be a communicating God. He spoke a universe of living things into existence. He spoke and fellowshipped with the living souls He had put in charge of the earth. God sent His Son as His Word—*Logos* (John 1:1)—to communicate His love and His will. He inspired faithful servants to record those things that are important for us to understand about His plan and purpose for us. The words of the Gospel writers contain power to bring people to salvation in Jesus Christ and sustain them as His followers.

Ministers who open the Scripture and proclaim its truth should be convicted by the realization they are *servants of the Word.* They must apply it, not for personal gain, but to serve the purposes of God in the lives of the listeners. In a broader sense, the Word of God is the voice of authority to all believers, and we become its servant as we follow its direction in our lives.

CHECKING OUT THE SOURCES

Like other interested persons, Luke read the early eyewitness accounts. He was not a casual reader who was only interested in surface speculations based on partial understanding. He was too thorough of a person for that. He was trained as a physician (Col. 4:14) and, as such, was committed to thorough investigation and analysis. All details were important, all alternatives had to be explored, and all implications had to be checked out. He could not be content to read what others said without checking the sources himself. **I myself have carefully investigated everything from the beginning** (Luke 1:3).

Scripture does not contain a record of his conversion. Did he place his faith in Christ as a result of his investigation? Or did his careful checking of the details come from the passion of his newfound faith as he sought to validate the commitment he had made? Both are possibilities, and we can approach the details of his record with the same motives. You may be searching for truth that can be found in this Gospel—truth that can lead you to Christ and transform your life. You may be looking to build a strong foundation for your faith—truths upon which your commitment to

Christ can rest as you live in a faithless world. You can be confident that Luke explored everything about Jesus and that God will use this Gospel to meet you where you are.

The careful investigation of the truth by Luke is an example for us. Sincere faith in Christ can never be secondhand. Luke was not content to read the accounts of others or try to live through their experiences of Christ. He could not be content until he could say "I myself . . ." Likewise, God encourages us to investigate, seek (11:9) and test the reliability of the truth, understand it, and count the cost of committing ourselves to it (14:28). Faith is never a blind, naïve, or mindless thing.

PROVIDING AN ORDERLY ACCOUNT

It seemed good to Luke to write his own record of the life and ministry of Jesus. This was not a personal decision based on emotional impulse. The Spirit of God moved on the spirit of Luke, as He used another human instrument to give us an additional perspective through another volume in the library of books written about Jesus. While we accept the Scriptures as being God's Word to us, we recognize that the personalities of faithful persons chosen by God show through the writings. They were not mechanical scribes, recording what they had not experienced or did not understand. They were inspired by God to write those things that seemed good to preserve for our benefit.

Since Luke was given to detail and thorough investigation, he wrote **an orderly account** (1:3). He was motivated to be sure the sequence of events was reported with accuracy, the stories were recorded in their historical context, and the persons involved were clearly identified.

FOR LOVERS OF GOD EVERYWHERE

Luke addressed his record to **most excellent Theophilus**. The book of Acts is also addressed to Theophilus, a name that means "lover of God." It would appear that Luke was providing a detailed account of the life and ministry of Jesus to a sincere seeker after God. Many books of the Bible were written to particular persons or groups with the intent that they also be shared with others. It would appear that Luke was inspired by God to address his record not only to a specific person who was a lover of God, but lovers of God in all times and places.

Theophilus was a Gentile, like Luke. Throughout the Gospel, Luke uses Greek terms, not Hebrew, and attaches events to Roman personalities rather than Jewish prophecies as Matthew does. The book was written so Gentiles could easily understand and come to place their faith in Christ. Luke wrote for people like us. Without question, Luke had become a lover of God, and it was his desire that others become lovers of God too.

Luke accompanied Paul for two years while he was in prison in Caesarea and most likely wrote his Gospel from Caesarea or Rome. Since Luke was a companion of Paul, it could be that Luke became acquainted with Theophilus while with Paul in Rome. If that is true, the writing of this book would be dated around A.D. 60.

IT'S TIME TO BE SURE

Luke prepared this record so Theophilus, and people like him, might know the certainty of the things they have been taught through thorough investigation, verification, and careful documentation. It is wonderful when head knowledge becomes heart experience. It is great to grow up with matters of faith passed on through the teaching of parents and churches. But the time comes when faith must become the conviction of a person's heart, not an accumulation of teaching in a person's head. Luke wanted Theophilus to have full understanding about the person of Jesus and have no doubt about his relationship to Him.

LIFE CHANGE

TRANSFORMATIONAL TRUTH

Life transformation begins by personally receiving the truth about Jesus Christ and placing faith in Him. It is the truth that sets us free (John 8:23) and that truth is found in a person—Jesus Christ.

This book was written with you in mind. Read on and become certain in your faith and a more committed lover of God.

2

YOU ARE GOING TO HAVE A BABY

Luke 1:5–80

Firstborn children bring a lot of excitement to waiting parents. But if an angel were to tell you that you were going to give birth after being barren your whole life—and it would be a son in a culture where not having a son was disgraceful—you would have reason to be speechless with unbridled joy.

But what kind of emotions would you have if you were not yet married and an angel were to tell you that you were going to give birth to a son? And not just any boy, but the Son of God conceived by the Holy Spirit. This is not your typical birth announcement and may not be met with the greatest level of excitement, since sex outside marriage was a capital offense.

This is not entertaining soapbox drama, but the unfolding of God's eternal plan, surrounded by miracles and charged with emotion.

1. BIRTH ANNOUNCEMENT OF JOHN THE BAPTIST (1:5–25)

A BLAMELESS PRIEST WHOSE PRAYER WAS ANSWERED

Zechariah and Elizabeth were good people: descendants of the high priest Aaron and **upright in the sight of God, observing all the Lord's commandments and regulations blamelessly** (Luke 1:6). They were the kind of people God loves to bless. But **they were both well along in years** and **had no children** (1:7). They had often prayed for a child, but this was a blessing withheld from them. Not having a male child was more than a missed blessing. In their culture, it bordered on a disgrace for a woman to be unable to bear a man-child to carry on the family name and to support the family. For Elizabeth, disappointment turned to despair, and despair turned to hopeless resignation. They would never have a son.

Have you been faithful to God, but have not seen prayers answered the way you would hope? We know His delays are not always denials, but waiting is difficult when we see no evidence that God even hears our prayer or will ever answer it.

Zechariah was selected to **go into the temple of the Lord and burn incense** (1:9). This was an honor for which many priests would wait a lifetime. Worshippers gathered in the Temple court to pray while Zechariah went inside the holy place to appear before God as a representative of the people and to offer the incense offering symbolizing the prayers of the people rising up to God. Zechariah's prayers had been sent toward God many times, but now he was appearing before God on behalf of the prayers of others. He did not anticipate that a representative of God would appear to him.

He was startled and was gripped with fear when **an angel of the Lord appeared to him** (1:12, 11). The angel's message was simple: **"Your prayer** is answered. You are going to have a baby!" (1:13). Even though Zechariah's prayers for a son went years without being answered, he remained blameless before God. It was while he was faithfully carrying out his spiritual responsibilities in the house of the Lord that God spoke to him and answered his prayer: "You will have **a son** and **give him the name John.**"

What a lesson for us—to be faithful to God and duty regardless of circumstances or personal disappointments!

A PREPARER OF THE WAY

The angel told Zechariah that his son, John, would have a special mission. What appeared to be a delay in answering their prayer made possible a birth that perfectly fit into God's timing for the coming Messiah. Since John would have a special role to play, he would have to live a special life. He was **never to take wine or other fermented drink, and he** would **be filled with the Holy Spirit** (1:15). This Nazirite vow indicated separation unto God (Num. 6). Samson was another notable person who was consecrated to God as a Nazirite prior to his birth (Judg. 13).

John was to have a mission of bringing **many of the people of Israel . . . back to the Lord their God** (Luke 1:16). Israel had a cyclical history of drifting away from God, experiencing judgment for their sin, repenting, turning back to God, restoring their relationship with Him, and enjoying His blessings again. In His faithfulness, God always sent a messenger who would warn of God's judgment and call the people to repent and return. Once more Israel needed to be called back to God, and He chose John as the instrument **to make ready a people prepared for the Lord** (1:17). Luke 3 covers the ministry of John as he filled the critical role of preparing the way for the coming Messiah. So dynamic and dramatic was his ministry that some thought he must surely be the Messiah. Not only would John **be a joy and delight** (1:14) to his parents who had waited so long for him, but **many** others would **rejoice** as he prepared the way for the Messiah for whom they had waited so long.

Angels are quite active in the Gospel of Luke, with this being the first of many appearances. We are given a brief glimpse into the world of angels when this one announced to Zechariah that he was **Gabriel** (1:19). He said, **"I stand in the presence of God, and I have been sent to speak to you."** Angels are ministering spirits who reside within the presence of God and who are sent to perform tasks at the command of God. It appears that God entrusted Gabriel with special messages to be delivered on special occasions. Gabriel's name appears four times in the Bible (Dan. 8:16; 9:21; Luke 1:19, 26) and on each occasion, he spoke as the appointed messenger of God.

We could imagine that Zechariah was ready to shout for joy when he learned God had answered his prayer, but when he asked Gabriel for some sign to verify that this was not a cruel hoax, the angel said, **"You will be silent and not able to speak until the day this happens, because you did not believe my words"** (1:20). What a time to lose your voice! Even as a righteous man of faith, Zechariah had difficulty believing the message of the angel. Perhaps, like Thomas a few decades later (John 20), Zechariah's doubt was born out of amazement that God could or would do such a thing. His lack of belief resulted in his inability to verbally communicate with others what God was planning.

2. BIRTH ANNOUNCEMENT OF JESUS (1:26–38)

A FAVORED VIRGIN

Six months after telling Zechariah his prayer had been answered, **God sent the angel Gabriel to Nazareth, a town in Galilee** (1:26), on another mission with another birth announcement. At the time, Israel was divided into three territories: Judea, Samaria, and Galilee. Nazareth was in Galilee, the northernmost of the territories. Nazareth did not have much going for it, except that two insignificant people lived there who would become very significant in the plan of God.

God is not limited to working within the same value systems we tend to elevate. Why Nazareth? Why Mary? Why Joseph? Because insignificant places and people are made significant when God shows up and leaves His fingerprints on them. Without His touch, those the world considers significant live in constant search for meaning and importance.

Gabriel had another miracle to announce. It might have seemed miraculous that an elderly couple would have a baby, but it could be explained that strange things sometimes do happen. However, a virgin having a baby is impossible. Even angels should know that.

This time, the miracle was not the result of prolonged prayer. In fact, this miracle might not be viewed as a blessing. The birth announcement was delivered to **a virgin**, whose **name was Mary** (1:27). Being unmarried and pregnant would pose a very disgraceful, critical problem. If an unmarried woman became pregnant, the

> ### KEY IDEA
> #### VIRGIN BIRTH
>
> It is reported that Larry King, television talk show host, was asked who he would most like to have interviewed over the course of history. He replied that he would like to interview Jesus Christ. "I would like to ask Him if He was indeed virgin born, because the answer to that question would define history." He was—and it has!

only conclusion would be that she was immoral and should be stoned to death as prescribed by Jewish law. If she were to claim her innocence by saying she was a virgin whose pregnancy was caused by the Holy Spirit, the charges of lying, insanity, and heresy could be added.

The angel said, **"Greetings, you who are highly favored! The Lord is with you"** (1:28). Why was Mary so highly favored? Why was the Lord with her in some special way? Why did God choose her to bear His only Son? Mary was certainly a remarkable young woman. There is no indication, however, that she was immaculately conceived herself, as some suggest, or that because of her role in God's plan she should be the channel through which our prayers reach God. She was chosen by the sovereign decision of God— separated out from others to be God's servant for a special task. God often works out His sovereign will by favoring common people like Mary—and us—to accomplish His purpose. The focus should never be on us but on the purpose of God that is being accomplished through us.

Mary **was pledged to be married to a man named Joseph** (1:27). Mary and Joseph were not yet married—only pledged to each other. In that culture, pledging or betrothal lasted for a year and was as binding as marriage. It could only be dissolved by divorce, which is why it was said of Joseph that because he "was a righteous man and did not want to expose her to public disgrace, he had in mind to divorce her quietly" (Matt. 1:19). Joseph was identified as being **a descendant of David** (Luke 1:27). Both of the genealogies of Jesus, recorded in Matthew and Luke, traced His lineage back through David, fulfilling the prophecy that the Messiah would be of the house of David.

ANNOUNCEMENT OF THE BIRTH OF THE SON OF GOD

Just as Gabriel had done with Zechariah and Elizabeth, he communicated God's choice for the child's name: **"You are to give him the name Jesus"** (1:31). The name Jesus is a form of the name Joshua (*Yeshua*) and means "Savior." The angel said that Jesus would be a king on **the throne of his father David** (1:32), and that He would be great and **called the Son of the Most High.** But of all of the names given to God's Son, the name *Jesus* most captures the heart of those who follow Him. It is not a name of heavenly royalty but of identification with humanity and its needs. It is at the name of Jesus that "every knee should bow, in heaven and on earth and under the earth, and every tongue confess that Jesus Christ is Lord, to the glory of God the Father" (Phil. 2:10–11). We must first know Him as Savior before we can know Him as Lord.

God's divine plan of salvation would be accomplished through a never-to-be-repeated miracle. Gabriel told Mary that **the Holy Spirit** would **come upon** her **and the power of the Most High** would **overshadow** her (Luke 1:35). This rather simple message contained complex realities that mystified Mary and around which we cannot fully wrap our understanding. The angel was telling Mary that the baby she would carry would be of divine origin. Her conception would not be the result of human action but of Holy Spirit action.

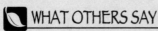

WHAT OTHERS SAY

INCARNATION

"In the moment of conception, the Holy Spirit took deity and humanity and, fusing them together, made possible the Lord Jesus, who came as the God-Man. The Spirit was the love-knot between our Lord's two natures."

—Herbert Lockyer

Mary's response was, **"How will this be?"** (1:34). She would have every reason to question the validity of the message. Yet her question seems to be more for understanding the process than of accepting its truthfulness—"Given what you say, how will it happen, **since I am a virgin?"** We may believe and accept the Word from God, but when viewed through the lens of our circumstances and our understanding of the laws of nature, the plan and promise of God can appear impossible. The word given to Mary needs to be spoken into the life of every follower of Christ: **"Nothing is impossible with God"** (1:37). Our circumstances may make the transition difficult, but this Word needs to move from being intellectually believed to being the conviction of our hearts. We will face things in our lives that have no resolution, and we will see them as impossible. But when God is included in the equation, possibilities show up. **Nothing is impossible with God!**

Mary's response to the plan of God was remarkable. Knowing the potential for personal embarrassment and disgrace, she said, **"I am the**

Lord's servant . . . May it be to me as you have said" (1:38). Though
Mary was favored by God, it did not insulate her from difficulty and hurt.
In fact, obedience to the plan of God would lead her into the potential of
experiencing serious problems. But she viewed herself to be the Lord's
servant, and servants serve their masters.

After delivering his message, **the angel left her.** Times of divine visitation are wonderful, but the moment comes when we are left alone.
There are no angels. There is no further word from God. There is no one
else with whom we can share our thoughts or questions. No doubt Mary
would wake up tomorrow with a new set of questions, but who would
answer them? Who would walk with her through the days of uncertainty
that lay ahead? The words of the angel would become her assurance:
"The Lord is with you." When we follow the plan of God, we experience
the presence and receive the provisions of God.

3. MARY AND ELIZABETH MEET (1:39–56)

Mary visited her relative Elizabeth while both were expecting. The
excitement they shared caused both to break out in song. Even
Elizabeth's **baby leaped in her womb** (1:41), as unborn John knew
something special was happening.

Elizabeth exclaimed to Mary, **"Blessed are you among women, and
blessed is the child you will bear!"** (1:42). She further referred to Mary as
the mother of my Lord (1:43). Mary would be the human means by which
the divine Jesus would be born. She was special in that she was chosen by
God for a special task, not unlike many others who have answered the call
of God, believing **that what the Lord has said . . . will be accomplished!**
(1:45). There is no greater privilege than to hear God call you to a particular task, believe that He will accomplish it through you, declare yourself
to be His servant, and allow Him to use you as He wishes.

Mary burst into what has become known in the Church as the
Magnificat, from the first words of her song: **"My soul glorifies the
Lord"** (1:46). Her song is rich in notes of rejoicing in God and the great
things He has done, in His holiness, mercy, mighty deeds, and help to
Israel. God fills the hungry, lifts up the humble, and remembers to be

merciful. He also scatters those who are proud, brings down rulers from their thrones, and sends the rich away empty. **"Holy is his name"** (1:49).

Elizabeth's song was one of declaring Mary to be blessed. Mary's song was one of declaring God to be praised. Both were caught up in the wonderful privilege of being included in the unfolding plan of God's redemption of His people.

During the one-year betrothal period, it was customary for the bride-to-be to live with relatives until she would be formally married to her husband. **Mary stayed with Elizabeth for about three months** (1:56) before returning to Nazareth. Meanwhile, what must Joseph have been going through? He too was being asked to believe that God would accomplish His plan through him. Our commitment to pursue God's purpose for us will affect our relationships with others. God's plan for Mary needed to be accepted by Joseph as well. She could be pleased that in spite of big risks, he stood with her in her journey of faith. If your resolve to follow Christ is supported by spouse, family, and friends, you are a blessed person and should thank God that He is working in the lives of those around you while He is working in you.

4. THE BIRTH OF JOHN THE BAPTIST (1:57–80)

HIS NAME IS JOHN

The time came for Elizabeth to give birth to her son, and **her neighbors and relatives . . . shared her joy** (1:58). They knew she had been childless beyond the normal time for having children, and they **heard that the Lord had shown her great mercy**. Her husband, Zechariah, was still unable to speak, so Elizabeth must have given the Lord credit for her miraculous pregnancy as she talked to friends and family. **On the eighth day they came to circumcise the child** (1:59), which was according to Mosaic law and symbolized the covenant between God and the child. The naming of the child usually occurred at this time since, in Jewish thought, the child became an independent person on the eighth day.[1]

It was anticipated that the baby would be named after his father, but Elizabeth said, **"No! He is to be called John"** (1:60). Up to this time

Zechariah was unable to speak, but he gave the final word on the matter when **he wrote** on **a tablet, "His name is John"** (1:63). As soon as Zechariah obeyed God's instruction regarding the naming of the baby, he was able **to speak**, and he began **praising God** (1:64). If you had not spoken a word in nine months, what would be the first thing you would say? The greatest words to roll off the tongue of any person are words of praise to God.

The whole event was amazing to the neighbors, and **throughout the hill country of Judea people were talking about all these things** (1:65). John became the talk of the town even before he took up residence in the desert and began his remarkable ministry.

A PURPOSE-DRIVEN LIFE

The people who heard about the events surrounding the birth of John began to ask, **"What then is this child going to be?"** (1:66). Parents believe God has a plan and purpose for their children that is unique and special. But will they follow God's plan? Will they fulfill God's purpose? What will they become as they take their place in the world? To those close to the family, it was evident that **the Lord's hand was with** John and would make his ministry effective. There is no substitute for the hand of God. Charismatic personality and dynamic communication skills can only take a person so far. Unless the hand of God is evidenced, that person's ministry will not fulfill its full potential.

ZECHARIAH'S SONG

It was time for Zechariah to break out in song, and the words that had been held inside for all these months came pouring out. His song is called the *Benedictus*, based on the first word that came from his lips: ***"Praise be to the Lord"*** (1:68, italics added). Zechariah believed that the Messiah was about to emerge, that God had **come and redeemed his people,** and that his son was going to prepare the way.

The redemption of Israel would be made possible because God had **raised up a horn of salvation** (1:69). This is the only place in the New Testament where Jesus is referred to as the "horn of salvation." The instruction from God for the construction of the altar in the Temple where the atonement for the sins of the people was to be made called for a horn at each of the four corners (Ex. 27:1–2). Blood was applied to the horns of the altars for atonement (Ex. 30:10). Adonijah, in fear of Solomon, fled to the altar and hung on to the horns as a place for refuge and salvation (1 Kings 1:50–53). Upon deliverance from his enemies, David sang, "The LORD is my rock, my fortress and my deliverer; my God is my rock, in whom I take refuge, my shield and the *horn of my salvation*. He is my stronghold, my refuge, and my savior . . ." (2 Sam. 22:2–3, italics added). Zechariah was inspired to proclaim Jesus to be the one to whom humankind could flee for refuge—the one who would become the atonement for sin— the one who would become **salvation for us and** (Luke 1:69) the strength of our life (see Ps. 28:7–8).

Zechariah anticipated God's salvation would be for the nation Israel in that he saw it as **salvation from our enemies and from the hand of all who hate us** (Luke 1:71). As others who longed for the Messiah, he believed Christ would deliver Israel from Roman control as a part of God remembering **his holy covenant** (1:72). However, Zechariah also saw God's salvation to be personal, not just national. God would enable people **to serve him without fear in holiness and righteousness** (1:74–75). Salvation includes personal moral and ethical transformation—holiness toward God and righteousness toward people.[2]

Zechariah understood the mission of his son, John, would be twofold: first, to **go on before the Lord to prepare the way for him** (1:76); and second, **to give his people the knowledge of salvation through the forgiveness of their sins** (1:77). John's ministry would call people to repentance and to seek the coming kingdom of God.

John **grew and became strong in spirit; and he lived in the desert until he appeared publicly to Israel** (1:80). Just as there is no substitute

LIFE CHANGE

GOD'S CALL

All believers are called to use their abilities and gifts to serve God in and through the church. God calls certain people to specialized vocational service within the church to equip God's people for effective ministry (Eph. 4:11–13). We find our highest fulfillment when we respond to God's call to service and engage ourselves in the purpose and place He has chosen for us.

for the hand of God, there is no substitute for preparation. John was being prepared in the desert by God for his public ministry. We can tend to either rush ahead of or lag behind the plan of God. Rushing ahead of God usually means we shortchange personal preparation and have to unnecessarily deal with circumstances that would not exist if we allowed God to establish His timing in us. "Desert living" can eliminate distractions and allow us to focus on God as well as our spiritual development. If you are led through the desert, as Jesus was (4:1), don't break the speed limit trying to get out of it. We will emerge—in God's time—into the fertile place where God wants to plant us for future harvests.

Two babies were born in Israel within months of each other, and together they would change the religious landscape of the people of Israel. One of them would prepare the way for the Christ—one who would call Israel back to God and announce the coming of the kingdom of God. The other, Jesus, would be the Christ who would fulfill God's promise to provide a redeemer.

ENDNOTES

1. Merrill Unger, *The New Unger's Bible Handbook* (Chicago: Moody Press, 1984), p. 207.

2. Ralph Earle, *The Wesleyan Bible Commentary: The Gospel of Luke* (Grand Rapids, Mich.: Eerdmans, 1964), p. 218.

3

HE BECAME FLESH AND DWELLED AMONG US

Luke 2:1-52

M any Christmas celebrations miss the enormity of Christ's birth. This was not just another baby or another birthday. God was born in human likeness—the Divine taking upon himself the limitations of humanity (Phil. 2:7). This event is understood by us to be the *incarnation*.

The mystery of the incarnation should always override our tendency to turn Jesus into a cuddly baby we can handle and control. He is Emmanuel—God with us—wrapped in human flesh (Isa. 7:14; Matt. 1:23). It is hard to wrap our minds around it, but it is true. He became flesh and dwelled among us (John 1:14). He was made like us so we could be made like Him.

1. THE BIRTH OF JESUS (2:1-20)

THE TIME HAD COME

The letter to the Galatians states that "when the time had fully come, God sent his Son" (Gal. 4:4). The time was right, and God used the Roman Empire to help make it so. Its conquests had created the infrastructure for travel and communication to spread the good news throughout the known world. Luke presents Jesus as the Son of Man by which he emphasizes His humanity and His appeal to all people of the world. This places

Jesus into the context of world history in a way the other Gospel writers do not.

Caesar Augustus was emperor in Rome, and **Quirinius was governor of Syria** (Luke 2:1–2). Evidence suggests that Quirinius was governor of Syria on two different occasions, the first time around 8 B.C.[1]

Palestine, under the emperor Caesar Augustus, was part of the **Roman world**. Caesar Augustus provided forty-four years of leadership of the Roman Empire and secured peace and order for the region, which also assisted in the rapid spread of Christianity. A godless empire and its ruler were used by God to fulfill His plan, and the timing was right.

A **census** was ordered that required every man go **to his own town to register** (2:3) for tax assessment and to determine those who were to be drafted into military service. The Jewish men were exempt from military service, but certainly not from paying taxes. **Joseph went up from the town of Nazareth** to his hometown of **Bethlehem**, the hometown of David and the place where all those of the **line of David** (2:4) were to go for the census, thus fulfilling two prophecies. The first was that the Messiah would come out of Bethlehem (Mic. 5:2) and that God's Anointed One would come out of the line of David (Jer. 33:15). Both Joseph and Mary were in the lineage of David.

Joseph took Mary with him, **who was pledged to be married to him and was expecting a child** (Luke 2:5). The distance from Nazareth to Bethlehem was around seventy to eighty miles, with Bethlehem being seven miles south of Jerusalem.

WHAT OTHERS SAY

INCARNATION

"I do not think of Christ as God alone, or man alone, but both together. For I know He was hungry, and I know that with five loaves He fed five thousand. I know He was thirsty, and I know that He turned the water into wine. I know He was carried in a ship, and I know that He walked on the sea. I know that He died, and I know that He raised the dead. I know that He was set before Pilate, and I know that He sits with the Father on His throne. I know that He was worshipped by angels, and I know that He was stoned by the Jews. And truly some of these I ascribe to the human, and others to the divine nature. For by reason of this He is said to have been both God and man."

—John Chrysostom

A KING IS BORN

The time came for the baby to be born (2:6). God's entrance into our world in human form began as naturally as the arrival of any other baby. The normalcy of nine months of gestation and then delivery gave little evidence of the supernatural conception and divine nature of the baby. The time was right, both naturally and within God's design, and Mary **gave birth to her firstborn, a son** (2:7). The setting may not have been as they would have anticipated for the arrival of the Messiah, but everything was unfolding just as God had told them through Gabriel. The use of the term firstborn suggests Mary later gave birth to other children, a possibility supported by Mark's gospel (Mark 6:3).

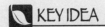

KEY IDEA

BIRTHDAY OF JESUS

December 25 was established as the birth date of Jesus by the Western church in the fourth century. January 6 is the date recognized by the Eastern church. The actual date is unknown and is not important as a matter of faith. Neither is it important whether the cavelike structure covered by the Church of the Nativity is the actual birthplace of Jesus. The fact that God became flesh in the person of Jesus is the important reality. That is what we celebrate.

Mary **wrapped** the infant Jesus **in cloths and placed him in a manger, because there was no room for them in the inn** (Luke 2:7). All accommodations for out-of-town visitors were full, and the inn to which Mary and Joseph went had no room. The innkeeper has become notorious for not providing room for an obviously expectant woman. Traditionally, several families crowded into the inn's rooms, so he actually provided the couple with a private area where the animals were sheltered, which tradition says was a cave.

WHAT OTHERS SAY

NO ROOM FOR JESUS

"That there was no room in the inn was symbolic of what was to happen to Jesus. The only place where there was room for Him was on a cross. He sought an entry to the over-crowded hearts of men; He could not find it; and still His search—and His rejection—go on."

—William Barclay

Humbly, the messianic mission began: Jesus, "being in very nature God, did not consider equality with God something to be grasped, but made himself nothing, taking the very nature of a servant, being made in human likeness" (Phil. 2:6–7). The arrival of the King of Kings came without fanfare or any of the trappings usually assigned to royalty.

BIRTH ANNOUNCED TO SHEPHERDS

However, the good news of the birth of God's Anointed One could not be confined to the stable. God chose to inform the common person first. He interrupted the stillness of the countryside by sending angels to **shepherds living out in the fields . . . , keeping watch over their flocks** (Luke 2:8). **An angel of the Lord** brought the message—the **good news of great joy** (2:9–10).

The glory of the Lord shone around them. The Old Testament speaks of the majestic presence or manifestation of God (glory) as a cloud (Ex. 16:10) and a consuming fire (Ex. 24:17), filling the Tabernacle, the Temple (Ex. 40:34; 2 Chron. 7:1–2), and the whole earth (Num. 14:21). This manifested presence of God, represented by light, surrounded the shepherds and angels as the good news was pronounced: the Light of the World had appeared to shepherds in the darkness of night.

The good news about the birth of Jesus was more than sharing congratulations with proud parents. The good news was—and is—that **a Savior has been born** (Luke 2:11). The birth of Jesus became the hinge pin of human history, and the religious landscape would never again be the same. All that God had asked His people to do under the law of Moses to relate with Him was preparing them for this moment.

It has been suggested that the shepherds near Bethlehem may have been caring for the sheep that were used for the sin offerings in the Temple sacrifices. If this were true, it would be fitting that these shepherds would be the first to visit the Lamb of God. The name Jesus means "Savior," and Luke is the only Gospel writer who specifically calls Jesus "the Savior," which he does five times within the first two chapters (1:31, 47, 69; 2:11, 30). The humble shepherd was the first to hear that salvation was personally available, and that message remains current and applicable to each of us.

There may be a lot of things from which we wish God could save us— political oppression, physical ailments, emotional stress, or unjust prejudice—but Jesus came to save us from the one thing we are totally incapable of handling ourselves: our sin.

This newborn child is Jesus **Christ the Lord** (Luke 2:11). His human name is to be *Jesus*. But the angels, who knew Him before He came to earth, knew that He was **Christ the Lord**. *Christ* means "the Anointed One," and this was the first announcement that Jesus was the Messiah, the chosen one of God. He was the one for whom the Jews longed, but sadly, "He came to that which was his own, but his own did not receive him" (John 1:11). *Lord* acknowledges His sovereignty, His supremacy, and His authority. Each of the three titles carries another dimension of the marvelous incarnation.

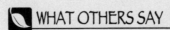

> ## WHAT OTHERS SAY
> ### GOD IN HUMAN FLESH
>
> "What a paradox! *The Eternal One* caught in a moment of time. *Omnipresence* corralled in a cave manger. *Omnipotence* cradled in a helpless infant who could not even raise His head from the straw. *Omniscience* confined in a baby who could not say a word. The Christ who created the heavens and the earth cradled in a manger in a cave stable. What condescending love!"
>
> —Ralph Earle

The messenger from God was joined by **a great company of the heavenly host** (Luke 2:13) as they offered praise to God and proclaimed **peace** to those **on whom God's favor rests.** All of heaven joined in praising God for what was happening on earth.

LET'S GO SEE

After coming face to face with the Lamb of God, the shepherds glorified and praised God **for all the things they had heard and seen** (2:20) and **spread the word . . . , and all who heard it were amazed** (2:17–18).

For Mary, life was coming at this young mother in major doses, and all she could do was treasure **up all these things** and ponder **them in her heart** (2:19). Luke sought firsthand observers of the events surrounding Jesus, so all that we have come to know about what led up to Jesus' birth and the birth itself likely came to Luke straight out of the treasury of Mary's heart.

2. THE PRESENTATION OF JESUS (2:21–38)

FULFILLING THE LAW

Galatians 4:4 reminds us that Jesus was "born of a woman, born under the law, to redeem those under the law." Jewish law required a number of things following the birth of a male child: circumcision, naming, purification of the mother, and presentation to the Lord. **On the eighth day** (Luke 2:21), the male child was to be circumcised and named. When that time arrived, **he was named Jesus, the name the angel had given him before he had been conceived.** The custom of the day was to name children after significant circumstances surrounding their

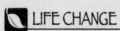

LIFE CHANGE

SENT BACK TO THE WORK

Spiritual encounters with God, as amazing as they may be, should always make us more fit for dealing with life's routines and more focused for handling life's responsibilities. God draws us away from this world to reveal things of the spirit to us and then sends us back into the world to live out the truth we have seen.

birth or for anticipated contributions they would make through their lives. God chose the name, and it was a promise of the contribution Jesus would make through His life, death, and resurrection. Jesus, *Savior*, would become the Lamb of God who would take away the sins of the world.

According to the law (2:22), a woman who gave birth would be ceremonially unclean for seven days and would need to wait thirty-three days before she could be declared purified from her bleeding (Lev. 12).

Mary and Joseph took Jesus **to Jerusalem to present him to the Lord.** As will be developed throughout the Gospel of Luke, Jerusalem was the center around which the life of Jesus would orbit and would be mentioned ninety-six times in the record of Luke and Acts. This would be Jesus' first visit to the Holy City to begin the fulfillment of the law of Moses and the mission of His life. He would ultimately return to complete all the requirements of the law and to complete the plan for purifying His people from their sin.

According to Exodus 13, God asked that all firstborn males be presented to Him for consecration as a reminder of the deliverance He provided Israel from Egyptian bondage. In this same spirit, it is a significant moment in church life when parents bring a child before the congregation to present it to the Lord. This is no casual event or meaningless ritual. We declare that our children belong to God, that we are stewards of their lives, and that we seek the assistance of God and His people as we raise them up in the nurture and admonition of the Lord.

The law also required new parents to **offer a sacrifice in keeping with what is said in the Law of the Lord** (Luke 2:24) as ordered in

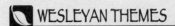

WESLEYAN THEMES
BAPTISM OF INFANTS

Male Jewish infants were circumcised as a part of God's covenant with Israel. It was an initiatory sign of belonging to God and being a recipient of the benefits of the covenant. Christian parents in the Wesleyan tradition may present their children to the Lord in an act of dedication or witness to their faith for the salvation of their children by presenting them for baptism. Infant baptism is rooted in the benefit of the Atonement and God's prevenient grace that covers the original sin of the innocent until they are capable of making moral choice. Later, those baptized as infants are encouraged to affirm the faith of their parents in a public ritual of personally declaring their commitment to Christ.

Leviticus 12. The woman who had given birth was to bring a year-old lamb and a young pigeon or dove as an offering. However, "if she cannot afford a lamb, she is to bring two doves or two young pigeons" (Lev. 12:8). The fact that Mary presented the lesser offering—**a pair of doves or two young pigeons**—would indicate she was a person of little means.

THE LONGING OF RIGHTEOUS PEOPLE FULFILLED

In Jerusalem lived **Simeon,** who was a very **righteous and devout man** (2:25). He, along with other people of the faithful remnant, waited for **the consolation of Israel**. *Waiting* suggests patient anticipation and faithful longing. Simeon felt the pain of his people, and he longed for the Messiah who would come to comfort embattled Israel with spiritual, if not political, deliverance. The prophet Isaiah had written, "Comfort, comfort my people, says your God. Speak tenderly to Jerusalem, and proclaim to her that her hard service has been completed, that her sin has been paid for, that she has received from the Lord's hand double for all her sins" (Isa. 40:1–2). Simeon longed for the Comforter to come and pay for the sin of his nation.

Simeon's relationship with God was such that the **Holy Spirit was upon him, revealed** things **to him** (Luke 2:26), and **moved** him (2:27). The desire of our hearts should be to have this kind of intimacy with God. Simeon was told by divine revelation that **he would not die before he had seen the Lord's Christ.** He would begin every day with the exuberant expectation that this could be the day. Where would he see Him? The Temple courts seemed appropriate, and that is where he was **when the parents brought in the child Jesus to do for him what the custom of the Law required**.

Simeon's "song" is the last of the four nativity songs including those of Mary, Zechariah, and the angels. This song is sometimes referred to as the *Nunc Dimittis*, which are the first words in Latin: **"Sovereign Lord, as you have promised, you now dismiss your servant in peace. For my eyes have seen your salvation, which you have prepared in the sight of all people, a light for revelation to the Gentiles and for glory to your people Israel"** (2:29–32).

The first words from Simeon were to extol the sovereignty and faithfulness of God. Rather than the common word for *Lord*, he used a word found nowhere else in the Gospels, a word that Thayer says "denoted absolute ownership and uncontrolled power."[2] Simeon acknowledged he was a servant or slave of the Sovereign Lord. If God gives birth to a hope that resides deep within the human heart, He will satisfy that hope. Some could only hope that they would witness the coming of the Messiah, but Simeon had the promise from God that he would see Him in his lifetime. God fulfills what He promises, and it is time to celebrate when salvation hoped for is experienced—when what is promised is seen.

Simeon recognized the universal accessibility of God's salvation when he said Jesus would be a light for revelation to Gentiles. Jesus' incarnation was to provide atonement for all people: Jew and Gentile. The Jews were looking for *their* deliverer, not a savior of all people. We too can keep Jesus too close to ourselves, as *our* Savior.

Mary and Joseph **marveled at what was said about** Jesus (2:33). What they did not understand about Him had been revealed to Simeon and now communicated to them: **"This child is destined to cause the falling and rising of many in Israel"** (2:34). We are reminded of this aspect of Jesus when Peter wrote that to those who believe, Jesus is precious, but to those who reject Him He is "a stone that causes men to stumble and a rock that makes them fall" (1 Pet. 2:7–8). The destiny of individuals will be determined by their acceptance or rejection of Jesus.

Simeon directed a prophetic word to Mary: **"A sword will pierce your own soul too"** (Luke 2:35). This is perhaps the first word received by Mary that would temper her joy of giving birth to God's Son. The angel said Jesus would be a Savior, but not that He would have to die to be that Savior. Mary would experience this intense sorrow years later as she watched nails driven through her Son's hands and feet, and then a spear thrust into His side. There are great joys and deep pains that accompany being a parent, but nothing like what Mary would experience.

Anna (2:36), an eighty-four-year-old widow, was another faithful person who longed for the Messiah and who also spent her life around the Temple. She is described as **a prophetess**: one who lived close to God and was used by Him to speak to the people in His behalf. Anna **never left the temple but worshiped night and day, fasting and praying** (2:37). When Anna saw Joseph, Mary, and Jesus, she came **up to them** and **gave thanks to God**, speaking **about the child to all who were looking forward to the redemption of Jerusalem** (2:38). God revealed to her that she was in the presence of the object of her worship and the reason for her fasting and praying.

3. THE GROWTH OF CHILD JESUS 2:39–52

After **Joseph and Mary** completed the requirements of the law in Jerusalem, **they returned to Galilee to their own town of Nazareth** (2:39). There could be a significant amount of time between verses 38 and 39. It is possible that Mary and Joseph remained in Bethlehem for a period of time before fleeing to Egypt to escape Herod's slaughter of infant males (Matt. 2:13). They were devout persons, which they demonstrated by carefully doing **everything required by the Law of the Lord**. They were devoted to their child, as demonstrated in that under their nurture, Jesus

grew and became strong; he was filled with wisdom, and the grace of God was upon him (Luke 2:40). Physically, mentally, and spiritually He was being shaped for His redemptive mission. What an awesome sense of responsibility Joseph and Mary must have carried as they knew they were custodians of God's Son. We will never have the responsibility of nurturing the child Jesus, but every child is a God-given trust whose raising should be seriously undertaken. You never know what God has planned for the child in your care.

VISITING HIS FATHER'S HOUSE

The piety of Joseph and Mary was further demonstrated in that **every year** they **went to Jerusalem** (2:41). If possible, male Jews were to make the trip to Jerusalem for the three great feasts of Passover (or Unleavened Bread), Pentecost (or Weeks), and Tabernacles (Deut. 16:16), of which Passover was considered the most important. At age twelve or thirteen, every Jewish boy was to go through the ceremony that transitioned him into manhood—*bar mitzvah*. At this time, the young man would be allowed to move from the court of the women in the Temple and to worship with the men. Because of His age, it is reasonable to believe this visit to Jerusalem would become Jesus' bar mitzvah.

The Feast of Passover lasted for seven days and **after the Feast was over, . . . his parents were returning home** (2:43). After a day of travel, they discovered Jesus was missing from the group that was traveling together. It should not be considered that Joseph and Mary were negligent to travel some distance before noticing that Jesus was not with them. Pilgrims to Jerusalem often traveled in groups, with men walking separate from the women. If He had just had His bar mitzvah, Jesus would be considered to be a man and could have traveled with the women, the men, or relatives and friends in the caravan. Consequently, Joseph could have thought He was with Mary, and Mary could have thought He was with Joseph. Regardless, as soon as they realized He was not with them, **they went back to Jerusalem to look for him** (2:45). After three frantic days of searching, **they found him in the temple courts** (2:46).

Most twelve-year-olds do not intentionally hang out at church. It was no oversight that caused Jesus to miss the trip home. He *stayed* **behind** (2:43, italics added), suggesting He made an intentional choice. If your twelve-year-old intentionally missed the ride home and it took you three days to find him, what would you say when you found him? You are overjoyed that your child is safe, but upset that he put you through this. And you want to make sure he never does this again. It is probably good that Luke did not fill in all of the blanks regarding the reunion, but we are given a frantic mother's question: **"Son, why have you treated us like this?"** (2:48). Of course, this concern for their personal feelings followed a quick check to be sure He was okay.

The young man Jesus was not overly concerned that his parents were not around. He was found **sitting among the teachers, listening to them and asking them questions** (2:46). He would soon be a rabbi or teacher himself (Mark 9:5), so He was quite comfortable sitting with them and entering into their discussions. Even at age twelve, **everyone who heard him was amazed at his understanding and his answers** (Luke 2:47). Usually children His age are full of questions, but Jesus was full of answers.

When confronted by His parents, Jesus responded, **"Didn't you know I had to be in my Father's house?"** (2:49). This is the first record of an awareness of Jesus of His divine Sonship. In the presence of His earthly parents, He acknowledged that God was His Heavenly Father. He also served notice, through this event, that the work of His Heavenly Father would always take priority over any other work or any other relationship. Joseph and Mary **did not understand what he was** **saying to them** (2:50), but they must have realized that they could not and should not try to control His destiny. Though He had been fully subject to them, there was something about Him that was beyond their parental or control.

Jesus viewed the Temple as His Father's house. Solomon's Temple was built to replace the Tabernacle and was to be a dwelling place for God. It was destroyed by the Babylonians in the sixth century B.C., and the second Temple was constructed after the Jews' return from Babylonian captivity—only for it to be desecrated by the Romans in their occupation of Israel. A little over a decade before Christ's birth, Herod restored and expanded the Temple. It was the most sacred site in all Israel, and throughout Luke's gospel, Jesus demonstrated great affinity for the Temple—His Father's house. It might be called *Herod's* Temple, but it was in reality the *Father's House*.

BEGINNING THE SILENT YEARS

The visit to the Temple in Jerusalem is the last insight Luke gives us into the childhood of Jesus. He would now enter into eighteen years of silence. The only information we are given is that Jesus went back **to Nazareth with** His parents **and was obedient to them** (2:51). He was fully subject to the guidance and nurture of His earthly parents. We know nothing regarding the activities of His life during these years, only that He **grew in wisdom** (mentally) **and stature** (physically) **and in favor with God** (spiritually) **and men** (socially) (2:52). He lived a balanced life as He developed as a model for us in how to become fully human.

The picture Luke gives us of Jesus is that He grew up as a normal child. Joseph is described in Greek as a *tekton*, which is most commonly translated "carpenter" but can mean a stoneworker or any craftsman. Regardless of the trade, Jesus probably grew up learning that trade and working alongside His earthly father. As the Son of God, He dignified common labor. Though there was so much Mary did not understand, she cherished her relationship with her child, the Son of God, and the memories she built with Him. There was so much she could not talk about to others, so she **treasured all these things in her heart.**

ENDNOTES

1. Merrill Unger, *The New Unger's Bible Handbook* (Chicago: Moody Press, 1984), p. 403.

2. J. H. Thayer, *A Greek-English Lexicon of the New Testament* (Grand Rapids, Mich.: Associated Publishers and Authors, Inc., 1981), p. 130.

Part Two

Ministry in Galilee

LUKE 3:1–9:50

Luke 3:1 through 9:50 chronicles the ministry of Jesus in His home area. In Roman times, the region was divided into Judea, Samaria, and Galilee, which comprised the northern section of the country. Herod Antipas, son of Herod the Great, ruled Galilee as tetrarch during Jesus' ministry. Following Jesus' birth and time in Egypt, Joseph took his family back to Nazareth of Galilee, which was home to Jesus during at least thirty years of His life and was the first area on which He focused His ministry. The first three Gospels of the New Testament are chiefly taken up with Jesus' public ministry in this region, particularly in the villages of Nazareth and Capernaum.

The region of Galilee contained some very fertile areas, unlike Judah, which tended to be more barren. Many of Jesus' parables that utilized agricultural themes and illustrations taken from nature occurred in Galilee.

4

THE KINGDOM OF HEAVEN IS AT HAND

Luke 3:1-38

The Word of God came to John (3:2). There was good and bad news in this message from God: The kingdom of heaven was at hand, but repentance was required to be a part of that kingdom.

John would discover that preaching the convicting word from God can sometimes be costly. Nonetheless he received the Word of God and faithfully delivered it to anyone who would listen.

1. THE MINISTRY OF JOHN THE BAPTIST (3:1-20)

A CALL TO REPENTANCE

With his characteristic commitment to detail, Luke identified the beginning of John's ministry as being **in the fifteenth year of the reign of Tiberius Caesar** (3:1), along with a list of both political and religious leaders. Several of these individuals would become major players as the ministry of John and Jesus unfolded. Tiberius Caesar was a half-son of Caesar Augustus and ruled the Roman Empire. **Pontius Pilate** was appointed governor of Judea and would later be called upon to determine the fate of Jesus. Tradition says that Pilate was quite sensitive to the feelings and traditions of the Jews. Tetrarchs were persons appointed by Rome to give leadership to specific regions under the appointed governors. Several persons carried the name or title of **Herod**: Herod the Great was the brutal king who ordered the deaths of male children after the birth of Jesus and was the father of Herod Antipas; Herod Antipas was tetrarch of Galilee at this time and would later order the death of John the Baptist and mock Jesus before His death. There was only to be one high priest who was selected by God from among the descendents of Aaron, but the religious life of the Jews had become so politicized that two high priests, **Annas and Caiaphas** (3:2) are identified. Annas was most likely the Jewish-appointed high priest who was replaced by his son-in-law Caiaphas by Roman appointment. Both were to hear the trumped-up charges against Jesus that would lead to His crucifixion.

The word of God came to John (3:2). From the first chapter of the Bible, God establishes himself as one who communicates at various times using various means of getting His message to His creation (Heb. 1:1–2). It is an awesome responsibility to speak for God, which was the grand purpose of John's life—to be the carrier of God's Word. It may not appear that every so-called "messenger of God" receives the word of God before claiming to speak for Him, but John spoke with passion and power because he spoke the Word of God.

John began **preaching a baptism of repentance for the forgiveness of sins** (Luke 3:3). Jewish tradition practiced several ceremonial purification rites that involved washing with water that would result in a *declaration* of purity that was ceremonial, not actual. John's baptism called for something more radical. The water ritual of baptism was to be accompanied by true repentance and change of life.

The word *repent* is found thirteen times in Luke's gospel. Jesus said, "I have not come to call the righteous, but sinners to repentance" (5:32). Repentance is the prerequisite to forgiveness. It is twofold: a change of heart toward sin, and a change of direction away from sin toward God. He does not forgive those who are not sorry for their sin, and that sorrow must be strong enough to want to leave the practice of sin and never return to it.

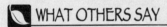

WHAT OTHERS SAY

REPENTANCE

"Repentance is a heart sorrow for our past misdeeds, and a sincere resolution and an endeavor to the utmost of our power, to conform all our actions to the law of God. It does not consist in one single act of sorrow, but in doing works meet for repentance; in a sincere obedience to the law of Christ for the remainder of our lives."

—John Locke

John's baptism was not the means of salvation, but the gateway through which persons would be prepared for the further revelation of God in Christ. John said there was something more and better to come (3:16).

In what we call the Great Commission, Jesus charged His disciples to baptize converts "in the name of Father, Son and Holy Spirit" (Matt. 28:19). John's baptism was a call for repentance. Christian baptism is a call for relationship with God, identification with Christ, and appropriation of all of the privileges of the Atonement through the ministry of the Holy Spirit.

The forgiveness of sins is the grandest possibility God could ever offer us. We are all sinners who need to be forgiven, and that need is greater than can be met with the sacrifice of an animal during an annual Day of Atonement. We need our sinfulness to be adequately dealt with by forgiving and cleansing grace. John called people to repent and pointed them to Jesus, "the Lamb of God, who *takes away* the sin of the world!" (John 1:29, italics added). The Scripture says that "The reason the Son of God appeared was to *destroy* the devil's work" (1 John 3:8, italics added), not just provide a temporary "fix." The reason John appeared was to prepare the way for the Son of God, not just to baptize people. He fulfilled a prophecy of **Isaiah . . . : "A voice of one calling in the desert, 'Prepare the way for the Lord'"** (Luke 3:4; Isa. 40:3). John became popular, but his purpose was to prepare the way for someone greater.

John preached that **all mankind will see God's salvation** (Luke 3:6). The Word of God was for all humankind, not just the Jews. Luke's immediate readers were Greeks—outsiders that he wanted to know were included in God's salvation. The Word from God is that salvation is for everyone—including you and me. Everyone can see and experience His salvation, regardless of ethnicity, culture, gender, status, or anything else that could be viewed to be a barrier.

John's preaching drew great crowds, but not everyone came with a desire to enter the kingdom of God. Some, whom he called a **brood of vipers**, were motivated by a desire **to flee from the coming wrath** (3:7). While a desire to escape punishment is legitimate, God wants us to be drawn to Him by love, not driven to Him by fear. Escaping the coming wrath requires repentance of our sin and acceptance of God's grace.

Relationship with God does not result from human heritage, and John warned that being **children of Abraham** would not save them. God's children are to **produce fruit in keeping with repentance** (3:8). Judgment will come to those who continue in sinful practices though claiming to be related to God: **every tree that does not produce good fruit will be cut down and thrown into the fire** (3:9). John's message was that salvation and righteousness are proven in the activities of life. If you are not demonstrating goodness in your actions, you are not a part of the kingdom of God. God's salvation is not ceremonial but transformational.

WHAT SHOULD WE DO?

Stung by John's rebuke and convicted by their sin, people in **the crowd asked, "What should we do then?"** (3:10). The Word of God is not intended to simply make people feel guilty. True conviction always leads to hopeful action. When the Holy Spirit convicts, "he will convict the world of guilt in regard to sin and righteousness and judgment . . . [and] guide you into all truth" (John 16:8, 13). No messenger of God should leave you in your guilt, because God's message always offers hope and help. Every convicted listener should ask, "What should I do then?" and every messenger of God should provide his hearers with God's remedy for sin and guilt. The preacher who majors in guilt and minors in grace is not a true messenger of God.

The Word from God demands a response. When people hear the Word of God they can respond in a variety of ways, but seldom can they receive it and remain neutral about it. You can receive it and act upon it; you can resist it; and you can ponder it in your heart and delay a response. The decision to delay is dangerous because over time you can become calloused and can silence the convicting voice of the Holy Spirit that is calling for you to respond; opportunities in which the influences and climate encourage your response may not return; and rationalizations and excuses can be developed that convince you to persist in directions and activities that are contrary to God's purpose. Immediate, obedient action in response to the Word of God is always best.

There were those who listened to John and responded, "What should we do?" Luke reports three different groups that asked that question: **the crowd** (Luke 3:10), **the tax collectors** (3:12), and **some soldiers** (3:14). John's reply was different in each case, but always involved an ethical action they needed to take, demonstrating that the kingdom of God involves concern for the social needs of others. The crowd was exhorted to look for the one among them who needed clothes or food and **share with him**. The tax collectors were exhorted not to **collect any more than** they were **required to**. The soldiers were exhorted not to **extort money** or **accuse people falsely**, and to **be content with** their **pay**.

LIFE CHANGE

TRUE TRANSFORMATION

Any lasting transformation of the human heart requires changes only God can make. However, God will not do His work until we have made the changes only we can make. Forgiveness, justification, and regeneration through the grace of God require us to first change our minds about our sin. Repentance is more than being sorry we got caught. We must be sorry that we violated the law of God and damaged relationship with Him. We must determine that with the help of the Holy Spirit, we will turn from our sin and turn toward God, never to go back to our previous unrighteous acts, attitudes, and associations.

The Holy Spirit accompanies the Word of God, producing conviction in the sinful heart and prompting the question, "What should I do?" When you learn what is required for entering the kingdom of God, you must take action.

A GREATER BAPTISM BY A GREATER PERSON

The history of the Israelites contains cyclical patterns of falling away from God, experiencing His corrective judgment, being challenged to repent, and returning to Him. Often, God's corrective judgment was implemented at the hand of a hostile power that would conquer and oppress them. These times of oppression would heighten Israel's longing for the Messiah, one who would deliver them and establish a reign of peace. This was the climate in Judah when John appeared on the scene: **The people were waiting expectantly** for the Messiah. Many of them wondered **if John might possibly be the Christ** (3:15). A lesser person might have seized an opportunity to benefit by pretending to be someone he was not, but John was quick to establish his place and purpose in the plan of God. He said, **"One more powerful than I will come"** (3:16).

John said the One to come would baptize them **with the Holy Spirit and with fire** (3:16). Fourteen times the Holy Spirit is mentioned in Luke's gospel. Persons were filled with the Holy Spirit: John (1:15), Elizabeth (1:41), Zechariah (1:67), and Jesus (4:1). The Holy Spirit came upon persons: Mary (1:35), Simeon (2:25), and descended upon Jesus (3:22). The Holy Spirit revealed truth to Simeon (2:26). Believers will be baptized with the Holy Spirit (3:16) and receive Him as a gift from God (11:13). Jesus was full of joy through the Holy Spirit (10:21). He will teach us what to say when we need it (12:12).

It is clear that the presence and power of the Holy Spirit is essential to our lives as followers of Christ.

John's baptism was with water and was largely symbolic. Jesus' baptism was to be with the Holy Spirit and fire. It was transformational. One of the manifestations of the coming of the Holy Spirit on Pentecost was "tongues of fire" that rested on the heads of those in the Upper Room (Acts 2:3). Paul exhorted the Thessalonians, "Do not put out the Spirit's fire" (1 Thess. 5:19), which suggests the energizing, purifying ministry of the Holy Spirit. Beyond these two positive references, almost without exception the numerous other times *fire* appears in the New Testament suggests God's judgment against sin. "God is a consuming fire," the writer to the Hebrews said (Heb. 12:29). Jesus said, "I have come to bring fire on the earth, and how I wish it were already kindled!" (Luke 12:49). The good news of salvation is also a word of judgment against sin. John said God will **gather the wheat into his barn, but he will burn up the chaff with unquenchable fire** (3:17). Righteousness requires judgment that will separate wheat and chaff.

THE PRICE FOR SPEAKING THE TRUTH

John **exhorted the people and preached the good news to them** (3:18). The call to repentance is good news because it includes the message of forgiveness. But the call to repentance may cause the messenger to point out unrepented sin. John stopped preaching and went to meddling when he **rebuked Herod** for **all the evil things he had done**, along with evil he had tolerated by **Herodias, his brother's wife** (3:19). All of the Herods were infamous as being incestuous, murderous, and deceitful. John took aim at unrighteous behavior in the top levels of Jewish life, and found it a dangerous thing when he hit the target.

Pointing out a person's sin can lead that person to acknowledge and confess the sin, or it can cause the person to become angry and take revenge on the messenger. Herod did not take kindly to the rebuke, so **he locked John up in prison** (3:20), bringing his preaching and baptizing ministry to an abrupt end. John's name appears again in the seventh chapter when he sent some of his followers to Jesus for assurance that He was the Christ, and again in the ninth chapter when Herod said that he had beheaded John (9:9). We have to go to Matthew 14:3–11 to pick up the sordid story surrounding the John's death.

2. THE BAPTISM AND GENEALOGY OF JESUS (3:21–38)

FATHER, SON, AND HOLY SPIRIT

Obviously, the events of verses 21–22 occurred before John was imprisoned. Jesus joined the crowds who gathered along the banks of the Jordan River, listening, repenting, and being baptized. To the surprise of John, Jesus stepped out of the crowd and asked to be baptized. According to other Gospel records, John showed immediate resistance to the request. It is difficult to know how much he knew or understood about the nature of Jesus, but he sensed he was standing in the presence of One greater than himself.

The question must be raised as to why the sinless Jesus would join repenting sinners in being baptized. There are several reasons: (1) Jesus identified himself with humanity and sin; (2) as suggested in Romans 6:3–4, baptism was symbolic of His death and resurrection; (3) in taking upon himself the sins of the whole world, He was participating in the acts of repentance on behalf of all sinners; and (4) He endorsed baptism as an initiatory rite for all His followers. Primarily because of this endorsement, we observe baptism along with the Lord's Supper today as the two sacraments of the Church.

Something spectacular happened while Jesus was being baptized. Heaven **opened and the Holy Spirit descended on him in bodily form like a dove** (Luke 3:21–22). Then a voice from heaven was heard to say, **"You are my Son, whom I love; with you I am well pleased."** This is one of those few occasions in Scripture when the three persons of the Holy Trinity are all recognized—the Father, the Son, and the Holy Spirit. This was an inaugural event in the ministry of Jesus, and each person of the Godhead was visibly or audibly present. Jesus had earlier indicated His awareness of His Heavenly Father when He visited the Temple at twelve years of age (2:42–49). Earthly children need the affirmation, affection, and assurances that come from their father and, whether the only Son of God *needed* it or not, His Heavenly Father affirmed His relationship, declared His love, and assured Jesus of His Father's pleasure. What a fire this must have kindled in the spirit of Jesus. Armed with the word from heaven, He was ready to begin His ministry.

The Father has provided the same assurances to us that He did to Jesus. His Spirit comes to bear witness to us that we belong to Him, that He loves us, and that we please Him.

Following the Temple visit recorded in Luke 2 when Jesus was twelve years of age, nothing is known about Him except that He "grew in wisdom and stature, and in favor with God and men" (2:52). He **was about thirty years old when he began his ministry** (3:23), leaving his earthly father's workshop to give himself to His Heavenly Father's business. Numbers 4:3 suggests that priests may have begun their ministry when thirty years of age. Regardless, Jesus engaged himself in patient preparation for His public ministry, spending thirty years experiencing those things that would qualify Him for His priestly ministry: "For we do not have a high priest who is unable to sympathize with our weaknesses, but we have one who has been tempted in every way, just as we are—yet was without sin" (Heb. 4:15).

ROOTS OF THE FAMILY TREE

Next-door neighbors thought nothing more but that Jesus **was the son . . . of Joseph**. It may have been that for over thirty years only Mary and Joseph knew the secret that Joseph was not the real father. Luke has reason, in his commitment to detail, to include the family tree of Jesus in his record. Matthew's gospel contains a family tree as well, but it is different, tracing through Joseph back to Abraham, the father of Israel in whom all the families of the earth are blessed (Gen. 12:3). Luke's gospel emphasizes the unique God and man nature of Jesus—He was God in the flesh—and his genealogy traces the human ancestry of Jesus through Mary back to Adam. **Heli** was actually the father of Mary—the father-in-law of Joseph. Jesus **was the son . . . of Joseph . . . the son of Adam, the son of God** (3:23, 38). Jesus is the second Adam (1 Cor. 15:45), the Son of God.

The family tree contains the names of notables of Jewish history such as **Levi, Judah, Joseph, David, Jesse, Boaz, Isaac, Abraham, Noah, Methuselah, Enoch,** and **Adam** (3:24, 30–32, 34, 36–38). It also includes unknown persons, such as **Jannai, Maath, Semein,** and **Cosam** (3:24, 26, 28). Jesus identifies with all of us, regardless of status or notoriety. Because of what Jesus has done, we can be grafted into the family of God and have our names included in the spiritual lineage of Jesus.

5

FULL OF THE SPIRIT

Luke 4:1-44

As Jesus began His ministry, He was "full of the Holy Spirit" (Luke 4:1). This is a blessing we, too, can experience. Ephesians 1:23 speaks of "the fullness of him who fills everything in every way." It is in the nature of God to fill things, and it is in the nature of sin to empty things. Ephesians 3:19 exhorts us to know the love of God so that we might "be filled to the measure of all the fullness of God." God is entirely self-sufficient—He lacks nothing—and out of His fullness and adequacy, He imparts fullness to us. We are instructed to be filled with the Spirit as a part of the blessings provided to us through God's grace (Eph. 3:18).

We might expect that since Jesus was one with the Father and the Spirit, He would be "full of the Holy Spirit." However, having been "made in human likeness" (Phil. 2:7), He was subject to the same struggles faced by each of us. He demonstrated for us the need for the power of the Holy Spirit in dealing with them. The fullness of the Spirit is needed if we are to experience full salvation, be victorious over human weaknesses and sins, and be effective in our service. It is not a take-it-or-leave-it option, but a don't-go-without-it necessity.

1. THE TEMPTATION OF JESUS (4:1–13)

LED BY THE SPIRIT

When the time had arrived for Jesus to begin His earthly ministry, He was **full of the Holy Spirit** and was **led by the Spirit** (4:1). It was during this spiritual highpoint of Jesus' life that He was **tempted by the devil** (4:2). Temptation often comes to us on the heels of spiritual highs, as illustrated by Elijah, who experienced extreme depression immediately after the great display of his God's reality and power on Mount Carmel (1 Kings 18–19).

One of the activities of the Holy Spirit is to lead us. Jesus **was led by the Spirit in the desert** (4:1). Our first inclination is that if the Spirit leads us, our path will always be along pleasant streams, but there are occasions when we enter the desert as a part of God's plan. It is good to know that even there we are led by the Spirit.

Most likely, Jesus was baptized in the Jordan River near where it empties into the Dead Sea. It would not be far to the desert or wilderness area of Judea where He was led by the Spirit and where His temptation would begin. The desert would be a place for Jesus to prepare himself for His ministry in solitude, away from distraction.

Jesus spent **forty days** in the desert where **he was tempted by the devil** (4:2). It was not a momentary, fleeting temptation, but intense and long lasting. The Scripture identifies the source of His temptation as being the devil. We often give the devil credit for showing up in our lives and doing bad things to us, but he is not omnipresent, and temptation does not necessarily come directly from him. However, it would seem the devil appeared to Jesus personally, in a visible form, or at least he was spiritually perceived by Jesus. James says that the genesis of sin resides within our fallen natures and does not need the devil to be present for us to be tempted: ". . . each one is tempted when, by his own evil desire, he is dragged away and enticed" (James 1:14). Jesus was the unique God-man who had taken upon himself human nature without our fallen nature, so he had no inner "evil desire" to become the focus of the devil's enticement. The devil would direct his temptation toward issues surrounding Jesus' divinity and the natural human appetites that were a part of Jesus' God-man nature.

Temptation is not sin, but rather an enticement *to* sin. As long as we resist temptation and do our best to cultivate a pure life in thought, association, and habit, we should not carry guilt because we are often tempted. The experience of temptation is common to all humankind and does not preclude falling into sin. We have the great promise: "No temptation has seized you except what is common to man. And God is faithful; he will not let you be tempted beyond what you can bear. But when you are tempted, he will also provide a way out so that you can stand up under it" (1 Cor. 10:13). We may consider our time of temptation to be unbearable, but God not only promises to help us bear it, but He will provide a way out of it that retains our moral, ethical, and spiritual purity.

Why was Jesus tempted? Was it possible for Him to sin? If He would fully understand our humanity and participate in it, He would have to experience what we experience, including temptation. We are encouraged in our struggles with temptation through the realization that Jesus was "tempted in every way, just as we are—yet was without sin" (Heb. 4:15). He did not crumble under temptation's pressure. He is now our High Priest who, because of His identification with human weaknesses, is able to intercede with the Father on our behalf. He left us an example, and we are to "follow in his steps. 'He committed no sin, and no deceit was found in his mouth'" (1 Pet. 2:21–22). However, it is sobering to realize that if Satan believed he could cause the Son of God to fall, he surely must think we are easy prey.

LED BY THE DEVIL

It may be difficult for us to read within the same paragraph that Jesus was "led by the Spirit" and "led by the devil," but that's the way it was with Him, and that's the way it often is with us. It is the earthly struggle of the immortal soul, and our destiny is determined by which leading we allow to establish our direction.

Jesus observed a forty-day fast during which **he ate nothing . . . and at the end of them he was hungry** (Luke 4:2). Moses also fasted forty days when he met with God in the mountain (Ex. 34:28). Fasting is a spiritual discipline that often accompanies a deep and sincere desire to know God more intimately and experience His intervention in difficult situations.

71

Fasting is voluntarily abstaining from eating any food, or selected foods. It is the denial of a natural appetite with the intent of creating a greater sensitivity to and appetite for spiritual things. Though the denial of the natural appetite for food may temporarily dull the desire for food, the body must have food to survive and the fast must ultimately be broken. It is obvious that after forty days Jesus would be hungry, and the devil approached Him at this point of human need and physical weakness. Jesus had a natural appetite that needed to be met, and the devil tempted Him to meet it through illegitimate means—which is a tactic the devil often uses with us.

The devil said to Jesus, **"If you are the Son of God, tell this stone to become bread"** (Luke 4:3). Jesus could easily have turned a stone into bread and met a real need in His life, which would not have violated any law of God. But if He did, He would be responding to a challenge from the devil rather than responding to the leading of the Spirit. He would act because of a challenge to prove His divinity—"*If* you are the Son of God"—but the devil already knew He was the Son of God, and turning stones into bread would not prove anything. The devil wasn't looking for evidence in order to believe, but for an opportunity to force Jesus into a misuse of His power to meet personal human need. Our strengths can cause our fall as easily as our weaknesses. If our enemy cannot cause us to fall by attacking our weaknesses, he will attempt to get us to use our strengths inappropriately.

Jesus answered the challenge of the devil by saying, **"It is written: 'Man does not live on bread alone'"** (Luke 4:4; see Deut. 7:2–3).

Jesus reached back into Jewish history to quote a word from God that had direct application to the present situation. Our sword of defense against the attack of Satan is the knowledge and application of the Word of God (Eph. 6:17). The psalmist said, "I have hidden your word in my heart that I might not sin against you" (Ps. 119:11). Jesus provided an example for dealing with temptation by responding to each of the temptations by quoting Scripture.

The devil did not stop with one unsuccessful attack. He took Jesus **up to a high place and showed him in an instant all the kingdoms of the world** (Luke 4:5). Some think that it was to the summit of Mount Pisgah that Jesus was led, the same place where Moses was taken to see the land

God had promised His people (Deut. 3:27). From this high place Moses was allowed to see the land in each direction—land that, though governed by several different powers, was promised to be the possession of the children of Israel. Now Jesus stood on that summit and heard the devil say, **"I will give you all their authority and splendor, for it has been given to me, and I can give it to anyone I want to. So if you worship me, it will all be yours"** (Luke 4:6–7). Moses saw the land but was not allowed to enter into it. It was a promise fulfilled under the leadership of his successor, Joshua. The suggestion might have been strong that Jesus, though sent to be King, would look out over the kingdoms of the world but never become King unless He would worship the devil.

Jesus did not deny the devil's claim that the authority and splendor of the world had been given to him. He later called Satan the "prince of this world" (John 12:31), and Paul called him the "ruler of the kingdom of the air" (Eph. 2:2). Our fallen world, except where the kingdom of God is allowed to reign, lives under the "dominion of darkness" (Col. 1:13). The temptation presented to Jesus was for power and authority over the kingdoms of the world. He would later say, "All authority in heaven and on earth has been given to me" (Matt. 28:18), not because the devil gave it to Him, but because the Father bestowed it upon Him as the King of a Kingdom that is not of this world (John 18:36).

Jesus again quoted Scripture, responding to the temptation with **"It is written: 'Worship the Lord your God and serve him only'"** (Luke 4:8). There are occasions when minor ethical or moral indiscretions may seem to us to be necessary to gain power and authority. These indiscretions would not seem big enough to say that we *worship* the devil, but they do constitute the "devil's schemes" (Eph. 6:11) that are designed to bring us under his dominion. No indiscretion that causes us to move from being led by the Spirit to being led by the devil is small.

For his third attempt to bring Jesus down, the devil led Jesus to the highest point of the Temple in Jerusalem—the center of the worship of God. The tactic of the devil now became, "Okay, if You say You worship God, let's go to the place of worship and see if God will respond to You." Standing at this high point, the devil said, **"If you are the Son of God, . . . throw yourself down from here. For it is written: 'He will command**

his angels concerning you to guard you carefully; they will lift you up in their hands, so that you will not strike your foot against a stone'" (Luke 4:9–11). Jesus had quoted Scripture as a response to each temptation. The devil knew Scripture, too, and decided to use it as a means of testing both Jesus and God. Original sin grew out of Satan tempting Adam and Eve to question the word of God. His approach toward Jesus was to again put the Word of God to the test.

The enemy of our soul would like to use God's Word against Him by twisting its meaning or confusing its application. You have to cringe at times when believers take a promise in the Bible out of its context and apply it indiscriminately to their situation, believing God will respond in their lives exactly like He promised to do in a person's life in the Bible. The question is not whether God *can* respond in the same way; it is whether He *will* or whether His commitment to act in the situation in the biblical account in any way applies to the present situation. God's promises are true, when spoken by Him to specific persons in specific situations. To open your Bible, point at a promise, claim it for yourself, and hold God to it is a dangerous practice.

If Jesus would have thrown himself off the high place, could God have sent angels to catch Him before He reached the rocks below? Yes, He *could* have. *Would* He? *Should* He? It would be a mistake for us to take the biblical encouragement to trust in the care and protection of God to mean we could jump off any high place and believe God has committed himself to always catch us so we won't get hurt. It doesn't work that way. But if the devil can cause us to question God's care and protection, he has driven a wedge in our trust of God's Word. Again, Jesus quoted Scripture and said, **"It says: 'Do not put the Lord your God to the test'"** (4:12). Our inappropriate application of Scripture might well constitute a test of God.

Three strikes and you are out is a rule that is not exactly practiced when it comes to temptation. This was only the first inning, and the devil was only temporarily defeated. **When the devil had finished all this tempting, he left him until an opportune time** (4:13). The season of severe temptation was over, but the devil would be back—in other forms and in other ways. There are opportune times for the enemy to tempt us, and his best times may correlate with our worst times. The time Jesus

74

spent with the Father in the desert prepared Him for the time with the devil, a practice He repeated throughout His ministry that should be our practice as well.

2. THE ANNOUNCEMENT OF HIS MISSION (4:14–21)

BEGINNING A TEACHING MINISTRY

Jesus was "full of the Holy Spirit" and was "led by the Spirit." From the time of temptation, **Jesus returned to Galilee in the power of the Spirit** (4:14). The word *power* is the same word used in Acts 1:8, where Jesus promised His disciples, "You will receive *power* when the Holy Spirit comes on you; and you will be my witnesses in Jerusalem, and in all Judea and Samaria, and to the ends of the earth." The same power of the Spirit that brought dynamic effectiveness to the ministry of Jesus is promised to us as we minister in His name. We too can experience the fullness, leadership, and power of the Spirit. The fullness of the Spirit relates to our spiritual formation—issues of character. The leadership of the Spirit relates to our agenda—issues of motivation and direction. The power of the Spirit relates to our service—issues of ability and effectiveness.

The anonymity of Joseph's shop quickly disappeared as **news about** [Jesus] **spread through the whole countryside. He taught in their synagogues, and everyone praised him** (4:14).

LIFE CHANGE
POWER OF THE SPIRIT

Christians do not have to face temptation or the challenges of service in their own strength or limited abilities. The power of the Holy Spirit is available. Paul prayed that believers would be strengthened by God's power in their inner being, where life's real battles are won or lost (Eph. 3:16), and he gave the assurance that God "is able to do immeasurably more than all we ask or imagine, according to his power that is at work within us" (Eph. 3:20).

The world is hungry for good news, and good news can travel far and fast. Jesus taught in synagogues, which were located in every village where a significant number of Jews lived. Large cities in Palestine might have had more than one synagogue where Jews gathered each Sabbath for prayer and reading God's Word, and during the week when people would congregate for study and worship. The synagogue was the spiritual and social center of the community. Jesus had a regular pattern of going to the synagogue, joining others in the traditions of worship, reading the Scriptures, and teaching the Word and way of God. Since He is the Truth (John 14:6), He knew the subject matter well, and He taught it as a master teacher.

ANNOUNCING HIS MISSION

Jesus went to Nazareth, where He had been brought up, **and on the Sabbath day he went into the synagogue, as was his custom. And he stood up to read** (4:16). Nazareth was His hometown, so He had gone to this synagogue all of His life. Apparently, those who offered to read the Scripture would stand and be given the prescribed lesson to read to those assembled.

The person in charge of the synagogue handed a scroll to Jesus, who unrolled it so He could read. The scroll was that of the prophet Isaiah, and Jesus found where it was written: **The Spirit of the Lord is on me, because he has anointed me** (Luke 4:18). The Scriptures consisted of the Law, the Prophets, and the Writings. Jesus chose one of the significant messianic passages in the Prophets, Isaiah 61:1–2, from which to read. This passage and its context would have been familiar to the listeners—a favorite reading because it spoke of judgment against Israel's enemies and redemption for God's people. Just prior to the passage that was read by Jesus, the prophet said, "The Redeemer will come to Zion" (Isa. 59:20). "Arise, shine, for your light has come, and the glory of the LORD rises upon you" (60:1). "Lift up your eyes" (60:4). The people longed for prophecies like these to be fulfilled, and Jesus was about to tell them that He was the Redeemer about which Isaiah spoke.

Isaiah wrote that the Spirit of the Lord would be upon the Redeemer and He would be *anointed* for His ministry. Anointing was a rite performed by a representative of God, usually involving oil poured on the head of an individual who was set apart for divine use. The anointing conferred divine empowerment to accomplish the assignment. The

Messiah—the Anointed One—is a direct derivative of the Hebrew word used in this passage. Luke would later record, "God *anointed* Jesus of Nazareth with the Holy Spirit and power, and . . . he went around doing good and healing all who were under the power of the devil, because God was with him" (Acts 10:38, italics added).

The Redeemer was anointed **to preach good news to the poor** (Luke 4:18). Reference to the "good news" is prominent throughout Luke's gospel. The angel proclaimed good news of great joy upon the birth of Jesus. John preached the good news. Jesus repeatedly spoke of His mission to preach "the good news of the kingdom of God" (4:43; 7:22; 8:1; 16:16). A world lost in the consequences of its own sinfulness was hungry for good news.

Good news often is delayed in getting to the poor. The rich have their own set of difficulties, but Jesus had great affinity for the needs of the poor, perhaps because He was raised in relative poverty. Luke's gospel speaks often of the plight of the poor—and their privileged place in the kingdom (6:20). Those who wanted to follow Christ were instructed to give to the poor (11:41; 12:33; 18:22). The poor were to be given special invitation to banquets (14:13), including the great banquet of the Kingdom (14:21). Jesus took special notice of the offering of the poor widow (Luke 21:2–3), saying that she gave more out of her poverty than any of the rich worshippers. With few things to celebrate, it was time that the poor hear the good news that the kingdom of God was within their reach.

The Redeemer was sent **to proclaim freedom for the prisoners** (4:18). Every person's heart yearns to be free, but freedom is not always experienced because sin imprisons and enslaves. Our sin results in self-destructive behaviors, harmful habits, webs of deceit, dysfunctional relationships, and inescapable consequences—prisons of our own making. Jesus would later say, "Everyone who sins is a slave to sin . . . if the Son sets you free, you will be free indeed" (John 8:34, 36). The ministry of the Messiah is to free the imprisoned, of which all of us qualify.

The Redeemer was sent to proclaim **recovery of sight for the blind** (Luke 4:18). Jesus would fulfill this ministry in both the physical and spiritual arena. In His healing ministry, "Jesus cured many who had diseases, sicknesses and evil spirits, and gave sight to many who were blind" (Luke 7:21). After healing a blind man, Jesus said, "For judgment I have come into this world, so that the blind will see and those who see will become blind. Some Pharisees who were with him heard him say this and asked, 'What? Are we blind too?'" (John 9:39–40). Jesus left the question dangling without an answer, exposing the greater issue of spiritual blindness. Zechariah spoke of the Savior's ministry of recovery of sight for the blind when he said, "the rising sun will come to us from heaven to shine on those living in darkness and in the shadow of death, to guide our feet" (Zech. 1:78). John also wrote, "In him was life, and that life was the light of men. The light shines in the darkness, but the darkness has not understood it" (John 1:4–5). There is no greater blindness than in those who have eyes that do not see because they love darkness rather than light (John 3:19).

The Redeemer was sent **to release the oppressed** (Luke 4:18). The Jews had a history of oppression at the hands of those who conquered them in battle. The occupation of their land by the Romans was most recent, having been preceded hundreds of years earlier with captivity by the Babylonians. Israel longed for a Messiah who would release them from the oppression of hostile kingdoms and governments. This longing and expectation would cause many to reject Jesus because He was not the political liberator for whom they waited. However, oppression can be spiritual as well as political. Beyond demonic oppression, people endure the oppressing affliction of worry, stress, and relational hostility. It is wonderful to experience the release that comes when the peace of Christ occupies your mind and spirit. His promise to everyone who places trust in Him is "Peace I leave with you; my peace I give you" (John 14:27).

The Redeemer was sent **to proclaim the year of the Lord's favor** (Luke 4:19). Every fiftieth year the Jews celebrated the favor of God in their lives with the Year of Jubilee, during which wonderful things happened. If you had a mortgage against your land, it was forgiven. If you had become enslaved, you were set free. If you owed money, the obligation was erased. The people were to live in peace, plenty, and freedom. In fulfilling Isaiah's prophecy, Jesus was fulfilling the blessings of the Year of Jubilee, declaring it to be the year of the Lord's favor.

Jesus recited this litany of blessings that were to be available to God's people through the coming Redeemer, and it caused everyone in the synagogue to focus on Him. Then the shocking pronouncement was made: **"Today this scripture is fulfilled in your hearing"** (4:21). Customarily, after the Scripture was read it was time for teaching and making application of what had been read. The reader would take his seat, and the rabbi would stand to teach. But with the attention of those in the synagogue focused on Him, Jesus declared himself to be the fulfillment of the prophecy. He was the Redeemer, God's Anointed One.

Isaiah's prophecy beautifully captured the essence of Jesus' ministry. He came as God's Chosen One, anointed and empowered by the Spirit, to bring release, recovery, and a reason for rejoicing. His mission was at the same time present and physical as well as future and spiritual. He would spend three years teaching, preaching, and healing—offering hope, freedom, and wholeness. But this was only a part of, and symbolic of, His greater mission of redemption that would be made possible through the cross. He was more than a good teacher. He was more than a miracle healer. He was to be the Savior of His people.

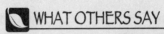

WHAT OTHERS SAY

TRUTH IS A PERSON

"Fundamentally, our Lord's message was Himself. He did not come merely to preach a Gospel; He himself is that Gospel. He did not come merely to give bread; He said, 'I am the bread.' He did not come merely to shed light; He said, 'I am the light.' He did not come merely to show the door; He said, 'I am the door.' He did not come merely to name a shepherd; He said, 'I am the shepherd.' He did not come merely to point the way; He said, 'I am the way, the truth, and the life.'"

—J. Sidlow Baxter

3. REJECTED AT HOME (4:22–30)

All spoke well of him (4:22), but as He would later say, "Woe to you when all men speak well of you, for that is how their fathers treated the false prophets" (Luke 6:26). He was a true prophet, and too quickly the crowds would turn against Him. **They were amazed at the gracious words that came from his lips** (4:22), but truth can also have a sharp side to it. Jesus was "full of grace and truth" (John 1:14), the perfect blend of the two. Truth can sometimes be harsh; grace can sometimes be soft. Effective teaching tempers truth with grace and toughens grace with truth.

While the people were amazed at the gracious words of Jesus, He knew they were unprepared to listen to and accept the truth about themselves and their need for a Savior. He said to them, **"no prophet is accepted in his hometown"** (Luke 4:24). Israel was God's chosen people, and they expected Him to come through for them when they were in trouble. They were *insiders* with God, and all others were *outsiders*. Jesus reached back into their history to remind them of two occasions when God's blessing was given to outsiders rather than insiders. Elijah was sent to a widow in Zarephath during a time of severe famine throughout the land of Israel, and while she entertained Elijah, her oil and flour were miraculously multiplied, though she was not a Jew. And Elisha was God's instrument to bring healing to Naaman the Syrian, while many with leprosy in Israel went without healing. There were others who needed Jesus, and if He were rejected in His hometown, and He would go to the outsiders.

Things began to turn bad in the synagogue as the people became upset by the words of Jesus, and they **drove him out of the town** (4:29). The adoration and amazement quickly turned to anger and rejection when Jesus suggested they were not prepared to accept Him and His teaching. They took Him up a hill and intended **to throw him down the cliff** (4:29).

Miraculously, Jesus **walked right through the crowd and went on his way** (4:29). Sadly, He was rejected by His hometown people and moved on with no record that He ever returned to the town. "His way" would not bring him back home. God comes to us where we are, but if we reject Him, He may go on His way, leaving us in our sin. Salvation occurs when God comes to us and we come to Him. When we persist in going our way, He may also go on His way.

4. THE AUTHORITY OF JESUS (4:31–41)

AUTHORITY IN HIS MESSAGE

From Nazareth, Jesus **went down to Capernaum, a town in Galilee**. The town was located on the northern side of the Sea of Galilee and was a center for much of Jesus' ministry, along with Bethsaida. Matthew records, "Leaving Nazareth, he went and lived in Capernaum" (Matt. 4:13).

As was His custom, Jesus went to the synagogue on the Sabbath and **began to teach the people. They were amazed at his teaching, because his message had authority** (Luke 4:21–32). Matthew records that multitudes followed Jesus after His Sermon on the Mount "because he taught as one who had authority, and not as their teachers of the law" (Matt. 7:29). Jesus taught with authority because He taught truth; He knew His audience; He did not whitewash the truth to accommodate His audience; and the power of the Holy Spirit accompanied the delivery of the message, applying its truth to the listeners. The result was that those who listened "praised him" (Luke 4:15) and "were amazed" (4:22, 32) by His teaching.

AUTHORITY OVER EVIL SPIRITS

Not only did Jesus speak with authority, He demonstrated His authority within the spirit world. **In the synagogue there was a man possessed by a demon, an evil spirit** (4:33). Thirty-nine times demons, evil spirits, the devil, and Satan are referenced in Luke's gospel. At least five cases of deliverance of persons possessed by demons or evil spirits are referenced, besides the word in verse 41 that "demons came out of many people." When Jesus ". . . called the Twelve together, he gave them power and authority to drive out all demons" (Luke 9:1). It would appear that demon possession was real and somewhat prevalent in Jesus' day. With authority Jesus spoke to the demon—**"Come out of him!"**—and the demon **came out**, amazing the people that Jesus could do this **with authority and power** (4:35).

AUTHORITY OVER SICKNESSES

Jesus left the synagogue and went to the home of Simon (4:38), where He would demonstrate His authority over sickness. When He arrived at Simon's house, He found **Simon's mother-in-law** sick with a very **high fever.** Jesus **rebuked the fever** in her, **it** immediately **left her,** and **she got up at once and began to wait on them** (4:39). This is the first physical healing recorded by Luke, and it demonstrates the compassion Jesus had for the sick along with His ability to heal. Hearing about this, **people brought . . . all who had various kinds of sickness, and laying his hands on each one, he healed them** (4:40). There did not seem to be any prerequisite for their

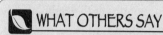

WHAT OTHERS SAY

HEALING

"Ultimate healing and the glorification of the body are certainly among the blessings of Calvary for the believing Christian. Immediate healing is not guaranteed. God can heal any disease, but He is not obligated to do so."

—Warren Wiersbe

healing and no selection process for who could receive it. Jesus simply laid His hands on the sick and healed every one of them.

Throughout His ministry, Jesus demonstrated that He had complete authority over everything in the world. Whether in the natural or spiritual world, He was God and He had authority.

5. FOCUSED ON THE KINGDOM (4:42-44)

The demands of people can be draining, and **at daybreak Jesus went out to a solitary place** (4:42). As much as Jesus loved people, He needed regular times of solitude for renewal and to maintain focus. However, Jesus would not be alone for very long, because **the people were looking for him and when they came to where he was, they tried to keep him from leaving them** (4:42). You want to keep the Miracle Worker with you as long as you can. However, to those who tried to hold on to Him, He said, **"I must preach the good news of the kingdom of God to the other towns also, because that is why I was sent"** (4:43).

His mission was not to heal all those who were physically or emotionally sick—as much as He cared for them—but to inaugurate the kingdom of God that would bring healing to the spiritually sick. **And he kept on preaching in the synagogues of Judea** (4:44). A key to effective leadership is to know your mission and resist being led away from it, as legitimate as another direction might seem to be. Jesus knew His mission and would maintain His focus. He kept on preaching. Up to this point His

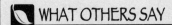

WHAT OTHERS SAY

AUTHORITY

The authority and power of Jesus are demonstrated in Luke's gospel by His

- overcoming evil (4:12, 35; 9:38; 11:14)

- controlling the elements of nature (8:22–25; 9:12–17; 5:4–11)

- overcoming death (8:41–42; 7:11–15)

- healing people (5:12–13; 7:1–10; 4:38–35; 5:18–25; 6:6–10; 18:35–43)

- forgiving sins (5:24; 7:48)

- blessing people (6:20–22)

- giving people eternal life in heaven (23:43)

ministry had been in regions of Galilee, but now He took His teaching ministry to the synagogues of Judea. The message of the kingdom of God was needed in that region as well, so He was led there by the Spirit, in the Spirit's power and authority.

6

WILLING AND ABLE

Luke 5:1–6:16

A leprous man called out to Jesus, **"Lord, if you are willing, you can make me clean."** Jesus' response was **"I am willing"** and He commanded, **"Be clean!"** (Luke 5:12–13). He had a ministry of compassionate willingness and divine ability. What a powerful combination!

Jesus taught with authority because He is the Truth. There was power in His words because He embodied the omnipotence of God. The combination of truth and power can have an edge that drives people away rather than draws them. In Jesus, loving compassion joined truth and power to create a magnet that drew people to Him. He was willing to touch the untouchable and associate with outcasts. Some people have the ability to help others but do not have the will to do it. Others have the desire to help but do not have the ability or capacity. Jesus had the ability to make a difference in people's lives, and He had the compassion to make Him want to. He was both willing and able. He sought those who would be willing to join Him and to whom He could impart some of His authority, ability, and compassion. He is still looking for those who are willing to be made able.

1. JESUS CALLS DISCIPLES TO FOLLOW HIM (5:1–11)

Wherever Jesus went crowds were sure to gather. Some people came out of curiosity and some came to witness or receive a miracle. Others came to listen to His teaching, which He did anywhere people would congregate.

A crowd gathered to listen to the word of God at the edge of the **Lake of Gennesaret** (5:1), which is another name for the Sea of Galilee.

There was no question in Luke's mind regarding the authority of Jesus' teaching. He did not speak words *about* God or words *for* God, but He spoke **the word of God** (5:1). What a privilege it must have been to sit at the feet of *the* Word as He taught the word of God.

It was on the shore of the Sea of Galilee that Jesus gave the first invitation for persons to follow Him. **Simon** (5:3) was first, a fisherman whose boat became a platform from which Jesus addressed the crowd. Jesus asked Simon to **"Put out into deep water, and let down the nets for a catch"** (5:4). The Lord of all nature put the professional fisherman to the test. Simon's retort was, **"We've worked hard all night and haven't caught anything"** (5:5). Had his fisherman's ego gotten in his way, there is a good chance he would never have become a disciple. Amazingly however, Simon said, **"Because you say so, I will let down the nets"** (5:5). Obedience is more important that reasonable action, if God is the one who gives the command.

Already Simon sensed an authority emanating from this man that commanded his respect and obedience. A night of futile fishing was transformed into a bonanza catch so large that the **nets began to break** (5:6). Simon had fishing partners nearby, and he called for them to bring their boat to help with the catch, **and they came and filled both boats so full that they began to sink** (5:6). If there is such a thing as being too successful, they were.

Simon saw something more going on here than a miraculous catch of fish. He fell on his knees before Jesus and said, **"Go away from me, Lord; I am a sinful man!"** (5:8). Jesus was more than a teacher or wannabe fisherman. Simon may not yet have come to the conviction of Jesus' divine nature (Luke 9:20), but he did sense a holiness that exposed his own imperfections. We cannot be in the presence of the Lord and remain unaware of our sin. Like Isaiah, when we see the Lord and become aware of His holiness, we immediately become aware we have "unclean lips" (Isa. 6:5). Encountering Jesus causes us to marvel at His nature and to become aware of our own. Perhaps we would be less tolerant of our imperfections if we would more frequently enter His holy presence.

Jesus said to Simon, **"Don't be afraid; from now on you will catch men"** (Luke 5:10). Jesus met people where they were. He entered into their world and spoke to them in terms they could understand. To the woman at the well He spoke of living water (John 4:6–15). To people of the country He spoke of the soil (Luke 8:4–8). To hungry people He spoke of the bread of life (John 6:35, 48). To fishermen, He got their attention and respect by showing them how to catch fish, and then told them they would transfer their fishing skills to that of catching men.

James and John, the sons of Zebedee, were **Simon's partners** (Luke 5:10)—the ones who had been invited to join in on the miraculous catch. Their previously empty boat was filled with the spillover from Simon's catch.

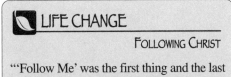

LIFE CHANGE

FOLLOWING CHRIST

"'Follow Me' was the first thing and the last thing Christ said to Peter. It is for us, as well, the beginning and the end of everything."

—Joseph Stowell

Our obedience to God often results in spillover blessings that benefit others. Simon's influence and associations were already being used to catch other men. Three men gave up their fishing franchise that day for a new adventure: **they pulled their boats up on shore, left everything and followed him** (5:11). Sometimes, spontaneous actions are short lived, shallow, and emotionally based. When the euphoria wears off, doubt and regret about the decision comes. But this was the kind of commitment Jesus demands, and He provides new substance to life that keeps doubt and regret away. The three fishermen showed no hesitation or reservation, but they left everything and followed Jesus. This dimension of discipleship is explored more in chapters 9 and 15 of this book. It is enough to say at this point that the first three of Jesus' disciples provided a model of commitment for those of all generations who would follow Jesus. Perhaps their immediate and complete commitment is why Peter, James, and John became the inner circle of Jesus' friends and disciples.

Jesus made the leaving of their nets a bit more difficult by asking them to follow Him when the nets were full of fish rather than when they were empty. It would seem easier for a fisherman to leave his nets after an unsuccessful night of fishing than after swamping a couple of boats with a miraculous catch. It is harder to leave full nets than empty ones, but Christ may call us to follow Him when life is going great and our nets are full. What nets did you leave behind in order to follow Christ, or are you hanging on to some nets and boats that you should let go of? You will never be an *able* disciple until you are a *willing* disciple.

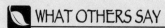

WHAT OTHERS SAY

LEAVING EVERYTHING

"Luke's model for his readers is a person having position, power and possessions, who, having considered the invitation fully, thoughtfully decides to surrender everything to the lordship and mastery of Jesus."

—Melvin Shoemaker

2. JESUS TOUCHES THE UNTOUCHABLE (5:12–16)

WILLING TO TOUCH THE LEPER

Luke was a doctor, and he understood diseases. He recorded that a man **covered with leprosy** (5:12) saw Jesus. Leprosy was a dreaded disease that carried social as well as physical implications, and evidently the disease was in extreme stages so that it covered and disfigured the man's body. Lepers were considered unclean and were kept isolated from others. Jewish law required lepers to call out, "Unclean!" wherever they went so others would steer clear of them, lest they be made unclean as well.

The leper begged Jesus, **"Lord, if you are willing, you can make me clean"** (5:12). He did not question the ability of Jesus to heal him, but there is the hint of a question as to whether Jesus would be willing. Jesus went beyond demonstrating His willingness, and He **reached out his hand and touched the man** (5:13). Most likely, the leper had not experienced a human touch since he showed the first sign of leprosy, since touching him would cause that person to also become unclean. Jesus was willing and able, because at His word, **immediately the leprosy left** (5:13) the man. Leprosy was a disease that disfigured, and evidently the healing not only destroyed the bacterial infection that caused the disease, but also removed the disfigurement caused by the disease. A man who had no future, now had one. A man who could have no association with family or friends could now move freely among others. The healing was immediate and complete, initiated because Jesus was willing to touch an untouchable man.

When you are experiencing difficulties, what challenges your faith the most—wondering if God cares or if He is able to make a difference? Whether He *wants* to help you or if He *is able* to help you? If you ever question God's ability, do a search through the Scriptures for references to "He is able." Let the truth of words such as "to him who is able to do immeasurably more than all we ask or imagine" (Eph. 3:20) soak into your spirit. He is able. He is willing. He is willing to put His power to work in your life in the most perfect way to bring you good and Him glory.

TRYING TO CONTROL THE CROWDS

Usually, when a "miraculous" cure is discovered for a disease, or a doctor is found who has skill beyond the normal, promotional campaigns begin to attract those who need the cure. Rather than promoting His miracle of healing, Jesus ordered the cured leper, **"Don't tell anyone, but go, show yourself to the priest and offer the sacrifices that Moses commanded for your cleansing, as a testimony to them"** (5:14). Three things were at work here. First, Jesus wanted the cured man to follow the prescriptions of the Law so he would be fully functional in society, having met the requirements and practices that would officially declare him to be clean. Second, Jesus wanted this miraculous healing to be a testimony to the priests. Third, Jesus had other things to do besides healing the sick, and He did not want only those who were sick to come to Him.

In spite of Jesus' desire to minimize word about the healing of the leper, **news about him spread . . . , so that crowds of people came to hear him and to be healed of their sicknesses** (5:15). The mission of Jesus was to draw people to Him for salvation not miracles. He told the healed leper not to tell anyone, but it is hard to keep news of a miracle quiet. Crowds pressed against Jesus seeking hope and help, **but Jesus often withdrew to lonely places and prayed** (5:16). The demands of people can draw energy from you, and the one who loved people deeply often withdrew from them. The hands that healed with a touch would be found clasped in prayer. The power and authority of the human Jesus came from His vital connection with God the Father, and throughout Luke, we witness Jesus regularly practicing the disciplines of prayer and solitude. This practice will be referenced later in this chapter (6:12).

The authority of Jesus over physical disease is prominent in Luke's gospel. The physician and writer would certainly have an eye for the sick and would marvel at the healings performed by the Great Physician. Jesus healed people because He cared about them and their needs, and He healed people because dealing with their physical need often provided opportunity to deal with their spiritual need. He was always aware that He was not just a healer but a Savior on a mission to redeem fallen humanity. So when needy people came to Him, "He welcomed them and spoke to them about the kingdom of God, and healed those who needed healing" (Luke 9:11). Truth and compassion met perfectly in Jesus. Truth without compassion can be hard, unyielding, and uncaring. Compassion without truth can be sentimental, shallow, and compromising. Jesus cared about people enough to heal their diseases, but He cared more about their spiritual sicknesses, which compelled Him to teach them about the kingdom of God.

It would be a mistake for any of us to believe that every person should or will be healed from every disease, every time—*if* they have enough faith. God can and does still bring the miracle of healing to suffering people, but healing is the sovereign act of a sovereign will that does not result from our self-centered demands. We cannot command God to do anything, even in the name of faith. Healing may come as the result of our request, but not as the result of our demand. As a sovereign act, it is a gift wrapped in the purposes of God, which are not always fully understood by us. Healing is not a result of the quantity of our faith, so if we have "enough" of it a miracle is guaranteed, and if a miracle doesn't happen it is because we do not have enough of it. Many believers have been severely damaged by well-meaning but misguided people who have told them that the absence of a healing miracle meant either there was sin in their lives or they did not have enough faith.

3. JESUS FORGIVES SIN (5:17–26)

Pharisees and teachers of the law (5:17) were prominent players in the unfolding drama of the redemptive story. The Pharisees were a religious sect of Judaism whose focus was on strict adherence to the laws of Moses. Their passion for the law led them to interpret, expand, and codify the law. Another sect, the Sadducees, was often in conflict with the Pharisees. They held a strict obedience to the *written* law of Moses that did not include the oral traditions of the Pharisees. The Sadducees did not believe in the resurrection of the dead, as did the Pharisees. The Sadducees were more politically oriented than the Pharisees, and generally appealed to the wealthy and powerful. Luke references the Sadducees only once, and it relates to their resistance to the resurrection of the dead (Luke 20:27). Jesus admonished the people to be on "guard against the yeast of the Pharisees and Sadducees" (Matt. 16:6).

JEWISH CUSTOMS

RELIGIOUS AND POLITICAL GROUPS

Pharisees	"Separated Ones" who maintained separation from anything non-Jewish; meticulously followed the Old Testament laws and historic oral traditions; were criticized for being legalistic and hypocritical
Sadducees	Accepted the Pentateuch (Genesis—Deuteronomy) as God's law; did not believe in the resurrection; more political than the Pharisees
Publicans	Jewish tax collectors
Herodians	Jewish political group who supported Herod Antipas, who played up to the Roman occupation in order to keep his job
Sanhedrin	Seventy-one-member supreme council of the Jews
Levites	Descendents of the tribe of Levi; assigned the duty of caring for details that surrounded worship at the Temple
Scribes	Primarily writers of the law; often associated with the Pharisees

It was among these religious leaders that Jesus was found in the Temple during His first visit to Jerusalem (Luke 2:46). The Pharisees and teachers of the law were formidable opponents of the teaching of Jesus, and they often came to listen to Him, not because they accepted His teaching, but because they wanted to catch Him teaching heresy that they could use to discredit Him.

Jesus continued His healing ministry, and crowds gathered either to witness or receive a miracle. Among them were men who cared enough about a paralyzed friend that they came to Jesus, carrying the **paralytic on a mat** (5:18). Too many people were crowded in and around the house where Jesus was, so **they went up on the roof and lowered him on his mat through the tiles into the middle of the crowd, right in front of Jesus** (5:19). Houses of that day were built of stone with flat roofs and often had stairs that led to the roof. These men were committed enough to their friend that they were prepared to pay to repair a man's roof in order to get their friend to Jesus. They believed that if they could just get their friend to Jesus, He would be willing and able to do something for him. What great friends they were!

Jesus took note of the paralytic and his friends, and when He **saw their faith, he said, "Friend, your sins are forgiven"** (5:20). Their friend was now His friend. It was not the faith of the paralyzed man that brought the response of Jesus, but the faith of his friends. They believed Jesus could make a difference in their friend's miserable life, and they did everything within their power to get him to Jesus. Nothing would stand in their way, whether people or roofs. But an amazing thing happened. They brought their friend so he could experience a physical healing, but they heard his spiritual need addressed. Jesus forgave the man's sins through the faith of his friends. There certainly had to be faith in the paralyzed man's heart as well, since every person must respond to Christ in his or her own faith, not that of someone else. But this occasion points to two important truths. First is the importance of bringing others to Christ—of making it possible for others to be in a position for Jesus to touch them. Some will never experience Christ if we do not take action on their behalf. Second is the realization that our greatest need is always spiritual, and there are times when spiritual healing may be the vehicle through which physical and emotional healing comes to us. Jesus wants to straighten out our priorities when our concern over our physical condition is greater than our concern over our spiritual condition.

This was a moment the Pharisees and teachers of the law had been looking for. It sounded like blasphemy to them, and they **began thinking to themselves, . . . "Who can forgive sins but God alone?"** (5:21). They were experts in the law, and they knew sin when they saw it. They knew what a person needed to do to get forgiveness and who had the authority to offer it. This was not the way, and this man was not the one. Only God could forgive sin, and this man was usurping the place of God. That was blasphemous.

Jesus knew what they were thinking, and He asked if it would be easier to tell someone their sins were forgiven or to cause someone who was paralyzed to get up and walk. The claim that sin was forgiven could be discounted as meaningless or blasphemous words, but an obvious miracle like causing a paralyzed man to walk could not be as easily pushed aside. So Jesus said, **"That you may know that the Son of Man has authority on earth to forgive sins. . . ."** He said to the paralyzed man, **"I tell you, get up, take your mat and go home"** (5:24). The ability to perform the miracle was exercised to support the authority to forgive sins. The visible and tangible was evidence for what was invisible and spiritual.

The healing was immediate and complete, and the healed man **stood up in front of them, took what he had been lying on and went home praising God** (5:25). As a doctor, Luke must have marveled every time he heard evidence of a miraculous healing. He knew that his best treatments, if effective, usually took time. Jesus' healings were usually instantaneous. Luke does not tell us the cause of the paralysis, whether by birth, accident, or disease. If caused by genetic defect, the genes were repaired and the man learned to walk immediately. If caused by disease, what had come gradually was reversed instantly. Not every healing is immediately recognized as a miracle, but instantaneous healings are most easily claimed by us to be miracles. This is the kind of healing we hope for and the kind for which we are ready to give God credit. It is only appropriate that we give praise to God when He has done something great in response to our need—whether it happens immediately or over a period of time.

The effect of the healing of the paralytic was that **everyone was amazed and gave praise to God. They were filled with awe** (5:26). The focus of attention should not be on the miracle itself or on the instrument of healing, but on a merciful, caring, and powerful God. Perhaps if we were quicker to recognize the hand of God at work and give Him praise, we would have more occasions to be amazed and filled with awe.

4. JESUS CALLS LEVI: WILLING TO RECEIVE SINNERS (5:27–32)

Jesus gathered around Him quite a varied collection of people who would become the Twelve. They were different in temperament, background, and vocation. Jesus **saw a tax collector by the name of Levi sitting at his tax booth** (5:27). Levi, who would become known as Matthew, did not go looking for Jesus. He was "discovered" while performing his daily responsibilities as a tax collector. Tax collectors were usually Jews employed by the occupying Roman government to collect taxes from their countrymen. Whatever they could collect beyond what Rome required could line their own pockets and further bring disdain from their countrymen. The Pharisees usually said "tax collectors" and "sinners" in the same breath.

God comes to each of us and meets us where we are. Sometimes God is found because we go seeking for Him. Sometimes He is found because He came seeking us, and where He finds us may not be the most favorable condition to be considered for discipleship. He does not choose us on the basis of our position, heredity, or record of achievement. He seeks us because He loves us, and He knows what we can become through His transforming grace.

Jesus invited Levi, **"Follow me"** (5:27). The invitation was simple and straightforward. He didn't give extensive information on where they would be going or what the journey would be like. We often want to see a *plan*, but God offers us a *person*. Plans have details, but the invitation to follow Jesus doesn't come with details, only the opportunity to trust in the nature and mission of the person. **Levi got up, left everything and followed him** (5:28). Five times in the book of Luke Jesus said, "Follow me," and each time it involved willingness to pay a price. Being a disciple of Christ always requires *leaving* before *following*. Both are conditions of discipleship. Levi did not appear to hesitate, but like Peter,

94

James, and John, who immediately left their boats to follow Jesus, he got up from his tax-collecting table, left everything, and followed Jesus. Leaving everything may be more painful for some because in their minds they have more to leave. But even little things can be held on to and can become chains that bind us to that which is unimportant and prevent us from following Christ. Note two amazing things: that Jesus would invite Levi into the group of disciples He was forming, and that there was such an immediate and complete obedience to the call on the part of Levi.

Levi was a new follower, and he **held a great banquet for Jesus at his house, and a large crowd of tax collectors and others were eating with them** (5:29). New followers still have old friends, so Levi invited his "cruddy buddies" to celebrate his new vocation and meet his new Master. He was no longer a tax collector, he was a follower of Christ, and he wanted to introduce Him to his friends. This is the way it is supposed to work. A person decides to follow Christ and becomes so excited about it that he shares the experience with his friends and introduces them to Him. This is the way revivals begin. This is the way churches grow—one forgiven sinner showing other sinners where they can find forgiveness.

The Pharisees and the teachers of the law addressed their complaining question to the disciples and got their answer from Jesus: **"Why do you eat and drink with tax collectors and 'sinners'?"** (5:30). This was more than a question. it was an accusation that would come up again: "The Pharisees and the teachers of the law muttered, 'This man welcomes sinners and eats with them'" (Luke 15:2). For a Pharisee, righteousness was possible only through disassociation from sin and those who committed it. Associating with sinners would make them sinners. Jesus was on a redemptive mission, and the only way to accomplish it was to get close to those who needed to be redeemed. Jesus responded to their accusing question by saying, **"It is not the healthy who need a doctor, but the sick. I have not come to call the righteous, but sinners to repentance"** (5:31–32).

The response of Jesus pointed out two things. First was His reason for associating with sinners: to heal their spiritual sickness by bringing them to repentance and forgiveness. Second was the inference that there will always be those, like the Pharisees and teachers of the law, who do not see themselves as being sick or as being sinners. Jesus came to those who knew they needed a Savior. Sin that is overlooked, minimized, excused, or denied will remain sin that is un-forgiven. Jesus comes to those who need Him and stays with those who want Him.

5. NEW WINESKINS: WILLING TO BREAK WITH TRADITION (5:33–39)

The Pharisees and teachers of the law were big on tradition. They confronted Jesus over the fact that **"John's disciples often fast and pray, and so do the disciples of the Pharisees, but yours go on eating and drinking"** (5:33). Jesus said the day would come when fasting would be appropriate, but not now while the **bridegroom** was with **his guests** (5:34). This was the day for new and exciting things that would break out of the stereotypes and restrictions of tradition. There may be patterns in how God works, but He is unpredictable. He can't be boxed in to only work within walls constructed by the minds and wills of humankind. Something new was happening, and those who were bound by tradition were going to miss it. So He told them a parable about patching garments.

Sometimes old things cannot be fixed but must be replaced with something new. You don't ruin a new garment by cutting it up into pieces to use to patch something old. The new garment is destroyed, and the old garment is obviously patched with something that does not match. It doesn't make sense to ruin the new in a fruitless attempt to salvage the old.

Jesus continued the point with another illustration: **"No one pours new wine into old wineskins. If he does, the new wine will burst the skins, the wine will run out and the wineskins will be ruined"** (5:37). Goatskins were commonly used as containers for wine. New skins would be flexible and could expand with the fermentation of the wine. Old skins would be inflexible and would not move with the expansion of the wine. They would burst. In its worst sense, tradition can become inflexibly bound to the past. Tradition was at one time spontaneous and new, but when it becomes prescriptive, it becomes limiting and rigid. In Jesus, something new was happening that could not be contained by the restrictions of the old.

The truth of this illustration, that **new wine must be poured into new wineskins** (5:38), is not difficult to understand and accept. However, the church has always wrestled with how this truth is applied. Our faith is rooted in historical fact, and we celebrate God's work in the past. It is rather easy for the church to prefer the old and the predictable. New is suspect; old is safe.

Tradition is the established way of doing things. Jesus was the new Way toward which the old way was to lead. But because the Pharisees and teachers of the law saw the old way as most familiar and comfortable, and they maintained authority and control in the old way, they would say, **"The old is better"** (5:39). Their taste for the old kept them from accepting the new wine of the Spirit that was available in Christ. As attractive as Jesus might be, some find the hold of the old life to be so strong that they prefer it to new life in Christ, even thought they know the old no longer works.

New life in Christ cannot consist of doing a patch job on the old life or trying to contain it by making it fit into the old patterns. New wine can be lost by forcing it into old wineskins or by providing no wineskin at all.

6. JESUS CONFRONTS THE LAW: WILLING TO BREAK SABBATH REGULATIONS (6:1–11)

On one hand, Jesus came to fulfill the Law, so He meticulously kept its requirements, as illustrated in His circumcision, presentation to the Lord, and visits to Jerusalem on feast days. On the other hand, He came to free people from the unreasonable demands and religious bondages that grew out of the Law. So, while respecting the Law and keeping the moral aspects of it, He was willing to confront its abuse and the hypocrisy that accompanied many pious persons who hid behind strict adherence to the Law but who had lost sight of personal righteousness.

The religious leaders gave great attention to God's command to "Remember the Sabbath day by keeping it holy" (Ex. 20:8). They took the simple command of God and expanded it to include thirty-nine categories of activities that were forbidden on the Sabbath.[1] During **one Sabbath Jesus** and His disciples were walking through fields of grain **and his disciples began to pick some heads of grain, rub them in their hands and eat the kernels** (6:1). God had instructed harvesters to leave grain around the edges and corners of their fields so travelers and needy people could find food. The disciples were not stealing, however they were breaking one of the expanded versions of the Law that identified this activity as one of the thirty-nine prohibited activities on the Sabbath. They were not breaking God's law, only man's law.

Always on the lookout for violations of the Law, some Pharisees asked, **"Why are you doing what is unlawful on the Sabbath?"** (6:2). Jesus answered by pointing back in their history to when **David . . . and his companions were hungry** and **entered the house of God, and taking the consecrated bread, he ate what is lawful only for priests to eat** (Luke 6:3–4; see 1 Sam. 21). Tabernacle worship included placing showbread, or bread of Presence, on a table in the Tabernacle. It was to be eaten only by the priests and only after seven days when they had replaced it with fresh bread. David and his band of supporters were running from Saul and needed food. Nothing was available to them except the seven-day-old bread that by ceremonial law was limited to consumption by the priests. David demonstrated that occasions come when meeting human need is of more importance than keeping ceremonial law.

If this precedent were not enough, **Jesus said to them, "The Son of Man is Lord of the Sabbath"** (Luke 6:5). If Jesus was Lord of the Sabbath, He could determine how it could be used, not them. There is no indication that they caught the full meaning of what Jesus said, that He was the Son of Man and that He was Lord of the Sabbath. If they caught any of the meaning of the statement, it would be filed away as another one of the blasphemous claims of a man who said He was bigger than the Word of God and the law of Moses.

On another Sabbath, while **teaching** in a **synagogue,** Jesus was approached by **a man . . . whose right hand was shriveled. The Pharisees and teachers of the law were** already upset with how Jesus violated their Sabbath laws, **so they watched him closely to see if he would heal on the Sabbath** (6:6–7). Jesus knew what they were up to, so He stood the man in front of everyone and said, **"I ask you, which is lawful on the Sabbath: to do good or to do evil, to save life or to destroy it?"** (6:9). The keepers of the Law had determined it to be unlawful for a physician to practice on the Sabbath, therefore if Jesus healed the man with a shriveled hand He would break their law. Again,

Jesus appealed to the higher law of doing good and saving life. Willing to challenge the authority of the Pharisees and their prescriptive laws, Jesus promptly healed the man's hand, which infuriated the religious leaders, and they **began to discuss with one another what they might do to Jesus** (6:11). Already, in the early stages of His ministry, seeds of hatred were being planted that would eventually lead to the crucifixion.

7. JESUS CHOOSES THE TWELVE: WILLING TO KEEP IN TOUCH (6:12–16)

Jesus is found praying on thirteen different occasions in Luke. As earlier noted, "Jesus often withdrew to lonely places and prayed" (Luke 5:16). He prayed in gardens and on seashores and mountainsides. Sometimes He went to be alone with God, and other times He took chosen followers with Him to cultivate their prayer life. He prayed as a regular pattern of keeping in touch with His Father, and He prayed prior to making big decisions or facing big events. On one of these occasions, **Jesus went out to a mountainside to pray, and spent the night praying to God** (6:12). Perhaps, knowing the critical nature of choosing in whom He would invest His life, He sought the counsel of His Father. Perhaps, knowing what those He chose would have to face because of their commitment to follow Him, He interceded on their behalf. Perhaps, knowing the choice of the Twelve would launch Him into a new phase of His ministry, He sought the favor and blessing of the Father. Perhaps all of these things occupied His heart so greatly that He wanted and needed to spend the whole night in prayer.

If Jesus, being the Son of God, felt the need to spend time in prayer, how much more should the children of God feel this need? We should certainly use the circumstances that cause us concern to cause us to pray. Like Jesus, we should be willing to keep in touch with the Father.

After spending the night in prayer, **when morning came, he called his disciples to him** (6:13). We are not told the total number of followers that would be referred to as "his disciples," though we know that out of the larger group, He **chose twelve** (6:13) to become the apostles. He would pour His life into this small band of followers. The level of their

THE TWELVE DISCIPLES

Simon	Fisherman; renamed Peter by Jesus; became leader of the church in Jerusalem
Andrew	Fisherman; Simon's brother; known for bringing people to Jesus, including his brother Simon
James	Fisherman; son of Zebedee and brother of John; nicknamed "Son of Thunder"; martyred by Herod
John	Fisherman; son of Zebedee and brother of James; nicknamed "Son of Thunder"; referred to as "the disciple Jesus loved"; writer of Gospel of John and Revelation; exiled to Island of Patmos
Philip	Fisherman; told Nathanael about Jesus
Bartholomew	Also called Nathanael; brought to Jesus by Philip; initially rejected Jesus because He was from Nazareth
Matthew	Jewish tax collector; entertained Jesus in his home
Thomas	Nicknamed "Didymus," which means "twin"; often referred to as a doubter
James	Son of Alphaeus; nothing more known about him
Simon	Known to be a Zealot, which was a political activist group that opposed Roman occupation; nothing more known about him
Judas	Also called Thaddeus; son of James; little known about him
Judas Iscariot	Treasurer of the disciples; Satan entered him; betrayed Jesus; hanged himself in remorse

commitment had to be higher than others. They would have to leave other occupations and relationships to be with Him. The word *chose* is a word that can mean "ordained"—a word familiar to the church as it recognizes those called by God for specialized service and "endorses" them for that service. **He also designated** them to be **apostles** (6:13). Mark's record says, "He appointed twelve—designating them apostles—that they might be with him and that he might send them out to preach and to have authority" (Mark 3:14–15). Several things are implied here: (1) They would have a close special relationship with Jesus; (2) He would commission and send them out; (3) they would have a mission of preaching; and (4) He would give them authority. This could well become a working definition of *apostle*. They were *learners* (disciples) until Christ gave them authority and sent them out. Then they were apostles: *those who are sent forth*.[2]

From this point, this cadre of disciples would be known as the Twelve, until after the defection of Judas when they were referred to as the Eleven (Luke 24:33). Jesus chose a diverse group of men who basically were common, no-name people—like us. But why would He choose Judas Iscariot? Didn't He know at the time that he would become a traitor? If all of the rest of the names let us know that we have the potential of being a disciple of Jesus, the inclusion of Judas Iscariot lets us know we have the potential of betraying Jesus too.

Jesus was willing to invest himself in people who could carry out His mission after He was gone. He was willing to believe in and trust people like us.

ENDNOTES

1. *Life Application Bible* (Wheaton, Ill.: Tyndale House, 1989), p. 168.
2. Marvin R. Vincent, *Word Studies in the New Testament* (Grand Rapids, Mich.: Eerdmans, 1973), p. 57.

7

CORE VALUES OF THE KINGDOM OF GOD

Luke 6:17–49

The *kingdom* is referenced thirty-nine times in the Gospel of Luke. Kingdoms are where specific rulers exert their authority and establish a culture that is governed by rules that reflect the values of the ruler and, in turn, affect the quality of life of those in the kingdom. They differ from each other in the nature of their government and in the quality of life they generate.

Scripture speaks of two dominant kingdoms at work on earth. One is variously referred to as the kingdom of God, kingdom of heaven, kingdom of light, kingdom of Christ, and the eternal kingdom. The second is described as the kingdom of the air (Eph. 2:2), ruled by the "prince of this world" (John 12:31). Jesus often referred to it simply as "this world." On one occasion He said, "Now is the time for judgment on this world; now the prince of this world will be driven out" (John 12:31). He identified Satan as exercising his dominion over the affairs of this world, establishing a world order that opposed the kingdom of God.

The kingdom of God exists wherever His authority is recognized, His values are established, and His will is obeyed. Jesus taught the disciples to pray for the kingdom of God to come and His will be done, on earth as it is in heaven (Matt. 6:10). It is governed by values and practices that differ from earthly kingdoms. Living in the kingdom of God entitles you to special blessings that are not found in the kingdoms of this world, but in order to receive them you must live by kingdom rules.

1. BLESSINGS AND WOES OF THE KINGDOM (6:17–26)

LIVING WITH BLESSING

Large crowds gathered wherever Jesus went, and on one occasion He **stood on a level place** (Luke 6:17) to deliver a classic message. It is similar to Matthew's Sermon on the Mount, and it is quite possible that this is a composite of several messages delivered at different times and places. As a possible composite "sermon," Matthew provides a more complete record, but Luke retains the Beatitudes for his readers, although with slightly different wordage.

As on other occasions, some people came for the teaching and some came looking for a miracle. Jesus responded to the physical needs of the crowd and healed many. To some He directly addressed their need and healed them, while others **tried to touch him, because power was coming from him** (6:19). There will always be those who seek the blessings of God without relationship with Him or without submitting to His rule in their lives. For some, Jesus was more of a celebrity who could do miracles than the Lord to whom they owed allegiance.

Jesus came to proclaim the kingdom of God, where real blessings accompanied those who entered that Kingdom. It is an "upside down" Kingdom, where the conduct of its members and the values of the Kingdom often are opposite to the conduct and values of the kingdom of this world.[1]

This world puts high value on achieving wealth, but Jesus said, **"Blessed are you who are poor, for yours is the kingdom of God"** (6:20). In the values of this world, being poor is not perceived to be a blessing, but rather a curse. In fact, often in the Scripture, wealth is seen as an indicator of God's favor. God blessed the faithful with possessions, and if you had none, evidently God was not pleased with you. However, Jesus proclaimed a new order in which the kingdom of God can be the possession of the poorest person. Regardless of the depth of your poverty, you can experience God's blessings and know His favor. The kingdom of God may "belong" more to the poor than to the rich, since the rich will have much greater difficulty entering it (18:24–25).

Food is necessary for survival in this world and being hungry is undesirable, but Jesus said, **"Blessed are you who hunger now, for you will be satisfied"** (6:21). Matthew made fullness a blessing that was available to those who "hunger and thirst for righteousness." Whether the hunger is physical or spiritual, present or future, God promises to bless those who are hungry with a fullness that is completely satisfying. The kingdom of this world emphasizes the need to be satisfied **now**, while the kingdom of God promises **you will be**. Satisfaction in the kingdom of this world is based on what is presently being experienced. Satisfaction in the kingdom of God is based on the promise of God for what will be realized in the future. People pursue what they think will bring satisfaction *now*, only to be disappointed. Full satisfaction, both now and eternally, can only be found in the kingdom of God.

The kingdom of this world promises fun, pleasure, and happiness, but Jesus said, **"Blessed are you who weep now, for you will laugh"** (6:21). No one desires sorrow or painful experiences, but reality is that we live in a fallen world, and we all experience pain and suffering. It is a mistake to fall for the empty pursuit of pleasure as a means of dulling the pain of life in this world. When the fun wears off, the pain only intensifies. But for those who are in the kingdom of God, the pain and sorrow of life in this world will be forgotten in the joys of the next world. In fact, our present sorrows are modified by the comfort of God and the joy of His Spirit.

The kingdom of this world will compromise principles and values to gain the praise and support of others, but Jesus said, **"Blessed are you when men hate you, when they exclude you and insult you and reject your name as evil, because of the Son of Man"** (6:22). No one wants to experience hatred, exclusion, insult, or rejection. It is much easier to disassociate yourself from the person or cause in order to have people like you and include you. Jesus knew that those who chose to be a part of the kingdom of God would suffer because of Him. Unfortunately, we often invite people to follow Christ so they can experience happiness, peace, and His wonderful plan for their lives. But Jesus said that special blessing would come to those who are willing to endure hardship in this world because of Him: **"Rejoice in that day and leap for joy, because great is your reward in heaven"** (6:23).

Jesus began this section speaking of blessing and finished it speaking of reward. Blessing is a gift that is benevolently bestowed out of the goodness of the benefactor, not the worthiness of the recipient. Reward is recognition for accomplishment and completion based on meeting the requirements established by the reward-er. In this case, blessing is considered to be present and reward is considered to be future. Blessing may be experienced by both the just and the unjust, while reward is for faithful followers of Christ upon completion of their earthly journey. Between Jesus' pronouncement of blessing and His promise of reward is a lot of tough stuff that comes as a part of living in a fallen world, the kingdom of this world. At times believers experience the results of this world's fallenness, while also receiving blessings that come from the kingdom of God. That is the reality of being in the present. But the future holds promise of reward in heaven, the place where the fullness of the kingdom of God will be experienced with no residue of the fallen world. We persevere in this present world because of the blessings of God and the promise of reward. One day, we will be transported out of the kingdom of this world into the eternal kingdom of God and into the reward prepared for us for faithful completion of our time here.

LIVING WITH AWARENESS

Some people trade the future for the present, choosing to be rich on earth but poor in heavenly investments. To such people, Jesus said, **"But woe to you who are rich, for you have already received your comfort"** (6:24). Those who live for riches get all they are going to get here and now. They have more stashed away here than they have in heaven, making them earth rich and heaven poor.

For each of the blessings promised to those who live for the kingdom of God, Jesus spoke of woe to those who live for the kingdom of this world. They may be well fed, having fun, and be well spoken of now, but that will all change. Those who grab all they can get of this world's pleasures and profits may get it all now but have nothing for eternity.

2. A NEW WAY OF LIVING (6:27–42)

LOVE IS A CORE VALUE

The values and standards of the kingdom of the world differ from those of the kingdom of God. Love is a core value of life in God's kingdom—a love radically different from worldly love. Love may be expressed in legitimate ways and evidenced in relationship between family members, friends, or spouse. This world may place high value on these evidences of love as being normative and right. However, this world's love can be misused to exclude, and can be used for selfish purposes and self-gratification. Love in the kingdom of God calls people to a higher standard. The love of which Jesus spoke is a deep caring for and commitment to the well-being of the other person and a willingness to sacrifice for the other's benefit.

The idea of being more interested in the well-being of others than in yourself would be radical enough, but Jesus added a further dimension to it: **"Love your enemies, do good to those who hate you, bless those who curse you, pray for those who mistreat you"** (6:27–28). The standard of kingdom love is high, so high that at some point we can feel the need to explain the meaning of Jesus' words in ways that can give us a bit of wiggle room in dealing with not-so-lovable people. Praying for those who mistreat us, saying good things to people who say bad things to us, and doing good to those who want to do us bad may be a stretch for us, but we can do it, empowered by the Spirit of Christ. But to say that we deeply love our enemies is more than a stretch. As if that were not difficult enough, Jesus added physical abuse: **"If someone strikes you on one cheek, turn to him the other also"** (6:29). A strike on the cheek was intended to be as much an insult as it was to bring injury. Turning the other cheek was to invite further insult or injury. Love's first response to insult or injury is not to retaliate or find revenge, but to demonstrate being longsuffering and to return kindness.

Love seeks to give rather than take. Love's first response to someone wanting what you have is to see what their needs are, and if you have what can help them, you give it. People who live for this world often live with the rule "Do to others before they do it to you." But the rule of the kingdom of God is **"Do to others as you would have them do to you"** (6:31). Love requires you to treat others in a way you want them to treat you, rather than to treat them in the same way that they have treated you.

It might not be too hard for us to love people who love us and to do good to those who are good to us, but this does not make us any different from people of this world. Jesus said **even "sinners" do that** (6:33). But people of the kingdom of God are to love and seek the well-being of their enemies. If you live this way, **"then your reward will be great, and you will be sons of the Most High, because he is kind to the ungrateful and wicked"** (6:35). As children of God, we are to demonstrate the characteristics of our Father. We value what He values. We love because He loves.

MERCY IS A CORE VALUE

Genuine love is expressed in showing mercy. Mercy is the willingness to extend kindness and grace to those known to be guilty. Mercy suspends judgment in an effort to bring reconciliation. Jesus said, **"Be merciful, just as your Father is merciful"** (6:36). People of God's kingdom are to reflect the values and driving motivations of the Father, which He models in His actions toward us.

Jesus said, **"Do not judge . . . Do not condemn"** (6:37). Mercy is reflected in a nonjudgmental, noncondemning approach toward others. This does not mean that followers of Christ should lack discrimination and be tolerant of evil. Mercy does not ignore and excuse wrongdoing, but neither does it seek opportunity to be the judge of the behavior of others. It is easier to condemn than it is to extend mercy, so showing mercy is not a demonstration of weakness but of strength.

Mercy allows forgiveness to be possible, and the capability to forgive those who have sinned against you is a core value of the kingdom of God. Jesus said, **"Forgive, and you will be forgiven"** (6:37). If we want God to be merciful to us as sinners, we must be merciful toward those who sin against us. We cannot receive from God what we are unwilling to extend to others.

GENEROSITY IS A CORE VALUE

Greed is the creed of the world. Not so with people of the kingdom of God. Jesus said, **"Give, and it will be given to you"** (6:38). The mentality of the world is that to get ahead, you must get and hold on. It does not make sense that you become richer by giving away. The core value of the Kingdom is not just to give, but to give generously. If you are generous with others, God will be generous with you. **"For with the measure you use, it will be measured to you"** (6:38). We determine the dimension of what we receive by the dimension of our giving. If we are stingy, our reward will be meager. If we are generous, our reward will be abundant.

INTEGRITY IS A CORE VALUE

People of the Kingdom are loving, merciful, generous, and *authentic*. A hypocrite is someone who is not what he wants everyone to think he is, and no one wants to carry that label. God demands that His children be people of integrity—honest, authentic, and transparent.

Jesus spoke this way of the generation to which He came: "Though seeing, they do not see; though hearing, they do not hear or understand" (Matt. 13:13). Spiritual blindness results from the disease of sin and often manifests itself in the inability to see one's own faults while believing one can clearly see the faults of others. People with this blindness often view themselves as responsible to give direction to those who are obviously blind and to point out their problems to them. Jesus asked, **"Can a blind man lead a blind man? Will they not both fall into a pit?"** (Luke 6:39). Jesus was speaking to the Pharisees and teachers of the law who viewed themselves as leaders of those who were unrighteous, while they lacked righteousness themselves. Both they and those they viewed as blind would be lost.

Spiritually blind people have the tendency to minimize their personal faults and maximize the faults of others, which leads to judgmentalism and spiritual elitism, a problem of the Pharisees. They could easily see **the speck of sawdust in** their **brother's eye** but paid **no attention to the plank in** their **own eye** (6:41).

Jesus is not suggesting that Christians never be concerned about the sins or faults that may be obvious in our brothers and sisters. He said, **"First take the plank out of your eye, and** *then* **you will see clearly to remove the speck from your brother's eye"** (6:42, italics added). Likewise, Paul wrote, "If someone is caught in a sin, you who are spiritual should restore him gently. But watch yourself, or you also may be tempted" (Gal. 6:1). The word used for *restore* carries the meaning of setting a bone that is broken. We are to be engaged in helping others to deal with their sins and find healing, but do so humbly, gently, and with an understanding of our own capacity for brokenness and blindness.

3. FRUIT AND FOUNDATIONS (6:43-49)

Jesus quickly stacked up word pictures to illustrate the fact that people who follow Him are transformed. He drew connections between tree and fruit, heart and mouth, and house and foundation.

LIFE CHANGE

CHANGED BEHAVIOR

We become Christians through *belief*, not *behavior*. We cannot be good enough to merit salvation. However, our behavior is changed by our beliefs. Faith without corresponding good deeds is dead (James 2:26).

You can look at a tree and tell what kind it is by the fruit it bears. **"No good tree bears bad fruit, nor does a bad tree bear good fruit"** (Luke 6:43). Good people are recognized by the good things that come out of the good that is in their hearts. If you have evil in your heart, it will show up as clearly as bad fruit will on a bad tree. What is in a person's heart will be revealed in that person's speech and activity. Transformation of behavior begins with transformation of the heart, and we determine what we store there.

Transformation comes through internalizing the Word of God and incorporating its principles as the foundation of our lives. Jesus asked, **"Why do you call me, 'Lord, Lord,' and do not do what I say?"** (6:46). Jesus can only be Lord if His Word is obeyed. He was not just concerned that the crowds hear His message, but that people hear His words and put them into practice. He said that the person who does that is **like a man building a house, who dug down deep and laid the foundation on rock.** There is stability and strength, so when floods come the house cannot be shaken **because it was well built. But the one who** is only a listener and not a practitioner has **built** life **without a foundation.** The outcome is predictable: When the flood came **it collapsed and its destruction was complete** (6:48–49).

People who live in the kingdom of God live with different values than people who align themselves with the kingdom of this world. The values of the kingdom of God shape the lives of people in the Kingdom so they have strength and stability while they must deal with the issues that result from living in a fallen world.

ENDNOTES

1. Donald Krabill, *Upside Down Kingdom* (Scottdale, Penn.: Herald Press, 2003).

8

GOD HAS COME TO HELP HIS PEOPLE

Luke 7:1–50

G od helps those who help themselves" is not found in the Scriptures. In fact, He is particularly concerned for, and inclined toward, those who are unable to help themselves. "When [Jesus] saw the crowds, he had compassion on them, because they were harassed and helpless, like sheep without a shepherd" (Matt. 9:36). Salvation is made available to the helpless: "When we were still powerless [helpless], Christ died for the ungodly" (Rom. 5:6). God helps those who cannot help themselves.

God helps the helpless because He is the God of compassion. The psalmist wrote, "The LORD is gracious and righteous; our God is full of compassion" (Ps. 116:5). And God said, "With everlasting kindness I will have compassion on you" (Isa. 54:8). It was His love and compassion for us that

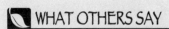

WHAT OTHERS SAY

VIRTUES OF JESUS

"Most men are notable for one conspicuous virtue or grace. Moses for meekness. Job for patience. John for love. But in Jesus, you find everything."

—J. Oswald Sanders

motivated Him to send His Son to meet needs in us that we are helpless to meet ourselves. God is love, and Jesus embodied that love.

As the people witnessed the compassionate activity of Jesus toward hurting people, it caused them to exclaim, "God has come to help his people" (Luke 7:16). We believe God cares about our "helpless estate."

He who cares is with us, and He has the power and authority to change our circumstances for His glory and our good.

1. COMPASSION FOR AN OUTSIDER (7:1–10)

Like metal responds to a magnet, Jesus and human need were quickly drawn to each other regardless of who the person was or what the need was. The first act of compassionate ministry in **Capernaum** was toward the servant of a non-Jew, a **centurion**, who had a **servant** he **valued highly** who **was sick and about to die** (7:1–2). By most Jewish standards the centurion and has servant were losers on two counts: The centurion was a Gentile, and his servant was a person of low status in the culture. Centurions were prominent soldiers of the Roman Empire, giving leadership to battalions of soldiers that occupied Israel at the time. This centurion would prove to be a man of unusual character—a man of compassion, faith, and humility. He had more than utilitarian concern for his sick servant. Sure, he would lose "property" if the servant were to die, as well as the service he provided, but his relationship with his servant ran deeper than that. He valued him highly. There is possibility that the servant was a Jew, which would make the relationship all the more interesting.

The centurion heard of Jesus and sent some elders of the Jews to him, asking him to come and heal his servant (7:3). What he had heard led him to believe that Jesus would care about his servant and that He had the capacity to do something about it. However, there was a problem in that he was a Gentile. The identification of *insiders* and *outsiders* was pretty clear within the Jewish community, who knew *they* were God's people and they often viewed non-Jews with contempt. Using his influence with Jewish leaders, the centurion asked some elders of the Jews to deliver his request to Jesus.

The Jewish leaders **came to Jesus** and **pleaded** the centurion's case, telling Him, **"This man deserves to have you do this, because he loves our nation and has built our synagogue"** (7:4–5). It is a wonderful thing when those who are outside of the kingdom of God are drawn to the Kingdom rather than driven from it by the lives of God's people. The centurion was an outsider who had learned to love the Jewish people and had earned their respect. He had even taken the initiative to see that a synagogue was built in Capernaum, showing more than a casual interest in the religion of the Jews. The elders of the Jews were so impressed with the man that they told Jesus that he *deserved* a miracle.

Impressed by the leaders' respect for the centurion, **Jesus went with them** (7:6). God's love is not limited to a single group or a status of people. While Israel was chosen by God for the special role of being a people through whom salvation might come to the world, the people of God includes all who acknowledge Him. Jesus went with them, but before He got to the house He was met by friends of the centurion who were sent with a message from the centurion: **"Lord, don't trouble yourself, for I do not deserve to have you come under my roof"** (7:6). The Jews considered the centurion deserving of a miracle, but he did not consider himself to be worthy of Jesus entering his house. In fact, he did not consider himself worthy of coming personally to Jesus with his need: **"I did not even consider myself worthy to come to you"** (7:7). Others might want to crowd Jesus to be seen with Him or to gain personal benefit, but not the centurion. His concern was for his servant, so he asked Jesus to just **"say the word, and my servant will be healed"** (7:7). The centurion knew that a strict Jew was forbidden to enter the house of a Gentile (Acts 10:28), but based on what he had come to know about this healer, he believed Jesus could do the healing from a distance by simply speaking a word.

The centurion was a man of authority who spoke with authority. He had soldiers who served under his direction, to whom he could say, **"'Go,' and he goes; and . . . 'Come,' and he comes"** (7:8). He also had a servant to whom he could say, **"'Do this,' and he does it"** (7:8). He understood authority because he had authority. He was appealing to an authority greater than himself to act where he was helpless. Some people who have a little authority do not know where that authority ends, but rather they try to extend it to cover far more than is their prerogative. The centurion had faith that Jesus had only to speak a word and that word would have authority over the sickness of his servant.

Jesus was **amazed** at the spirit of the centurion and said, **"I tell you, I have not found such great faith even in Israel"** (7:9). An outsider's faith was greater than that of many of the insiders. Faith is the recognition of authority in areas where you have none and submitting to it. The appeal of the centurion for his servant was heard by Jesus, who, from a distance, sent healing into the house of a Gentile. When the people **returned to the house** they **found the servant well** (7:10).

Luke's record would suggest that Jesus responded to the faith of a man with whom He had never met or spoken. He sent a miracle to a sick servant without ever seeing him. He responded with compassion and authority toward people considered outside of the ethnic boundaries of God's chosen people. The message is that God chooses all peoples to participate in His grace. It is up to us to respond in faith and choose Him.

2. COMPASSION FOR A GRIEVING MOTHER (7:11–17)

As **Jesus** approached **the gate** to **a town called Nain, . . . a dead person was being carried out—the only son of his mother, and she was a widow** (7:11–12). This woman had already suffered the death of her husband, and now her only son had died. Without a husband, the woman was dependent on her son for her livelihood, and now he too was gone. All hope for her son's return to health had disappeared.

When Jesus saw the woman and the depth of her grief, **his heart went out to her and he said, "Don't cry"** (7:13). The word translated in the NIV as "his heart went out" can also mean "moved with compassion" as translated in the King James Version.[1] Someone has defined compassion as experiencing your pain in my heart. Jesus had a great capacity for feeling the pain of others as if it were His own. The tears of others could quickly be reflected in His own eyes. With deep caring in His voice, He asked the mother to stop crying, which would appear to be a rather heartless request, unless you are able to remove the pain that caused the tears.

Jesus interrupted the death march and said, **"Young man, I say to you, get up!"** (7:14). It was customary for the townspeople and professional mourners to join the family procession as it made its way to the burial place, which could raise the level of sorrowful wailing. It was not customary for someone to tell people to quit crying and then tell the dead person to get up. But the son **sat up and began to talk**. **Jesus** reversed what was irreversible and **gave** the young man **back to his mother** (7:15).

This miracle was unrequested, but Jesus did it because His heart felt the pain of a sorrowing widow woman.

The people were **filled with awe and praised God** (7:16). Miracles should always result in praise being directed toward God. So-called modern-day "healers" who either take or are given undue credit for miracles are inappropriate. A miracle is divine intervention in what is humanly impossible. If God is the cause of a miracle, He should get the praise regardless of the human instrument that may be used. The people viewed Jesus as being **a great prophet** who had **appeared among** them, and said, **"God has come to help his people"** (7:16). The people were to believe that God was moving to help Israel by sending another great prophet, but Jesus was not just another prophet. He was *God* coming to help His people. When the angel informed Joseph that Mary was pregnant with the Son of God he said, "'and they will call him Immanuel'—which means, 'God with us'" (Matt. 1:23).

3. COMPASSION FOR HONEST SEEKERS AND A LOST GENERATION (7:18–35)

HONEST SEEKERS

This is the first reference to John the Baptist since Jesus' baptism. Luke informed us back in 3:19–20 that John was thrown into prison because he spoke out against the sins of Herod and his family. He was out of circulation, but he still had disciples who kept him informed about the activities of Jesus. John sent two of his disciples to ask Jesus, **"Are you the one who was to come, or should we expect someone else?"** (7:20). John had previously declared Jesus to be the "Lamb of God who takes away the sin of the whole world" (John 1:29). He had been given the mission of preparing the way for the Messiah, and he had declared that one was coming who was greater than he who would baptize with fire. He had baptized Jesus and was present when the heavens were opened and the Holy Spirit descended upon Him. Could it be that he was wavering in his belief that Jesus was the one for whom they were looking?

William Barclay offered three possibilities for John posing the question to Jesus. First, John may have sent the disciples for their benefit, not his.

He may have wanted them to connect personally with Jesus, transferring their commitments from him to the one who was greater. Second, John may have posed the question in an attempt to move Jesus to more publicly declare himself to be the Messiah, thereby speeding up His recognition and acceptance by the Jews. After all, John had prepared the way as much as he could and probably knew he did not have much time left to witness for himself the coming of the new kingdom. Third, John may have asked the question because sitting in solitary confinement in a dark, cold prison cell can shake up what a person has previously resolved in his heart.[2]

While John's disciples were present, **Jesus cured many who had diseases, sicknesses and evil spirits, and gave sight to many who were blind** (Luke 7:21). He didn't ignore their question, He just went about His ministry of compassion before responding to it. His answer was in the form of miraculous action, not words. He then told the men to report to John that they had witnessed **the blind receive sight, the lame walk, those who have leprosy are cured, the deaf hear, the dead are raised, and the good news is preached to the poor** (7:22).

John's message was a call to repentance and commitment to do the work of the kingdom of God. He was a man of action who could understand action, and Jesus was doing what Isaiah had said the Messiah would do (Luke 4:18–19). Many may have expected the Messiah's action to be that of gathering armies and staging strategies to overthrow the Roman occupation. But Jesus was changing lives and establishing a new spiritual Kingdom, just like God planned.

Perhaps it is most logical to believe John asked the question because he was an honest seeker who wanted to be sure, since the word of Jesus in dismissing the disciples was, **"Blessed is the man who does not fall away on account of me"** (7:23). Honest, seeking questions are never dismissed by Jesus as being inappropriate. There may be times when life throws a lot of stuff at us and we are moved to ask real, hard, honest questions, not born out of faithlessness or doubt, but out of a desire to experience again unquestionable assurance from God.

A LOST GENERATION

When John's disciples left, Jesus spoke to the crowd about John. He questioned them about why they went out into the desert to listen to John. John was quite a phenomenon—wild looking, dressed in animal skins, and dining on locust and wild honey. Were they drawn out to John to see **a prophet** (7:26)? Jews lived with the expectation that Elijah would return to herald the Messiah (Mal. 4:5). Jesus told the people that John was more than a prophet: He was the one God said He would send to prepare the way for the Messiah's coming. Jesus said, **"I tell you, among those born of women there is no one greater than John; yet the one who is least in the kingdom of God is greater than he"** (Luke 7:28). The greatest thing in all world is to be included in the kingdom of God. Jesus gave appropriate honor to John, but His heart reached out to a generation of people to whom John's message had been delivered and who now needed to respond to the good news that He preached.

When the people heard Jesus' words that day, they all **acknowledged that God's way was right** (7:29). There were those who had listened to John's call to repentance and were now ready to respond to the good news they heard from Jesus, **but the Pharisees and experts in the law rejected God's purpose for themselves** (7:30). You cannot listen to the message of the Kingdom and remain neutral. Either you acknowledge that God's way is right, or you reject God's purpose for yourself.

Jesus reached out to a generation who said of John the Baptist, **"He has a demon,"** and who said of Jesus, he **"is a glutton and a drunkard, a friend of tax collectors and 'sinners'"** (7:33–34). They rejected the message of the one who was to prepare the way for the Messiah, and they did not receive the one who came to be a redemptive friend of sinners, like they were. But His heart was still moved with compassion toward them. He still healed and preached the good news to a generation of needy people.

4. COMPASSION FOR A SINFUL WOMAN (7:36–50)

The Pharisees were quick to recognize sinners, and on several occasions they pointed out Jesus' habit of eating and associating with them (5:30; 15:1–2). They had less care about people than they did about keeping the law, as they interpreted it. Jesus usually went where He was invited, regardless of the motivation of the one doing the inviting, and a Pharisee **invited Jesus to have dinner with him, so he went to the Pharisee's house and reclined at the table** (7:36). Reclining around the table provided opportunity for social interaction during which significant things often happened. On this occasion, there was **a woman who had lived a sinful life in that town** (7:37) who heard where Jesus was and went to the house of the Pharisee. Evidently she had not sneaked off to another town and secretly engaged in sin and cover-up, but had sinned in their town, perhaps in open, shameful behavior. She came uninvited into the Pharisee's house, probably along with others who were free to gather whenever a rabbi spent time teaching. The presence of the sinful woman provided a perfect opportunity for the Pharisee to point out a sinner in the crowd.

But before her sinful presence could be pointed out, the woman **stood behind** Jesus **at his feet weeping**, and **she began to wet his feet with her tears** (7:38). Meals were customarily leisure events, with persons reclined on couches around the table. The woman moved close to Jesus, at his feet. She stood there weeping, and her tears fell on His feet. She was aware of her sin, and she was broken over it. Sometimes, like Nathan did with David, sinners need someone to point the finger of conviction at them and say, "You are the man" (2 Sam. 12:7). But sometimes, like with Isaiah, entering the presence of Holiness exposes one's sinfulness without the need of a condemning finger (Isa. 6:5). Pharisees liked to point, and they had gotten good at it. Jesus simply let His presence melt the heart of the sinful.

The woman **wiped** the feet of Jesus **with her hair, kissed them and poured perfume on them** from an **alabaster jar** she had brought with her (Luke 7:37–38). A similar event is recorded later in the ministry of Jesus (Matt. 26; Mark 14; John 12). Mary, the sister of Martha and Lazarus, is identified as the woman. On that occasion, it was an act of sacrificial devotion that raised criticism among the disciples as being wasteful. This is a different situation, a different woman, and a different criticism. The perfume may well have been a part of her trade, and prostitution may have been her sin. Perhaps she was out-on-the-town this night, loaded down with her perfume, and ready for business when she learned that Jesus was in a nearby house. What was intended to be used in sinful consumption was poured out as a sacrifice of repentance. A different kind of love had captured her heart. Her tears were symbols of her remorse, and her poured-out perfume was a symbol of repentance and adoration.

This was more than the Pharisee could handle. Religious men kept a safe distance between themselves and "sinners" lest they become contaminated. The Pharisee reasoned, **"If this man were a prophet, he would know who is touching him and what kind of woman she is—that she is a sinner"** (Luke 7:39). The *kind* of person an individual was did not keep Jesus from caring about or ministering to him or her. As Christians, we often try to carefully walk a line between associating with sinners but not wanting to be thought participants in their sin, and caring enough about them that we are willing to speak to them or reach out to them. It is not always easy to be "in the world but not of the world," at least when we live in fear of others' perception of us because of those with whom we associate. We can be afraid that people like the Pharisee will think that if we were either spiritual or smart we would not be caught in the same room with some people, let alone allow them to touch us. Jesus knew better than the Pharisee what kind of woman she was, and He knew this was a redemptive moment.

Jesus told the Pharisee about two men who **owed money to a certain moneylender** (7:41). One of the men owed twice as much as the other, but **neither had the money to pay back** the lender. In a gracious act of forgiveness, the lender **canceled the debts of both.** Jesus asked the Pharisee **which of** the two would **love** the lender **more** (7:42). The answer would seem obvious, and the Pharisee answered correctly, **"I suppose the one who had the bigger debt canceled"** (7:43).

It was common courtesy for hosts or their servants to wash the feet of guests as they entered the house, removing the dirt from the dusty pathways. Simon the Pharisee had not provided that common courtesy for Jesus, perhaps because he felt superior to Jesus. But the sinful woman, feeling the enormity of her sin, provided her tears and perfume to wash His feet. The Pharisee, who loved to point out sinners, was himself a debtor who was unable to pay his debt. But Jesus said of the woman, **"Her many**

sins have been forgiven—for she loved much. But he who has been forgiven little loves little" (7:47). It was Jesus' way of pointing a finger at the Pharisee who loved little because he had not experienced forgiveness. Jesus spoke to the woman, **"Your sins are forgiven . . . Your faith has saved you; go in peace"** (7:48, 50). The only sin that lies beyond the reach of forgiveness is the sin that is unacknowledged.

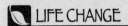

LIFE CHANGE

FORGIVEN

Our greatest need is to hear that we have been forgiven. Our debt is so big; our offence so great; our drift so far; and our guilt so devastating. The word *forgiven* is liberating. All that was lost because of our sin is restored because of His grace!

In Jesus, God had come to help His people. The heart of Jesus was moved with compassion toward the sick, the sorrowing, and the seeking. Most of all, He cared about the sinner. He felt their need deep in His heart, and that pain would take Him to Calvary, where He would fully carry the weight of the sin of the whole world—because He cares.

ENDNOTES

1. Thayer and Smith. "Greek Lexicon for Apostolos." The New Testament Greek Lexicon. http://www.studylight.org/lex/grk/view.cgi?number=6572.

2. William Barclay, *The Gospel of Luke* (Philadelphia: Westminster Press, 1956), p. 88.

9

MAKING DISCIPLES ONE AT A TIME

Luke 8:1–56

ollowers of causes come in all shapes, sizes, and levels of commitment. It was not hard for Jesus to draw a crowd, since people seemed to show up wherever He went. However, not everyone in a crowd could be called a *follower*. And not every follower could be called a *disciple*.

The word *follow* and its derivatives are prominent through Luke's gospel. Five times Jesus asked people to follow Him, and thirteen times it says that people followed Him, with many of those instances connected with people leaving everything, giving everything, or carrying a cross. Being a Christian means you are a *follower* of Christ, and being a follower means that you allow Christ to *lead*. Learning what it means to be a follower is perhaps one of our greatest needs in a culture that emphasizes independence and individualism.

The motives of the people in the crowds were varied. Some were followers, in that they were a part of an entourage of people who were interested observers. Some were disciples—persons whose lives were being transformed as they responded in obedience to the call of Christ. Some chose to follow *Him*, not just from village to village, but to really follow *Him*; to let His agenda become theirs; to internalize His teachings; and to live His life in such a way as to guide others into it. They were followers *and* disciples. Among them were twelve who left their homes and families to be with Him continuously.

This chapter gives us insight into types of followers and the level of their commitment to Christ. Chapter 9 speaks to issues surrounding the cost of following Christ, and chapter 14 focuses on how individuals respond to the invitation to follow Christ.

1. DIVERSE FOLLOWERS (8:1–18)

WOMEN FOLLOWERS

The group around Jesus included **the Twelve** (8:1). The level of their commitment to Christ ran deep. Christ had issued them the call, "Follow me," and they had left possessions and relationships to do that. Others might come and go from the crowd, but the Twelve were with Him all the time. Among other faithful followers were **some women who had been cured of evil spirits and diseases** (8:2). Women have a prominent place in Luke's gospel, and Luke portrays Jesus as one who showed great respect for women in a culture where they were often treated as property. These women had come to Jesus with spiritual and physical needs, and He had healed them. They followed Him out of gratitude and devotion.

This diverse group included **Mary (called Magdalene)**, from whom seven demons had been cast out; **Joanna**, the wife of the manager of Herod's household; and **Susanna** (8:2–3). Mary was a person with a sordid past. Joanna was a person of means. Susanna is not mentioned anywhere else in the Scripture. Mary and Joanna are mentioned later as the women who went to the tomb to care for the body of Jesus after His death (Luke 24:10). They were faithful followers to the end.

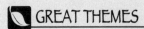 GREAT THEMES

WOMEN IN LEADERSHIP

The New Testament both dignifies the stature of women and affirms God's purpose to call, equip, and empower women for ministry and leadership in the church.

The work of God often rests on the shoulders of unknown persons. Luke says that **these women were helping to support** [Jesus and His disciples] **out of their own means** (8:3). Their commitment to the cause of Christ reached all the way to their purses. We don't know how much each of them would have been able to give, but this is the way it is in God's work—small gifts from unknown persons often outweigh the big gifts from prominent persons.

The point is that Jesus was able to do His ministry because of the financial support from people like this group of women.

DIFFERENT TYPES OF FOLLOWERS

The Twelve were there. The cluster of faithful supporting women was there. And a large crowd was **coming to Jesus from town after town** (8:4). People join crowds and follow leaders for a lot of different reasons, so Jesus used the gathering of a large crowd to tell them a parable that would identify some of the differences among followers. This is one of the few occasions in which Jesus interpreted a parable, providing in verses 9–15 the meaning of the story given in verses 5–8.

The parables of Jesus are often taken from nature or events that could be easily understood. On this occasion, He probably pointed to a field nearby where a farmer was sowing seed, a common scene in Galilee. There are three central elements in the parable: the *sower*, the *seed*, and the *soil*. Matthew records that when Jesus interpreted this parable, He said, "Listen to what the parable of the *sower* means" (Matt. 13:18, italics added).

The soil occupies the focus of the story, but we dare not miss what the story says regarding the sower. **A farmer went out to sow his seed** (8:5). The sower took the initiative and *went out*. He sowed *his seed*. He spread the seed "indiscriminately" yet deliberately, regardless of the type of soil. If God is recognized as the sower, He has faithfully sown the seed of His Word where people in all stages of receptivity have had opportunity. God—Father, Son, and Holy Spirit—are sowers of the Word of God. Every follower of Christ should also be a sower through life, testimony, and service.

The seed represents **the word of God** (8:11) that is sown in the soil of human hearts, where it is met with different conditions and responses. The human soul is like soil in which truth can be planted. How that truth is received, and what the outcomes are in life, depends on the condition of the soil. In the crowd being addressed by Jesus, the souls of the people were in varied degrees of preparation and receptivity to the truth. Some were there to listen, but they were not ready to believe. Some had heard the word before and were hungry to take it in and let it take root. Some had been hardened by life and were skeptical, ready only to reject what they heard.

In the parable, Jesus identified four kinds of soil. **Some** of the seed **fell along the path** (8:5); **some . . . on rock** (8:6); some **among thorns** (8:7); some **on good soil** (8:8). Jesus said the seed that fell along the path was quickly eaten by the birds. The ground would be hard there, and the seed would lie on top rather than penetrating the soil where it could germinate. It never had a chance to take root before it was taken away. Jesus said there will be those who hear the Word of God, but **then the devil comes and takes away the word from their hearts, so that they may not believe and be saved** (8:12).

The seed that fell on the rock withered and died. There was no depth of soil in which the roots could penetrate in order to get the necessary nutrients and moisture. Shallowness is the plague of many potential followers of Christ. They **receive the word with joy**, but when **the time of testing** comes **they fall away. They believe for a while** (8:13), but because of their lack of depth, they wilt when the heat is turned up on their faith. Their initial commitment to Christ is based more on emotion than on faith that is rooted in the Word of God. It is a painful thing to watch shallow people fall away after a joyful beginning. Sometimes the church has been guilty of thrusting new believers into the heat of the spotlight or in the pressure of leadership before they have opportunity to take root. When this happens, everyone loses.

The seed that fell among the thorns took root and grew up, but weeds grew up too and choked out the plants. The plants got a good start but ran into competition for space and nutrients. Jesus said this represented persons who are **choked by life's worries, riches and pleasures, and they do not mature** (8:14). God's objective in planting the seed is to see it grow, mature, and yield a harvest. Jesus never intended to simply draw crowds and tally up the number of people to whom He preached. He did not have to submit a report to His Father to show He had met His attendance goals. He was looking for transformed lives that were fruitful in godly graces and righteous living. But some people who start well do not finish well, because the life of God in them is choked out by things they allow to compete with it. Their lives are full, but not of the right things.

Their spiritual life gets more and more marginalized until it is covered up and pushed out by other concerns that are viewed to be more important.

However, some seed fell on good soil. These are people with **a noble and good heart, who hear the word** and **retain it** (8:15). The soil of their heart is ready to receive the Word, and it is allowed to take root. The Word is applied to their experiences in life, they mature, **and by persevering** they **produce a crop** (8:15). Perseverance is a necessary quality of a disciple. James says "that the testing of your faith develops perseverance. Perseverance must finish its work so that you may be mature and complete" (James 1:3–4). The seed that fell on the rocks withered and died when it experienced a time of testing. When the time of testing came to the seed that fell on the good soil, it survived and matured because the Word was internalized and enabled it to persevere, resulting in an abundant a crop. It fulfilled the purpose the sower had in mind when he sowed the seed.

Following Jesus and becoming a disciple involves receiving the Word of God into your life, allowing it to transform you so you can have staying power when you experience pressures, and demonstrating the fruit of God's grace through mature Christian living.

OPEN FOLLOWERS

Luke 8:16 is almost identical to what Jesus said later in 11:33, and 8:17 is almost identical to what He said in 12:2. In 8:16, He stated the obvious when He said a light is not meant to be lit only to be hidden, but it is to be placed where **those who come in can see the light.** In verse 17 He stated that **nothing** will be **hidden** but that will ultimately **be disclosed** and **brought out into the open.** When He said this later, it was in reference to those who were hypocrites, who pretended to be something they were not. When persons hear the Word of God, they are to receive it as light that exposes error and sin. When that Word is internalized and allowed to be light within them, it shines out, witnessing to others about their transformed life and leading others into the light. Paul said it like this: "It is God who works in you to will and to act according to his good purpose . . . so that you may become blameless and pure, children of God without fault in a crooked and depraved generation, in which you shine like stars in the universe as you hold out the word of life" (Phil. 2:13–16).

Faith in Christ cannot be hidden or pretended. Christians are to be open, authentic, and transparent before God and others. Only then can the light of Christ shine through them so others can see the light and move into it.

2. FAMILY OF FOLLOWERS (8:19–21)

While Jesus was teaching the crowd, His **mother and brothers came to see him** (8:19). This is the only reference to Mary in Luke's gospel between Jesus' visit to Jerusalem at age twelve and His crucifixion. His family included James, Joseph, Judas, Simon, and some sisters (Mark 6:3). At the beginning of His ministry when crowds began to press in on Jesus, His family tried to step in and take charge of Him because they said, "He is out of his mind" (Mark 3:21). At least early in His ministry, it appears that His family was not supportive, so perhaps Mary was kept busy at home keeping the others in line. There is no reason to believe Mary was unsupportive of Jesus' ministry, but she must have realized that He had a mission that she could neither control nor withstand. She had to let Him go, as all parents do at some point.

Once again, the crowds were pressing Jesus, so much so that His family could not get near Him. Someone carried the word through the crowd to Jesus, telling Him, **"Your mother and brothers are standing outside, wanting to see you"** (8:20). Luke does not say that Jesus ignored His family, but recorded that Jesus said that His real family is made up of **those who hear God's word and put it into practice** (8:21). A couple of things can come out of this exchange. First, sometimes a person's family can be a hindrance rather than a help in following Jesus. That is why He said that if we are going to follow Him we need to be able to "hate" our family, not in a literal and unrighteous way, but in a willingness to put Jesus ahead of any other relationship. Second, there may be brothers and sisters in Christ who become closer to us than blood relatives. "There is a *friend* who sticks closer than a brother" (Prov. 18:24, italics added) is often interpreted by us to be Jesus, which is a good thought, but it specifically refers to a human friend that can be closer than a blood brother. And third, if you do not have a family, or have been forsaken by your family, you have a new one in those who put God's Word into practice. You are a part of God's family. You have brothers and sisters in Christ who may be

LIFE CHANGE

A NEW FAMILY

When we join ourselves to Jesus, we also join ourselves to the family of God—the church. We are not alone in our spiritual journey. Our ability to persevere is enhanced by the support we receive from our brothers and sisters in Christ.

more important in your life right now than the human family into which you were born.

Disciples are those who have internalized the life and Word of God as well as having been adopted into a new family where followers of Christ find support and nurture.

3. FEARFUL FOLLOWERS (8:22–25)

Crowds can drain the energy out of those who are concerned about them and minister to their needs—even to one like Jesus. He needed occasional breaks from the people, so He gathered His disciples, **got into a boat and set out** (8:22) for the other side of the Sea of Galilee. The experienced seamen took over the sailing of the boat, and Jesus **fell asleep** (8:23). A sudden **squall came down on the lake** (8:23), which was not unusual on Galilee. Weather systems often moved over the mountains surrounding the Sea of Galilee and, without warning, dumped their energy in the form of heavy wind and rain. The rough waters began to swamp the boat, and even the experienced seamen were afraid.

The disciples woke Jesus and called to Him, **"Master, Master, we're going to drown!"** (8:24). The Greek word for *master* occurs only in Luke and was used to refer to the pilot of a ship and for one who had the right to give orders.[1] It is good that they recognized their limitations and went to the One who could take command of the situation. Often, it is only when our boat is in danger of sinking that we turn to the One who can navigate us through difficult waters so we come out safely on the other side. Fear must sometimes be experienced before we can find the foundation for our faith.

Jesus **rebuked the wind and the raging waters; the storm subsided, and all was calm** (8:24). He not only had the authority to command the boat, He could command the wind and water to obey Him. They had to submit to His authority. This power to command the elements amazed the disciples and caused them to ask among themselves, **"Who is this?"** (8:25). As much as they had already discovered about Him who had compelled them to follow Him, there were things yet that they did not know. They had been afraid of the storm; now they were **in fear and amazement** regarding Jesus (8:25).

Life often produces squalls that disturb our peace and trouble our spirit. In those times it is imperative that Jesus is in our boat and that He is the pilot. If He doesn't calm the sea, He can calm our spirit and deliver us safely through the storm. We are in good hands when we allow Jesus to be the pilot of our boat.

Disciples are those who know enough about Jesus to follow Him, but they remain *learners*. The more they walk with Jesus, the more they discover about Him that brings amazement and reverence.

4. LIBERATED AND BELIEVING FOLLOWERS (8:26–56)

LIBERATED FOLLOWER

When they reached the other side of the lake, they were in the **region of the Gerasenes** (8:26), which Mark says was in the area of the Decapolis (Mark 5:20). The Decapolis was a confederation of ten cities that included the city of Gerasa. The cities were founded by Alexander the Great and the inhabitants were largely Greek, so in culture and nationality they were more Greek than Jewish.[2]

Jesus was met by a man possessed by demons. His situation was so severe that he **lived in the tombs** and wore no clothes (Luke 8:27). Society had tried to control him with chains and guards, but under the powerful influence of the evil spirit in him, he broke the chains and was driven into a life of isolation. Demon possession was a very real problem in those days, either because of extraordinary spiritual warfare against the ministry of Jesus or a high level of superstition and openness to evil spirits; or perhaps demon possession has always existed at this level but has not been identified as such.

The possessed man fell at the feet of Jesus and begged Him not to torture him. Jesus responded by commanding **the evil spirit to come out of the man** (8:29). Jesus asked the name of the demon, and he replied, **"Legion," because many demons had gone into him** (8:30). This was no ordinary demon possession. Luke recorded numerous occasions in a rather matter-of-fact manner when Jesus and His disciples cast out demons. Jesus had power over all forces of evil and, "When Jesus had called the Twelve together, he gave them power and authority to drive out all demons and to cure diseases" (Luke 9:1). In most of the recorded exorcisms, the condition was addressed as being caused by a single demon. In this case, the term *legion* is used, likely a reference to a Roman military legion, which numbered six thousand men.

Jesus sent the demons into a large herd of pigs, which promptly **rushed down . . . into the lake and drowned** (8:33). Those who were tending the pigs rushed into town to tell everyone what they had just witnessed. When the crowds gathered, they found the previously possessed man **sitting at Jesus' feet, dressed and in his right mind** (8:35). His life had been radically changed—physically, socially, mentally, and spiritually—by the power of Christ. Regardless of how entrenched Satan may be in a person's life, God has the power to bring freedom. Whatever it is that keeps you from being the person God intends, He has the ability to break its hold on you.

A social misfit could now return to a productive life back in town with his family. Rather than being overjoyed by this, however, **the people . . . asked Jesus to leave them, because they were overcome with fear** (8:37). Why were they afraid? Were there other more "respectable" demons Jesus might expose, and exposing them would make the people uncomfortable? Were they afraid that if this cure cost a whole herd of pigs, how expensive might it be to have Jesus around? Were they afraid because they could not deal with the mystery and power of Jesus, this one who had authority in the spirit world? The cost of a miraculous healing was more than they wanted to bear, so they asked Jesus to leave. Some people find it uncomfortable to have Jesus around. His demands can be considered to be too great.

The response of Jesus is summed up in just a few sad words: **So he got into the boat and left** (8:37). Jesus came to seek and save those who are lost. He would go anywhere and endure anything to find a lost sheep. But He would not force himself on people who did not want Him. So He left, never to return to the area. They lost the opportunity to experience His life-changing truth and compassionate healing.

There was one person who was grateful that Jesus made the trip across the Sea of Galilee, even if He did pull up anchor and leave shortly after arriving. **The man from whom the demons had** been exorcised **begged to go with him, but Jesus sent him away** (8:38). Jesus had asked others to follow Him, and they turned Him down. Now a man begged to follow, but Jesus said he couldn't. Rather, Jesus told the man, **"Return home and tell how much God has done for you"** (8:39). Not all disciples climb into boats to follow Jesus. Some go home to tell their story and share their faith. Some people would prefer working for Jesus on the other side of the lake than having to go home and try to live out their faith with people they know. Though the man begged to go, he obeyed the command to stay, and he **went away and told all over town how much Jesus had done for him** (8:39).

Several things should be noted. First, Jesus went away, but He left a faithful witness behind. If the people listened, the opportunity they lost could be recovered through the witness of the faithful remnant. Second, those whom Christ has transformed have the responsibility of sharing the witness of their lives and lips with others. Third, we have a story of what Jesus has done for us that needs to be told. People may reject our logic and arguments, but they cannot argue with what Jesus has done for us. Fourth, when Jesus calls us out of our sin, He often sends us back into our situations to be His messenger and minister there. Transformed lives can be one of the most powerful verifications of genuine salvation—even among those who are not sympathetic.

BELIEVING FOLLOWERS

Jesus had escaped the crowds for just a little while by sailing across Galilee, but when He returned, they were waiting for Him. **Jairus, a ruler of the synagogue** (8:40), stepped out of the crowd and pled with Jesus to go to his house because his only daughter was dying. Most encounters between Jesus and rulers of the synagogue were antagonistic, and most references to them are negative. But here was one who believed Jesus could heal his daughter and was willing to step out of the crowd to make the request. When people reach the end of their ability to control or fix things, they are more likely to turn toward God. As the ruler of the synagogue, Jairus was responsible for administrating the synagogue and assisting the community in its worship. He occupied a place of prominence in the community, but none of that mattered when his twelve-year-old daughter was dying. Parents will especially turn to God when it involves desperate situations with their children. It is a wonderful picture of grace that even if people wait until a crisis drives them to Him, God responds to any sincere plea for His help. The **crowds almost crushed him** (8:42), but Jesus always focused on the needs of individuals, and He followed Jairus to his home.

The crowds followed too, and while they were en route, a woman **came up behind** Jesus **and touched the edge of his cloak** (8:44). Jesus asked who had touched Him, which Peter and the others thought was a foolish question. With people crowding Him, *many* had touched Him. However, her touch was different. **Jesus said, "Someone touched me; I know that power has gone out from me"** (8:46). The woman was **subject to bleeding** (8:43). Mark wrote that she had spent everything she had on doctors but had only gotten worse (Mark 5:26). The bleeding would make her, and anyone who came in contact with her, ceremonially unclean. This is why she would have tried to sneak through the crowd unnoticed. She probably figured that if Jesus usually healed by touching, He would never touch her. The woman had hoped to go unnoticed, but you cannot reach out in faith and touch Jesus without His being aware and responsive. Jesus pulled her out of the crowd and spoke to her as a valued individual. She had lived in embarrassment and shame, but Jesus treated her with dignity. She had no resources, but Jesus wasn't charging a fee for His services. She had interrupted Him while He was on His way to an important man's house, but in that moment she was the most important person in the crowd. She came in faith, and Jesus sent her home in peace, telling her that she had been healed because of her faith.

Meanwhile, Jairus's daughter was getting sicker. You could imagine Jairus getting a bit impatient with Jesus because his daughter was dying and Jesus had stopped to pay attention to a woman of no means or status. A messenger from home came with the dreaded news that the daughter had died, and he said to Jairus, **"Don't bother the teacher any more"** (8:49). Sometimes it seems obvious that conditions have reached the point where even God can't change them and there is no sense bothering Him. But, ignoring the hopelessness of the messenger, Jesus said to Jairus, **"Don't be afraid; just believe, and she will be healed"** (8:50). It is hard to believe when there is absolutely no indication the thing for which you believe could possibly happen. But faith is defined as "being sure of what we hope for and certain of what we do not see" (Heb. 11:1). There is no cure for death. But Jesus said to believe, so Jairus must have believed. Can you imagine the waves of hopeless that must have washed against his faith as this group hurried on to his house? You can believe while there is still life, but can you believe when life has gone?

When they **arrived at the house**, Jesus went in to the child, taking with Him the **father**, **mother**, and His inner three: **Peter, John and James** (Luke 8:51). There were mourners outside that Jesus quieted, telling them that the girl was **not dead**, only **asleep** (8:52). They thought they knew better, so **they laughed at him** (8:53). But when **he took her by the hand** and told her to **get up** (8:54), she did so immediately. Luke says **her spirit returned** (8:55), which would seem to indicate that she was indeed dead, and Jesus returned life to her.

Disciples come to Jesus one person at a time. Individuals are the most important people in the world to Jesus. He treats each with dignity, replacing shame with self-worth. He cares about each person, regardless of position in life. William Barclay said, "God loves each one of us as if there was only one of us to love."[3]

ENDNOTES

1. Ralph Earle, *The Wesleyan Bible Commentary: The Gospel of Luke* (Grand Rapids, Mich.: Eerdmans, 1964), p. 258.

2. William Barclay, *And He Had Compassion* (Valley Forge: Judson, 1975), p. 54.

3. William Barclay, *The Gospel of Luke* (Philadelphia: Westminster, 1956), p. 114.

10

MOUNTAIN PEAKS AND VALLEYS

Luke 9:1-50

Commitment to Christ must transcend the emotional ups and downs of life. Often, we experience spiritual mountain peaks one day only to slide into the valleys of human frailty and limitation the next day. Ideally, our time on the mountain peak should prepare us to deal with the issues we confront in the valley.

Jesus and those who followed Him moved rather quickly through the emotions that accompanied acceptance and rejection, praise and ridicule, as well as divine miracles and human inadequacy. In these verses, the disciples witnessed God's glory on the mountain peak and their inability to perform miracles in the valley. Like the disciples, we are called to follow Christ and witness His glory and His ability to make a difference in the lives of those He touches. We also experience being sent out in His name to make a difference in the lives of those *we* touch. We should want to be as effective as possible as we minister in His name.

1. THE TWELVE ARE SENT OUT ON THEIR OWN (9:1-9)

DELEGATED AUTHORITY

Up to this point, the Twelve had been observers—learners. The time had come for them to take the message and ministry of Jesus to the streets, so **he sent them out to preach the kingdom of God and to heal the sick** (9:2). They were to have a ministry of proclamation and compassion, which was to flow out of genuine concern for people. It has been said that people don't care how much you know until they know how much you care. However, as much as they might care about helping the sick, the ministry of healing was not an end in itself. It was to prepare people for the message about the kingdom of God; to bring people into spiritual wholeness, not just physical health.

Effective ministry requires something more than dynamic personality or polished talent. At our best, our abilities are limited and our authority in spiritual matters is nonexistent. Prior to sending out the Twelve, Jesus **gave them power and authority to drive out all demons and to cure diseases** (9:1). Their power and authority was not humanly derived but divinely delegated. They were to be emissaries of Jesus, ministering in His name and exercising His authority, without which their ministry would be ineffective.

The subtle temptation of service in the name of Jesus is to try to do it on the strength of our personal giftedness and through positional authority—authority that is derived from the office or position we hold. Positional authority may cause some people some of the time to do what you want them to do, but demons and diseases do not respond to such authority. Ministry in the name of Jesus involves engaging spiritual forces and strongholds that respond only to the power and authority of God.

Jesus knew the disciples would experience both acceptance and rejection. **He told them: "Take nothing for the journey—no staff, no bag, no bread, no money, no extra tunic"** (9:3). They were to find people who were receptive, stay with them, and receive from them what was needed for their support. However, not everyone would welcome them, and when they met with rejection Jesus told them to **"shake the dust off your feet when you leave their town, as a testimony against them"** (9:5). There will always be those who will reject the messenger and the message of God. Ministers become so much a part of the ministry that when their message is rejected, they can suffer personal rejection that can put a lid on their effectiveness. Knowing that rejection would happen, Jesus encouraged His disciples to move beyond their feelings of rejection to the next place where their message and ministry would be received. Many ministers need to "shake the dust off" of past failures, not in defiance of those who would not listen, but in dependence on the authority of Christ upon whom rests the ultimate matter of acceptance and rejection.

The Twelve were effective in their ministry as they **went from village to village, preaching the gospel and healing people everywhere** (9:6). Jesus delegated power and authority to them and they ministered out of it. What Jesus had been doing, they could now do. Power and authority like this was awesome and had the potential of multiplying the ministry of Jesus beyond the time and space limitations of one person. But power and authority like this can spoil those who have it if they are not careful. This is always the dangerous possibility of delegated authority.

THE DEATH OF JOHN

The ministry and notoriety of Jesus was spreading, and **Herod the tetrarch heard about all that was going on** (9:7). This is the same person who imprisoned John the Baptist in chapter 3 and later had him beheaded at the request of his niece (Matt. 14:3–11). When Herod learned about the miracles of Jesus, **he was perplexed, because some were saying that John had been raised from the dead, others that Elijah had appeared, and still others that one of the prophets of long ago had come back to life** (Luke 9:7–8). Talk around the town watering holes focused on who this man was who spoke with such authority and performed miracles. He had to be someone special, someone sent from God. Herod had seen John's head carried on a platter and knew he had killed him. If the man creating the stir was John come back to life, Herod was definitely in trouble. If it were Elijah or a prophet of long ago, he was in greater trouble. So, to see what he was up against, **he tried to see him** (9:9). But he would soon turn his attention toward eliminating Jesus just as he had John (Luke 13:31).

2. HUNGRY MULTITUDES (9:10–17)

The Twelve **reported** back **to Jesus** (9:10) the acceptance and rejection they had experienced, their successes and failures, as well as the joys and sorrows of their ministry. There were things to celebrate, and there were wounds to be healed. Ministry is demanding, and it depletes human resources. Jesus knew this, and **he took them with him and they withdrew by themselves to a town called Bethsaida** (9:10). The need to periodically withdraw from the crowds and the demands of ministry was regularly recognized by Jesus and was modeled to His disciples. The issues surrounding ministry needed to be discussed and tired bodies needed to be rejuvenated. Effective ministry results from the overflow of vibrant spirits not the overwork of exhausted servants.

It is difficult to escape the needs and demands of people, particularly if people know you are a link to God and you have a word of healing and hope for them. The time alone was short lived, because **the crowds learned about it and followed him** (9:11). There must be a balance maintained between appropriate care for oneself and the demands of others, and finding that balance is critical for effective ministry. Regardless of how tired Jesus might have been, He was never rude to needy people, rather **he welcomed them and spoke to them about the kingdom of God, and healed those who needed healing** (9:11). Jesus was about to give His disciples another lesson in ministry—that effective ministry flows out of compassion that is combined with resources that come from beyond what are obviously visible.

Not only had the crowds interrupted the retreat time of Jesus and His disciples, but they had come without provision for food or lodging. This was not a small gathering, since **about five thousand men were there** (9:14) plus women and children. Ministers have sometimes been known to exaggerate the size of their crowds, but in this case the actual number was far more than what was reported. It got **late in the afternoon**, and **the Twelve** began to worry. **"Send the crowd away so they can go to the surrounding villages and countryside and find food and lodging, because we are in a remote place here"** (9:12). The disciples thought the reasonable solution was to give the benediction and send the people away. The crowd had become a liability.

The effectiveness of ministry rapidly diminishes when people are viewed as liabilities. It's easier to send them away than try to find a solution for their problem. When their problem is allowed to become our problem, then we all have a problem. So, it is easier if they keep their problem as their own responsibility to solve.

However, Jesus was not yet finished healing those who needed healing and speaking to them about the kingdom of God. Matthew's record of this event says Jesus "had compassion on them" (Matt. 14:14). Human need always finds a response from the heart of Jesus. He assumed responsibility for acting on behalf of those needs. His response to the hungry multitude was not to send them away, but to do what He could to help them. So He shifted responsibility back to those who viewed the crowd as a liability and told them, **"You give them something to eat"** (Luke 9:13). He asked them to do something both He and they knew they could not do. The inventory of their supplies showed they had **only five loaves of bread and two fish** (9:13). Lesson number one: In ministry, people are opportunities not liabilities. Lesson number two: In ministry, when God asks you to do something, it becomes His responsibility to help you with the resources necessary to do it. We are not to excuse our inactivity by saying we do not have what is necessary to complete the task. We are to begin doing what we can with what we have and allow God to do what He can with what He can bring to the table.

It was Jesus who was moved with compassion, and it was His disciples whom He asked to take action. God often uses His people to meet the needs of those who need assistance. Often, when God miraculously provides in response to someone's prayer, He does it through the resources of one of His children. He doesn't create something out of nothing He directs one of His disciples to take action.

LIFE CHANGE

ANSWER TO PRAYER

God answers prayer, and it is great when you receive a positive answer to a prayer. It may be a greater experience to know that we can become an answer to someone else's prayer. God told Abram that He would bless him and that he would be a blessing (Gen. 12:2). Sharing your loaves and fish with someone in need may be God's way of answering their cry for help.

Jesus instructed the disciples to have everyone **sit down in groups of about fifty each** (9:14). To their credit, the disciples did not question the sanity of Jesus, but did what He told them to do. The first step in divine provision was purely an organizational, mechanical thing. The next step was His. **Taking the five loaves and the two fish and looking up to**

heaven, he gave thanks and broke them. Then he gave them to the disciples to set before the people (9:16). Who could imagine that a meager supply of five loaves and two fish could satisfy one hungry man, let alone provide even the smallest morsel for thousands? Sometimes God asks His ministers to do things that are obviously beyond their capability and capacity, which allows "God things" to become possibilities. Without God things happening occasionally, our ministry is always limited to what we are capable of doing and does not display the glory of God.

There are times when God demonstrates that He "is able to do immeasurably more than all we ask or imagine, according to his power that is at work within us" (Eph. 3:20). Not only was there enough to tide the people over until the next good meal, **they all ate and were satisfied, and the disciples picked up twelve basketfuls of broken pieces that were left over** (Luke 9:17). This was not an appetizer but a satisfier, not an hors d'oeuvre but a full meal. Each of the Twelve, who previously had nothing to share, now had a basket of leftovers for himself. Another lesson: Though God can fulfill our needs beyond our expectation and imagination, He does not waste His miracles. The disciples picked up the leftovers because they would need them another day. They should never presume upon the ability of God to provide bread for them tomorrow if they wasted what He provided for them today.

3. PETER'S CONFESSION AND THE TRANSFIGURATION (9:18–36)

THE BIG QUESTION

Jesus emphasized the importance of prayer and had a regular practice of praying. He prayed in "lonely places" (5:16), on mountains (6:12; 9:28), in a "certain place" (11:1), and in a garden (22:41). Sometimes it was in private, sometimes with His disciples, and sometimes with an inner core of friends. Jesus snatched some time away from the crowds, and while He **was praying in private and his disciples were with him, he asked them, "Who do the crowds say I am?"** (9:18). Jesus was interested in *what* the people were saying about Him, but He was more interested in *who* they thought He was. He was setting things up for the "big" question that would separate opinion from truth.

The time had come for Jesus to clarify who He was, so He began by asking His disciples who others said He was. Their response indicated there were several opinions about Jesus. Some thought He was **John the Baptist; others** thought He was **Elijah; and still others, that one of the prophets of long ago** had **come back to life** (9:19). The crowds had listened to His teaching and received His miracles, and they had come to their own opinions. Jesus pushed the question to those who had spent hours with Him, lived life with Him, and had listened in on His conversations with His Father. **"But what about you?" he asked. "Who do you say I am?"** (9:20). He did not force His divine identity upon them, but allowed them to come to their own discovery of His divinity as the Spirit revealed it to them. But truth is more than having an opinion. Jesus is not one option among individuals' opinions. Accepting the person of Christ is essential to finding relationship with God. The evidence is there, but He will not force himself on us. Who is Jesus? If He is the Messiah, He cannot be ignored. He must be either accepted or rejected.

Peter either had greater insight than the others or, more likely, he was first to express himself. He **answered, "The Christ of God"** (9:20). The word he used means "God's Chosen One" or the "Messiah". Matthew expands this conversation to include the following: "Jesus replied, 'Blessed are you, Simon son of Jonah, for this was not revealed to you by man, but by my Father in heaven. And I tell you that you are Peter, and on this rock I will build my

WHAT OTHERS SAY
WHO DO YOU SAY I AM?

"A man who was merely a man and said the sort of things Jesus said wouldn't be a great moral teacher. He would either be a lunatic on the level with a man who says he's a poached egg—or else he would be the devil of hell; you must take your choice. Either this was, and is, the Son of God, or else a mad man or something worse. You can shut Him up for a demon, or you can fall at His feet and call Him Lord and God. But don't come up with any patronizing nonsense about His being a great moral teacher. He hasn't left that alternative open to us. He did not intend to."

—C. S. Lewis in *Mere Christianity*

church, and the gates of Hades will not overcome it'" (Matt. 16:16–18). The foundation of the Church is the knowledge of Christ, and that knowledge is obtained through the revelation of God. This revelation would transform

Simon into Peter, the rock, who would give leadership to the emerging church in Jerusalem.

Though He must have been pleased that His disciples had come to understand who He was, **Jesus strictly warned them not to tell this to anyone** (Luke 9:21). Being the Messiah could only be fulfilled when He completed His redemptive mission. He was not just a great teacher and miracle worker, but He was the Lamb of God who came to take away the sins of the world (John 1:29).

A DIFFICULT ROAD TO TRAVEL

The road to the mountaintop runs through the valley. Not only was Jesus called to suffer, but those who followed Him would also pay a price. Jesus told His disciples, **"The Son of Man must suffer many things and be rejected by the elders, chief priests and teachers of the law, and he must be killed and on the third day be raised to life"** (Luke 9:22). They did not understand the full impact of these words, but Jesus told them the road ahead would be difficult. Even as He told them of His death, He told them of His resurrection. His life began with a miracle, and it would extend beyond the grave with a greater miracle.

There was a cross in the future for Jesus and for each of His followers. His cross was made of wood and was an instrument of physical death. Dying on it would have a redemptive effect upon all who would accept it. But to those who would follow Him, He said, **"If anyone would come after me, he must deny himself and take up his cross daily and follow me. For whoever wants to save his life will lose it, but whoever loses his life for me will save it"** (9:23–24). When some people talk of their daily cross, they speak of physical afflictions or difficult situations. This is not the cross of which Jesus spoke. Followers of Christ are asked to choose to deal with issues of self-centeredness and self-determination. Accepting Christ and His way requires us to deny ourselves and our way. It is a difficult road to travel, because it is in our nature to save ourselves and to please ourselves. The call to follow Christ involves a willingness to lose ourselves in Him and for Him. Only then can we really save ourselves.

Our lives can be spent trying to **gain the whole world,** and in the process we can **lose or forfeit** our very selves (9:25). Many people have accumulated what would be considered "gain," but have lost more important things while doing it—things that could have brought meaning, fulfillment, and eternal reward. What they lost was far more valuable than what they gained.

ON TOP OF THE MOUNTAIN

Again, Jesus sought out a place to pray away from the crowds. This time it was **up onto a mountain**, and **he took Peter, John and James with him** (9:28). These three were the inner core of the disciples. They had a special relationship with Jesus that went beyond the fact that John and James were cousins of Jesus. They were the first to respond to the call of Jesus to follow Him and were included in several special times when the others were not along. They were prayer partners with Jesus. Tradition identifies the mountain where they went as Mount Tabor, though the exact location is unknown. Mount Tabor sits at the eastern end of the Jezreel Valley, eleven miles west of the Sea of Galilee. As with most traditional sites, the true physical location is not as important as the event that took place there.

While Jesus **was praying, the appearance of his face changed, and his clothes became as bright as a flash of lightning** (9:29). Matthew and Mark use the word *transfigured* to describe what happened to the appearance of Jesus. Perhaps this is part of what John referred to when he said, "We have seen his *glory*, the glory of the One and Only, who came from the Father, full of grace and truth" (John 1:14, italics added). The glory of God's presence was considered to be more than Moses could endure. Maybe Jesus turned down the lumens of His glory enough for Peter, James, and John to endure and to witness ultimate purity and holiness.

Jesus was joined by two Jewish icons, **Moses and Elijah**, who **appeared in glorious splendor, talking with Jesus** (9:30–31). These two men occupied positions of greatest prominence in Jewish history. Their appearance placed Jesus in the mainstream of God's work with His people. But it also settled the matter that He was not either one of them returned from the dead. He was with them, but not one of them. They were previous instruments of God, but He was greater. Moses and Elijah did not appear with Jesus to talk about themselves, but **they spoke about his departure, which he was about to bring to fulfillment at Jerusalem** (9:31). An event was about to occur for which the patriarchs and prophets of old could only point to as a far distant act of God on behalf of His people. That time was now drawing close, and Moses and Elijah were the advance guard for Jesus' welcome-home party.

Jerusalem was a place of destiny for Jesus, and it loomed closer and closer on the horizon. His departure dominated the conversation, though the details of the conversation are not recorded, perhaps because it was missed by sleepy witnesses. **Peter and his companions were very sleepy, but when they became fully awake, they saw his glory and the two men standing with him** (9:32). How many wonderful revelations of God have His people slept through? The three became awake enough to see what was happening but slept through the conversation that may have prepared them for what was ahead for Christ and themselves. Their lack of understanding led them to misjudgments. Peter told Jesus how good it was to be up on the mountain with Moses and Elijah, and it would sure be great to **put up three shelters—one for** Jesus, **one for Moses and one for Elijah** (9:33). Luke added the parenthetical statement: **(He did not know what he was saying)** (9:33). The statement is Luke's assessment of Peter's exuberant building project that was not based on spiritual understanding. He would have Jesus, Moses, and Elijah equally prominent and equally worshipped in shelters, which were often constructed as places for worship.

God the Father interrupted Peter's building plan and set things straight about Jesus. While Peter was talking, **a cloud appeared and enveloped them, and they were afraid as they entered the cloud. A voice came from the cloud, saying, "This is my Son, whom I have chosen; listen to him"** (9:34–35). Moses and Elijah were *important* in God's redemption of His people, but Jesus was *superior*. Only Jesus was God's Son, and it was He they should listen to. Lest they remain enthralled with others and begin building structures in which to worship others, the others were removed and Jesus stood alone before them. The reality of all our spiritual enterprises is that they are about Jesus, alone. Without Him we have empty "shelters" and a misplaced focus. Like Peter, it is one thing to say Jesus is the Christ, and it is another thing to live like He is.

4. HEALING OF A POSSESSED BOY (9:37–45)

TROUBLE IN THE VALLEY

Jesus and the three disciples descended from the relative solitude of the mountain and were **met** by **a large crowd** (9:37). The glory on the mountain is quickly balanced by trouble in the valley. Much of life is lived in the valleys, not on the mountain. The crowds are waiting there in the valley with their needs and demands. **A man in the crowd called out, "Teacher, I beg you to look at my son . . . A spirit . . . scarcely ever leaves him"** (9:38–39). The son suffered **convulsions** that were **destroying him** (9:39). No cure was available to him, and the father blurted out to Jesus, **"I begged your disciples to drive it out, but they could not"** (9:40). Earlier Jesus had given them the power and authority to heal and to drive out demons, but in this case they were ineffective. Was the rebuke of Jesus directed to the ineffective disciples or to the crowd when he said, **"O unbelieving and perverse generation, how long shall I stay with you and put up with you?"** (9:41). Even Jesus must get frustrated with us when our unbelief and perverseness hinder the flow of His power and authority through us. Jesus **healed the boy and gave him back to his father** (9:42). What the disciples were unable to do, He did.

We can dream big dreams on the mountain, but can we get the job done in the valley? We can be better at constructing buildings than we are at meeting the needs of people by bringing hope and help to them in the name and power of Jesus.

AMAZED BY NOT UNDERSTANDING

Once again, the people were wowed by a miracle and **amazed at the greatness of God** (9:43). They were more amazed by the miracle than by the Man who performed it. They marveled **at all that Jesus did** (9:43) but continued to miss who *He* was. It is easier to get excited about *what* has happened than with *Who* made it happen.

Up on the mountain God had told them Jesus was His Son and they should listen to Him. Jesus had to get their attention again by telling them, **"Listen carefully to what I am about to tell you: The Son of Man is going to be betrayed into the hands of men"** (9:44). Jesus tried to shift their focus toward the inescapable future of His mission. **But they did not understand what this meant. It was hidden from them, so that they did not grasp it, and they were afraid to ask him about it** (9:45). Why didn't they understand? Why was it hidden from them? Why were they afraid to ask? From our perspective, they should have picked up on the recurring theme of Jesus' teaching to them. They should have had the spiritual blinders removed from their eyes by now. If they did not understand, they should have been driven to ask, to seek, and to knock until they received. But God's purpose in our lives and our world is often missed because we just don't get it, and then we fail to ask Him to reveal it to us. Our fear to ask may come from our fear that He might ask us to partner with Him, and the road down which He is traveling appears to be difficult.

5. AN ARGUMENT ABOUT GREATNESS (9:46–50)

Dissention is unattractive when it appears among followers of Christ. In this case, it was conceived in self-centeredness and grew into a petty argument. **An argument started among the disciples as to which of them would be the greatest** (9:46). Tragically, Jesus was talking about betrayal and suffering, while they argued about their importance and greatness. They were in the presence of greatness but could see nothing but themselves. We can only imagine which disciple thought he was the greatest and the reasons he gave to argue his case.

Ambition is an inner motivation that wants to achieve, but it can quickly go astray if it becomes misplaced. The word *ambition* appears seven times in the New Testament. Five of those times it is preceded by the word *selfish* (Gal. 5:20; Phil. 1:17; 2:3; James 3:13, 16). Effective ministers have goals and dreams that should contribute to their drive and determination. But when that fire is burning for personal gain rather than God's glory, it is misplaced, ugly, and dangerous. The goal of ministry is not to gain the most prestigious position, receive prominence and recognition, or receive the adoration of religious fans.

Jesus used **a little child** (9:47) to define greatness. If the arguing disciples did not feel small, they should have. Jesus said, **"Whoever welcomes this little child in my name welcomes me; and whoever welcomes me welcomes the one who sent me. For he who is least among you all—he is the greatest"** (9:48). Greatness is not defined by power or prominence. The word used for *least* can refer to size, age, or influence. The "least" is whomever you may consider less important or inferior to you. But by God's assessment, they may be greater.

John wasn't finished with his sense of superiority. He shifted the focus to a person who was not among the Twelve. He said that they had seen **a man driving out demons in** Jesus' **name**, and they told him **to stop, because he** was **not one of** them (9:49). Too often we view those who are "not one of us" as being less than us and certainly not on the same level with God. They may be doing good, but because they are of a different class, culture, country or communion they are not one of us; so they must be less than us. The response of Jesus was **"Do not stop him, for whoever is not against you is for you"** (9:50). Jesus was not giving license to waive matters of biblical orthodoxy or to approve the ministry of unbelievers, but rather to squash the notion of superiority and greatness that infected the spirit of His disciples. Misplaced ambition should have no place in the disciples of Jesus Christ.

From the glory on the mountaintop to trouble in the valley, the disciples demonstrated their propensity for missing the important words from Jesus that were meant to inform them about who He was and prepare them for what was ahead for both Him and them.

Part Three

On the Way to Jerusalem

LUKE 9:51–19:27

Jesus' journey took on greater intensity as He turned His face toward Jerusalem. He did not move aimlessly from village to village—He was on a mission that could only be fulfilled in Jerusalem. The King James Version says, "he stedfastly set his face to go to Jerusalem" (Luke 9:51). He would not be detoured from completing His redemptive journey. For Him, all roads led toward Jerusalem, and He was moving in that direction.

11

CHOOSING WHAT IS BEST

Luke 9:51–10:42

C hoices have consequences and carry costs, and each of us makes choices that carry huge consequences. When we choose a direction, we choose a destination. When we choose a master, we choose that master's values, which become the governing principles of our lives. We may try to avoid the cost and consequences of particular choices we make, but we cannot escape them; they come with the privilege of making choices.

A major change of direction in the ministry of Jesus takes place in this chapter. His mission could only be accomplished by traveling to Jerusalem, as difficult as arriving there might be. He chose to make the trip that would define His mission and make our salvation possible. The choice to go to Jerusalem would be costly, but it would yield eternal consequences to our benefit.

1. OPPOSITION AND THE COST OF FOLLOWING JESUS (9:51–62)

Jesus was keenly aware of His mission and of the progressive movement of the events that surrounded Him. Timing was extremely important in His birth and in the beginning of His ministry. **As the time approached for him to be taken up to heaven, Jesus resolutely set out for Jerusalem** (9:51). Luke did not say "as the time approached for him to die," though that was His mission, and it would have to happen before He could be taken up to heaven. Being taken up to heaven would indicate He had fully completed His earthly ministry. As much as He loved people and was committed to the completion of His redemptive purpose, He must have longed to be back with His Father. The road that would return Him to heaven must first go through Jerusalem, and He did not try to avoid the inevitable, but rather He moved toward the necessary.

There is strength and determination expressed in the words used by Luke. *Resolutely set out* means to "steadfastly fix oneself to an objective." Jesus was on a journey from which He would not be detoured, and it would ultimately lead to His departure from this life.

Jesus sent **messengers ahead** of His entourage **into a Samaritan village to get things ready for him** (9:52). Expressing hospitality to strangers was a custom of the day, and to refuse to provide food and lodging for travelers was a great offense. However, **the people** in the village **did not welcome** Jesus **because he was heading for Jerusalem** (9:53). Perhaps their lack of hospitality resulted from the tensions that existed between Jews and Samaritans, since "Jews [did] not associate with Samaritans" (John 4:9). Perhaps they sensed the resolution of Jesus, and sometimes people who are resolutely focused on a mission make others uncomfortable.

When properly focused, zeal for a cause and loyalty to a person are admirable qualities, but when they are misguided they can be destructive. James and John, nicknamed "Sons of Thunder" (Mark 3:17), sometimes lived up to their fiery reputation. Faced with the lack of hospitality from the Samaritans, they asked Jesus if they could **call fire down from heaven to destroy them** (Luke 9:54). Previously, Jesus had instructed the disciples to shake the dust off their feet and move on if a village was not receptive to their presence and message (9:5), but He had never encouraged them to call down fire from heaven.

People may make the choice to reject Christ, and when they do, consequences follow. The consequences may not take the form of fire from heaven, but they may be just as destructive. Sometimes opportunity only knocks once. Only eternity will reveal the opportunities that have been lost because people chose not to welcome Jesus into their lives when He first came to them.

Having been refused entry into one village, **they went to another village** (9:56). Jesus moved on. Opportunity lost at one village became opportunity offered at another.

As they traveled, **a man** approached and **said, "I will follow you wherever you go"** (9:57). Enthusiastic willingness to follow Christ would appear to be the exact opposite of the rejection expressed in the previous village, and Jesus should be glad to hear it. But people can appear to be enthusiastic about a cause without being fully committed to it. It is possible to want to follow Jesus because it seems to be a glamorous and exciting thing to do, and it is the journey, not Jesus, that attracts you. If you could be a part of the group of disciples, it could be possible to have a front-row seat at the next miracle. Caught up in the excitement surrounding Jesus, a man did not wait for an invitation to follow, but enthusiastically proclaimed his willingness, regardless of where Jesus would go.

Jesus sought to balance the man's enthusiasm with the realities of what life as one of His followers could mean. He **replied, "Foxes have holes and birds of the air have nests, but the Son of Man has no place to lay his head"** (9:58). This must have been enough to dampen the man's enthusiasm, since there is no further interaction with him, and Jesus turned **to another man** and issued the invitation, **"Follow me"** (9:59). That man indicated interest in following Jesus, but said, **"Lord, first let me go and bury my father"** (9:59). A son was responsible for this last act of sonship, but the father was probably not close to dying. Another wanted to **say good-bye to** his **family** (9:61). Jesus invites everyone, **"Follow me."** Two men who heard the invitation that day responded with interest, perhaps even desire, but with conditions. Earlier, when Peter, James, and John received the invitation, they *immediately* "left everything and followed" Jesus (Luke 5:11), as did Levi (5:28). How often do the requirements of the kingdom of God get pushed back in our agendas, not because we deny them but because we delay them? To delay a response is

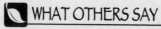

WHAT OTHERS SAY

FOLLOW ME

"Christ didn't spread out a road map showing where He would lead them. He never does that. We would like to negotiate a deal and evaluate the small print before we sign on to follow. But followers don't cut deals with Christ. They just follow. For followers, all the question marks fall into line behind Christ, who is the exclamation point."

—Joseph Stowell

often to choose not to respond, regardless of how reasonable the reason for delaying may appear. **"I will follow you, Lord, but . . ."** (9:61) expresses interest, but attaches conditions. Jesus is not interested in negotiating with our conditions.

To the second man, Jesus said, **"Let the dead bury their own dead, but you go and proclaim the kingdom of God"** (9:60). To the third, **"No one who puts his hand to the plow and looks back is fit for service in the kingdom of God"** (9:62). Being fit for service in the Kingdom includes a willingness to pay the price for unconditional acceptance of the invitation to follow Christ.

2. JESUS WAS ON A MISSION (10:1–24)

A SHARED VISION

The focus in the Scripture is often on the Twelve, the cadre of close disciples who shadowed Jesus in His ministry, yet a great number of others were a part of the entourage that accompanied Him as He moved from place to place. They had heard His teaching, had shared in His vision, and had committed themselves to be followers. Jesus commissioned them to go and minister in His name. He **appointed seventy-two others and sent them two by two ahead of him to every town and place where he was about to go** (10:1). The word *appointed* is found only here in the Gospels and means "to proclaim someone elected to an office."[1] The word *sent* is the word for *apostle,* and it means to delegate a mission to a person and dismiss that person with orders to accomplish that assigned mission.[2] All followers of Christ have a mission to accomplish, but God calls some to specialized tasks to assist the Church in fulfilling its mission in the world. God calls, appoints, and sends persons to function as *apostles*—persons who are divinely selected and sent out under orders of the King.

These appointed and sent persons were to go in groups of two ahead of Jesus to every place where he would be going. They were to **heal the sick . . . and tell them, "The kingdom of God is near you"** (10:9, 11). They were to be the advance guard, preparing the towns for the arrival of

Jesus, who was coming behind them. God's apostles always point people to Christ, not themselves.

Jesus had earlier sent the Twelve out with the power and authority to drive out demons and cure all diseases (Luke 9:1). Now there was a sense of urgency in the air. More messengers were needed, not only to address the physical needs of people, but to proclaim the kingdom of God. Not only did Jesus want these seventy-two to go, but they were to pray that others might be sent. Jesus said to them, **"The harvest is plentiful, but the workers are few. Ask the Lord of the harvest, therefore, to send out workers into his harvest field"** (10:2). The harvest into which the Lord sends His workers is more plentiful than they can even imagine. In sharing the gospel, we tend to minimize our opportunities and maximize the unresponsiveness of the people. The harvest field is His. And He says it is plentiful. There is more to be harvested than there are people who are willing to roll up their sleeves and work the fields.

Jesus prepared the seventy-two for their mission by telling them to be alert to the dangers they would face. He said, **"Go! I am sending you out like lambs among wolves"** (10:3). Matthew 10:16 records that Jesus gave this same warning to the Twelve when He sent them out to cast out demons and heal diseases (Luke 9:1). The image of lambs and wolves would be a sharp contrast in the minds of those being sent. Sheep and lambs, even more so, are defenseless when attacked by wolves. Jesus was sending them into potentially hostile and dangerous settings. The only safe place for a lamb is to stay close to the shepherd and the protection of the fold. But the Shepherd said, **"Go,"** not "Stay."

These sent ones were to travel light, not taking **a purse or bag or sandals** with them (10:4). As they traveled, they were not to **greet anyone on the road** (10:4). This was not telling them to be discourteous, but that they were to keep focused on their mission and not to waste time in frivolous conversations. (We get the word "trivia" from a famous Roman crossroad called the *Tri Via*, where people discussed inconsequential matters.) How often must God look upon our conversations and activities, both inside the church and outside, and think they are frivolous in light of the urgency of the mission! The urgency of the day called for them to look for places of receptivity and houses of peace in which to stay. There are times when God's messengers must work the hard and rocky soil, seeking to overcome resistance. But there are times, when the harvest is ripe, that the workers must concentrate on ripe, receptive places in which to harvest. There is a time to plant and there is a time to reap.

Jesus said that when they found a home or town that welcomed them, they should **"eat what is set before you"** (10:8). They were not to seek special treatment or pampering, but to graciously accept the hospitality of those who welcomed them. He established a principle that the apostle Paul echoed (1 Tim. 5:18), that **the worker deserves his wages** (Luke 10:7). Persons who are sent to do God's work are not in it for the money, but they do deserve reasonable and adequate compensation. Churches that neglect this principle do so at their own peril. God may move His worker to a field that obeys Him.

Jesus prepared the sent ones for the fact that they would enter some towns and not be welcomed. Rather than remain in a combative and unproductive situation, they were to wipe the dust of that town off their feet and move on. But before leaving, they were to tell everyone who could hear, **"The kingdom of God is near"** (10:9). When the kingdom of God comes near, the choice must be made whether to enter it or to reject it. If they chose to reject it they would suffer costly consequences. Jesus said, **"I tell you, it will be more bearable on that day for Sodom than for that town"** (10:12). Sodom was infamous for its sinfulness and was eventually destroyed by God with fire (Gen. 18–19). Jesus said that rejecting Him and the kingdom of God is a greater offense to God and will bring greater judgment.

The consequences of rejection can be sad and serious. Jesus pronounced "woe" on several cities for not accepting the kingdom of God. The word is an exclamation of great sorrow. Any condemnation and judgment against those who reject God is delivered with great sorrow and results in great sorrow.

Capernaum (Luke 10:15) became Jesus' home-away-from-home, a town in which he lived and out of which He did much of His ministry in Galilee. Because many people in Capernaum did not listen to Him, He said they **will go down to the depths** (10:15). The word used for *depths* is *hades*—the realm of the dead. A **woe** is pronounced on **Korazin**, a town in which it is reported that Jesus **performed** significant enough **miracles** that if they **had been performed in Tyre and Sidon, they would have repented long ago, sitting in sackcloth and ashes** (10:13). Though Jesus had significant ministry in Korazin, according to these verses, there is no record of that ministry in any of the Gospels. This simply adds to what John wrote as he completed his gospel: "Jesus did many other things as well. If every one of them were written down, I suppose that even the whole world would not have room for the books that would be written" (John 21:25).

The sent-out messengers met with both acceptance and rejection. Jesus said, **"He who listens to you listens to me"** (Luke 10:16). They were representatives of the King who carried the message of the Kingdom. What a great responsibility to know you are speaking God's words, and those who listen and obey them are connecting with God. Jesus also said, **"He who rejects you rejects me; but he who rejects me rejects him who sent me"** (10:16). Rejecting the messenger is to reject the one He represents, and to reject Him is to reject God.

Armed with the urgency of the message, instructions for the journey, and a warning about possible rejection, the messengers went out and met with great success. They **returned with joy and said, "Lord, even the demons submit to us in your name"** (10:17). In spite of sometimes being lambs among the wolves, there is joy in serving Jesus when we see the hand of God at work. The seventy-two engaged in warfare with demons in the name of Jesus, and they experienced victory. To which Jesus exclaimed, **"I saw Satan fall like lightning from heaven"** (10:18). It could be that Jesus joined in their joy that He too witnessed the defeat and downfall of Satan. Or, William Barclay suggests that Jesus was reflecting back on when He saw Satan fall from heaven because of pride and was warning these disciples lest they too lose themselves in pride over their accomplishments.[3]

To those whom God sends, He grants authority and power for the mission. Jesus said, **"I have given you authority to trample on snakes and scorpions and to overcome all the power of the enemy; nothing will harm you"** (10:19). The emphasis should be on God's ability to sustain those He sends, not on any promise that we should handle snakes and scorpions as a demonstration of our spirituality or to "put the Lord to the test" (Luke 4:12). At the same time, we will only discover in eternity how often the hand of God prevented evil from happening to us. For us to be effective in service, divine power and authority must accompany our acceptance of the responsibility. Jesus said, **"I have given you authority."** It is critical that we recognize that in our service, we have no authority on our own. All authority is His, and it is only delegated to us so we can be effective in our service.

In spite of all of the exuberance of experiencing the power and authority of Christ to be more than adequate for their ministry, they needed the additional caution from Jesus: **"Do not rejoice that the spirits submit to you, but rejoice that your names are written in heaven"** (Luke 10:20). Our greatest excitement should be that God has chosen and redeemed us, and He knows our names. It has been said that if God had a refrigerator, each of our pictures would be stuck on it. Our service may never be recognized or our names known by others, but we can glory in the knowledge that God has taken note, and He knows our names. William Barclay wrote, "It will always remain true that a man's greatest glory is not what he has done but what God has done for him."[4]

SPIRITUAL REVELATION

Throughout the Gospel of Luke, we can follow the priority and pattern of prayer in Jesus' life. We are seldom told the actual words of His prayers, but this time we are able to listen in as **Jesus, full of joy through the Holy Spirit** (10:21), prayed. He was moving toward Jerusalem, and death lay around a near turn in the road, yet He was full of joy. He demonstrated that joy is a matter of the spirit and not a reflection of circumstances. We are encouraged to look to Jesus when we experience tough times:

Let us fix our eyes on Jesus, the author and perfecter of our faith, who for the joy set before him endured the cross, scorning its shame, and sat down at the right hand of the throne of God. Consider him who endured such opposition from sinful men, so that you will not grow weary and lose heart (Heb. 12:2–3).

His joy was based on pleasing His Father and completing the mission committed to Him by the Father.

Understanding truth is more than an intellectual or academic exercise. Spiritual realities are only understood through spiritual revelation. Some realities are hidden **from the wise and learned, and revealed . . . to little children** (Luke 10:21). There are those who believe they are too smart to believe in God and His truth. Even children can accept and believe the simple things of the kingdom of God and trust in Jesus as their Savior. In His sovereignty, God both *hides* and *reveals* His truth; He conceals and He uncovers. To some people, the deep things of the Kingdom are hidden from their understanding because

LIFE CHANGE
TRUTH

Accepting God's truth and integrating it into our way of thinking and acting is transformational. Our capacity to understand God's truth, which is revealed by the Holy Spirit, grows out of our decision to accept Christ and to tune our spirit in to His frequency. We are given a new life by following a Person, not a new philosophy.

they can only be uncovered and made known as the Holy Spirit enlightens their mind and spirit. God's truth is spiritually revealed. It is so simple the learned cannot grasp it and so rich that little children can believe it.

Jesus, who knows the Father, came to reveal Him to the world (John 14:9). He claimed that if we want to see the Father, we have only to look at Him. He alone **knows who the Father is** (Luke 10:22), and He will reveal Him to those He chooses. He privately said to His disciples, **"Blessed are the eyes that see what you see"** (10:23). What prophets had longed for and kings had looked for, the disciples had seen and heard. Jesus is the fulfillment of the search of the human soul. Those of us who have heard the gospel need to recognize how blessed we are and express gratitude to God for revealing himself to us in Christ.

3. A SHORT QUESTION WITH A LONG ANSWER (10:25–37)

The religious leaders continued in their effort to test Jesus and discredit Him among the Jews or goad Him into saying something that would get Him in trouble with the Romans. An expert in the law asked Jesus,

"What must I do to inherit eternal life?" (10:25). As Jesus often did, rather than directly answering the question, He asked him a question that sent him to the law in which he was the expert. Jesus asked the man what the law said, and he replied, **"'Love the Lord your God with all your heart and with all your soul and with all your strength and with all your mind'; and, 'Love your neighbor as yourself'"** (10:27). The man quoted the greatest of the commandments, which was to love God with all of your heart (Deut. 6:5), and he added the command to love your neighbor as yourself (Lev. 19:18). He did well to connect the dots between loving God and loving others. Jesus told him, **"Do this and you will live"** (Luke 10:28).

In its simplest terms, eternal life belongs to those who love God with all of their being. The fulfillment of any and all law is found in our choice to lose ourselves in God. The highest attainment of righteousness is to engage the whole self, heart, soul, strength, and mind, in the love of God. That love in turn would cause us to have love for our neighbor. The love of self is at the heart of sinfulness, but the love of God is at the heart of holiness. Perfect love is only possible through the new birth and grace that is applied in our hearts as a gift of—and work of—the Holy Spirit (Gal. 5:22).

Though the religious leader answered well, **he wanted to justify himself, so he asked Jesus, "And who is my neighbor?"** (Luke 10:29). Jesus replied by telling a story that has universal appeal and provides us with a graphic lesson about loving others.

Jesus told a story about **a man** who **was going down from Jerusalem to Jericho** (10:30). The road between the two cities was well known. It was treacherous because of the terrain and dangerous because of the thieves who took advantage of those who traveled the road. The road went down from Jerusalem, dropping from around twenty-three hundred feet above sea level at Jerusalem to thirteen-hundred feet below sea level at Jericho, within a distance of just over twenty miles.[5] The road made its way along the rocks and precipices of the mountainside, which provided opportunities for injury as well as ideal hiding places for robbers. While the man was traveling, a band of robbers fell upon him, took his clothes, and **beat him, leaving him half dead** (10:30).

The first person to come upon the scene was **a priest**, who, **when he saw the man, passed by on the other side** (10:31). It could be that the priest lived in Jericho and was returning home after fulfilling his Temple duty in Jerusalem. He may have reasoned that if the man were dead and he came in contact with him, he would be declared ceremonially unclean for seven days and unable to perform any of his priestly duties (Num. 19:11). So he chose to pass on by without offering any help. Maintaining ceremonially cleanliness was more important than doing the messy work of responding to human need.

The second person who came by was **a Levite, and when** he **saw him, passed by on the other side** (Luke 10:32) just as the priest had done. Perhaps he thought it was too late to do the man any good—or too dangerous with more robbers in waiting. Both the priest and Levite were religious persons who were to do the work of God on behalf of the people, but neither made any connection between their duty to God and the need of the beaten traveler.

The third man who **traveled** that way **came where the man was; and when he saw him, he took pity on him** (10:33). Unlike those who preceded him, the pity he had for the wounded traveler was greater than the fear he may have had for his own well-being, or any inclination he might have had to not get involved.

The twist in the story was that the man who took pity on the traveler was a **Samaritan** (10:33). The Jews despised the Samaritans and had no dealings with them (John 4:9). The Jewish religious leader to whom Jesus addressed the story would have viewed the Samaritan as the bad guy in the story, perhaps even the perpetrator of the crime. But the one who was viewed as the bad guy turned out to be the good guy who showed compassion, while the Jewish religious leaders did not.

The Samaritan went further than to just feel bad about the condition of the traveler. He took action to help him. He **bandaged his wounds, put** him **on his donkey, took him to an inn and took care of him** (Luke 10:34). Charity is more than feeling pity for the unfortunate. It includes a commitment to get engaged with hurting people and their situations in an effort to make a difference. It includes a willingness to assume responsibility for the well-being of others and to use personal resources to help them. **The next day**, the Samaritan **gave** money **to the innkeeper** and asked him to look after the needs of the wounded traveler, with this added promise: **"When I return, I will reimburse you for any extra expense you may have"** (10:35). He cared. He got involved. He did what he could. He assumed responsibility.

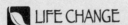

LIFE CHANGE

COMPASSIONATE MINISTRY

It has been said that the story of the Samaritan exposes three philosophies of life. The robbers had the philosophy, "What's yours is ours and we'll take it." The priest and Levite had the philosophy, "What's ours is ours and we'll keep it." The Samaritan had the philosophy, "What's mine is yours and I'll share it." Which perspective on life is yours?

Jesus ended the story with the question, **"Which of these three do you think was a neighbor to the man?"** (10:36). The religious leader had asked, "Who is my neighbor?" But Jesus asked him, "Who was a neighbor?" The religious leader wanted a narrower definition of *neighbor* so he could justify himself. Jesus caused him to define *neighborliness*, which would broaden his criteria for defining neighbor. He could only reply, **"The one who had mercy on him"** (10:37). So the question is not who is my neighbor that I am obligated to love, but who has a need to which I am compelled by love to respond?

Loving God with all of our hearts increases our capacity to love others and motivates our choice to do so. Love is a choice to respond to the well-being of another person with the same kind of mercy and compassion God has demonstrated toward us. The words of Jesus to the religious leader are directed to us as well: **"Go and do likewise"** (10:37).

4. CHOOSING THE GOOD, BETTER, OR BEST (10:38–42)

Jesus continued His movement toward Jerusalem, which took Him through Bethany, a village located about seven miles east of Jerusalem. It was the home of His special friends Lazarus, Mary, and Martha. The door of this home was always open to Him as a place of rest and escape from the crowds. He came to Bethany, and **Martha opened her home to him** (10:38). What was intended to be a quiet meal and a time to rest gave rise to a clash of personality types between Martha and her sister, Mary. Luke makes no mention of their brother, Lazarus, who was the focus of great drama in John 11 when he died and was restored to life by Jesus. You would have thought that out of gratitude, he would be in the middle of any visit from Jesus. But it was **Mary who sat at the Lord's feet listening to what he said** (Luke 10:39). Mary had a special devotion to Jesus. According to John's gospel, on one occasion she "poured perfume on the Lord and wiped his feet with her hair" (John 11:2). She is found again at the feet of Jesus, listening to His words.

Jesus was a guest in the house, and guests should be served a meal. While Mary showed her devotion by sitting at Jesus' feet, Martha showed hers by fixing the meal. Mary listened to Jesus, **but Martha was distracted by all the preparations that had to be made** (Luke 10:40). While Mary reclined, Martha worked and became more and more agitated by her sister's lack of assistance. Her joy over having Jesus in her home was lost in her rising frustration. There was an edge in her voice when she went to Jesus and said, **"Lord, don't you care that my sister has left me to do the work by myself?"** (10:40). Our frustration with the demands of life can cause us to say to God, "Don't you care?" Where is God when we are suffering injustice? How can God put up with people who take advantage of our goodness? Why doesn't He do something? Martha's frustration caused her to make a demand of Jesus: **"Tell her to help me!"** (10:40).

Too often our service to the Lord through the church can cause us to wonder where everyone else is who is supposed to be helping. Why are we left to do the work by ourselves? Our overload can lead to resentment toward God and feelings that He does not care. If we're not careful, we can start making ultimatums with God: "If you don't make them _____, then I am not going to _____."

Martha was probably not in the mood for a lecture. Mary was the one who needed to be lectured. But Jesus had a gentle rebuke for her: **"Martha, Martha . . . you are worried and upset about many things, but only one thing is needed. Mary has chosen what is better"** (10:41–42).

Mary chose **what was better**. The choices we face are not always neatly packaged as being between good and bad. Often we must choose between good, better, and best. When those are the choices, we can settle for something less than what is best. The problem with Martha was not that she was doing wrong things. She was worried, upset, and preoccupied with many things rather than with what was best.

We can look at the two sisters and see two different personality temperaments each with its own potential for choosing less than the best. There are personalities that do not see responsibility when it is right in front of them. They can appear to be irresponsible daydreamers who live off the hard work of others. There are personalities that can never relax to smell the roses or sit at the feet of Jesus. Busyness is their thing.

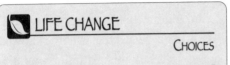

LIFE CHANGE

CHOICES

Choices have costs and consequences. It may seem costly to choose the very best, but the result is blessing beyond measure.

The fact is that there is a lot for all of us to do, and life can get frantic at times with all the demands that must be met. Someone has to do the work. Our devotion to Christ can suffer from distraction, worry, being upset, and doing many things. Balance may not be easy, but choosing to learn from Jesus about those things that cannot be taken from us is the best choice. Our goal should be to live like Mary in a Martha world. We should live with an appropriate balance between work and worship, but if we have to choose one over the other, we choose.

ENDNOTES

1. Marvin R. Vincent, *Word Studies in the New Testament* (Grand Rapids, Mich.: Eerdmans, 1973), p. 349.

2. Thayer and Smith. "Greek Lexicon for Apostolos." The New Testament Greek Lexicon. http://www.studylight.org/lex/grk/view.cgi?number=6572.

3. William Barclay, *The Gospel of Luke* (Philadelphia: Westminster, 1956), p. 137.

4. Ibid., p. 138.

5. Ibid., p. 141.

12

THE PROBLEM WITH PHARISEES

Luke 11:1-54

How do you define spirituality? Is it doing all the right things: faithfully attending church, paying your tithe, saying your prayers, reading your Bible, and making sacrifices at appropriate times? We would love to have people who do these things attending our churches, if we could only find them. Jesus found a group who zealously and meticulously did all of these things, but who lacked true spirituality. Some of the great teachings of Jesus, and some of His hottest words of rebuke, were generated out of His interaction with the Pharisees.

The spirit of the Pharisees lives on today and may show up now and then in our churches. If you have pharisaical tendencies, Jesus wants to have a word with you.

1. JESUS TEACHES ABOUT PRAYER (11:1-13)

A MODEL PRAYER

Jesus had a pattern of prayer in His life, and **one day** He was **praying in a certain place** (11:1). There were certain places for prayer that He frequented: a place on the mountain, a spot in a garden, and a retreat near the seashore. He prayed often because His priority was to maintain a close relationship with His Father. He prayed before He made important decisions, like choosing His disciples. He prayed when the demands of life crowded in and exhausted Him. He prayed when temptation was strong. He prayed when He struggled with the prospects of pain and death. He sought out time with the Father and the strength, perspective, purpose, will, and counsel He would gain from prayer. He prayed about the same things and for the same reasons that should cause us to pray.

Jesus was a master at modeling what He wanted others to learn. His disciples had observed the value of prayer in Jesus' life, and one of them said, **"Lord, teach us to pray"** (11:1). What followed was a thirty-four-word prayer we refer to as the Lord's Prayer. It may be short in length, but it is deep in meaning. The length of our prayers is not as important as the spirit and content of our prayers. This prayer of Jesus was probably not intended to be a model prayer that should be recited with slavish adherence to its form or words, but the content of the prayer reflects the kinds of things for which we should regularly pray.

Jesus opened His prayer by addressing God with the intimate term **Father** (11:2). We could understand Jesus addressing *His* Father in this manner, but He invites *all of us* to do so when He said, "Our Father . . ." (see Matt. 9:6). Prayer is the privilege of having intimate relationship with God. Prayer acknowledges and cultivates that relationship. Prayer is encouraged when you understand that "every good and perfect gift is from above, coming down from the *Father*" (James 1:17, italics added). God chooses to call us His children, which gives us the privilege and boldness to call Him our Father.

Our boldness to be intimate in our communication with our Father is balanced with reverence and awe. Even while calling Him Father, we acknowledge that His name is **hallowed** (Luke 11:2). If something is hallowed, it is considered holy and regarded with great respect and reverence. The boldness we have to enter into the holy presence of God (Heb. 10:19) should never mean that we are casual or disrespectful about it. When we lose our awe and reverential fear of God and treat Him as if He were our heavenly buddy, we lose an appropriate understanding of who He is. His name is *Father*, but His name is also *holy*. God considers the irreverent misuse of His name to be so offensive that He included it in His top ten things "thou shalt not" do (Ex. 20:7).

Our daily prayer should include inviting God to set up His rule in our lives and in our world. **Your kingdom come** (Luke 11:2) is the desire of every sincere Christian. We can rather enjoy our feeble attempts to control ourselves and the things around us, but the condition of our world shows us the disaster caused by the kingdoms that rival the kingdom of God. We pray that the rule of God will come and be realized in our lives and our world.

We experience real needs and wants that God asks us to tell Him about. But Jesus cut our prayer for needs and wants down to things quite elementary and simple when He prayed, **"Give us each day our daily bread"** (11:3). We would like to stockpile some things so we don't have to pray about them each day. However, our reliance on God noticeably suffers when we have abundance. We would like to have God supply us with some of the benefits of living in a land of plenty rather than have to ask Him to help us with such basics as bread. Ryrie says the literal translation of this phrase is "Give us for the day, or day by day, the bread which is sufficient for our subsistence."[1] We can have the perspective that our daily bread comes from the sweat of our brow rather than from the hand of our Father. To our discredit, we may more often need to pray that we'll be able to make this month's payment on the boat or condo than to pray for daily bread.

Any time we enter the presence of a holy God we are reminded of our lack of holiness. When Isaiah saw God on His throne and heard the angels calling out, "Holy, holy, holy is the LORD Almighty; the whole

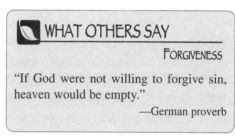

WHAT OTHERS SAY

FORGIVENESS

"If God were not willing to forgive sin, heaven would be empty."

—German proverb

earth is full of his glory," his immediate reaction was to cry out, "Woe to me! I am ruined! For I am a man of unclean lips, and I live among a people of unclean lips" (Isa. 6:1–5). We are all ruined and must throw ourselves on the mercy of God, who is gracious in forgiving us. Our fervent prayer is, "Father, **forgive us our sins**" (Luke 11:4). Of all of our wants and needs, forgiveness is our greatest need. We may think we can earn our daily bread by working hard, but there is no work we can do that will earn forgiveness. For that, we must throw ourselves on the mercy and grace of God.

Our need for forgiveness is matched with our need to be forgiving. Our prayer for forgiveness includes our commitment to **forgive everyone who sins against us** (11:4). The verses immediately following Matthew's version of this prayer say, "If you forgive men when they sin against you, your heavenly Father will also forgive you. But if you do not forgive men their sins, your Father will not forgive your sins" (Matt. 6:14–15). A forgiving spirit *must* characterize our relationship with others.

Beyond our concern that we have forgiveness for our sins should be an equal or greater concern that we not fall into sin through temptations, so our prayer should include the petition **"and lead us not into temptation"** (Luke 11:4). Matthew's version adds, "but deliver us from the evil one" (Matt. 6:13). We need the Holy Spirit to keep us sensitive to temptation's presence. We need God's help in developing the disciplines that will keep us strong in our fight against the schemes and devices of the devil (Eph. 6:10–18).

The King James Version includes a final phrase: "For thine is the kingdom, and the power, and the glory forever." These additional words appear in some late manuscripts, but are not considered to be a part of the original earlier manuscripts. It was added to make the Lord's Prayer more suitable for use in public worship and is customarily used when it is recited in worship. It certainly is within the spirit of the prayer and our need to ascribe honor to God.[2]

ANSWERED PRAYER

The Lord's prayer was short and simple, but shifting to His favorite means of teaching, Jesus began to unpack other underlying issues of prayer by telling a story. A man went to a friend at midnight and requested bread because a guest had dropped in to stay with him and he had nothing to feed him. The friend told him to go away because his family was in bed, and he didn't want to get up to give him anything. Jesus said, **"Though he will not get up and give him the bread because he is his friend, yet because of the man's boldness he will get up and give him as much as he needs"** (Luke 11:8). The story seems to teach that there are times when boldness and persistence in prayer are in order. However, it would not appear to be consistent with the whole of Scripture, or with the experience of the faithful, to conclude that even if God does not give us that for which we pray, we should harangue Him until, like spoiled children, we get our way. Adam Clarke suggests that "importunity," or "persistence," in prayer may be necessary to get our-selves "brought into a proper disposition to receive that mercy which he is ever disposed to give."³ Persistence suggests urgency, seriousness, and boldness that, when aligned with God's purpose, brings His response.

God has committed himself to care for His children in ways that bring ultimate good to us and glory to Him. This may not result in the kind of answers to our prayers that we anticipate, but when we look in the rearview mirror of life, the answers will testify to us that He has been faithful. Jesus encourages us, **"Ask and it will be given to you; seek and you will find; knock and the door will be opened to you"** (11:9). The first cause of unanswered prayer is an unasked prayer. "You do not have, because you do not ask God" (James 4:2). We are encouraged to ask, seek, and knock for God to open up His storehouse of spiritual blessings and give to us.

Jesus said that we should rest in confidence that God cares for us more than our natural father. No father would think of giving his **son** a **snake** when he asked **for a fish** or a **scorpion** when he asked **for an egg** (Luke 11:11–12). If **evil** fathers have enough goodness in them to know how to **give good gifts** to their **children, "how much more will your Father in heaven give the Holy Spirit to those who ask him!"** (11:13). When we ask, seek, and knock, the gift of the Holy Spirit should be at the top of our prayer list. God will not fail to answer that prayer, and quickly. Connection with God is possible and profitable not in a mercenary sense but in a relational sense. God is good and He desires good for us. The best gift He could ever give us is the gift of himself.

Prayer is a statement about our belief in God and our view of Him. What we pray for is a statement about us and our view of what we consider most valuable.

2. DEMONS AND PHARISEES (11:14–54)

THE FINGER OF GOD, NOT THE POWER OF BEELZEBUB

The existence of demons is verified in Luke's gospel with more than thirty references to the devil, demons, and evil spirits. Several of these references are to demon possession, which appears to have been prevalent in the day. Jesus and His representatives had a ministry of exorcising demons. One day **Jesus was driving out a demon** (11:14) to the amazement of the crowds who followed Him. **But some of them** declared that He was employing the power of **Beelzebub, the prince of demons** (11:15), to drive out demons. Their charge was ludicrous, and Jesus pointed out the impossibility of using the power of a demon to cast out a demon. Jesus suggested that He drove **out demons by the finger of God,** and if this were so, **then** the power and **the kingdom of God** (11:20) was among them. Jesus made the case that the weaker is overpowered by the stronger. If He cast out demons, He was demonstrating that He was superior in strength to the devil and his demons.

It is impossible to take a neutral position concerning Christ. He said, **"He who is not with me is against me, and he who does not gather with me, scatters"** (11:23). You are either with Him or against Him. You are either engaged in His work or you are opposing His work.

CLEAN BUT EMPTY

Jesus continued His teaching about demons by speaking to the condition of a person after **an evil spirit comes out of** him (11:24). He said that spirit will seek another place to inhabit, but finding none, will go back to the place it had left. There he **finds the house swept clean and put in order**, but empty (11:25). Jesus suggests that a heart can be cleansed of evil but not filled with something better. The human heart will be controlled or influenced by a dominant spirit. The apostle Paul said, "Those controlled by the sinful nature cannot please God. You, however, are controlled not by the sinful nature but by the Spirit, if the Spirit of God lives

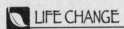

LIFE CHANGE
FILLED WITH THE SPIRIT

It is in the nature of sin to empty things. It is in the nature of God to fill things. Out of His fullness He "fills everything in everyway" (Eph. 1:23), and we are urged to "be filled to the measure of all the fullness of God" (Eph. 3:19). Our critical need as committed followers of Christ is to be filled with His Spirit. Our need is met by God's wonderful provision (Luke 11:13) if we ask for it.

in you" (Rom. 8:8–9). Godliness is not just getting rid of a sinful nature, but must include a new nature imparted by the indwelling Spirit of God.

When the evil spirit finds the house clean but empty, it brings in **seven other spirits more wicked than itself** to take up residence there again (Luke 11:26). The result is that the **condition of that man is worse than** it was before (11:26). Jesus was teaching several lessons. First, evil needs to be driven out of a person's life and it can be. Second, it is not enough to rid your life of evil. The Holy Spirit and all of His goodness needs to fill the cleansed heart. Third, it is possible for evil to return to an empty heart with such vengeance that it can be worse than it was before the cleansing. Jesus was stressing the importance of an inner fortification that is possible through the indwelling of the Holy Spirit.

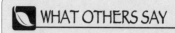

WHAT OTHERS SAY

LIFE CHANGE

"Even purely psychological considerations render it imperative that, when a person has passed through a crisis which has contributed to his renunciation of former sins and evil practices in his life, he must immediately in place thereof let his life be filled with what is beautiful and noble, otherwise the old sins and evils will return in renewed violence. . . . There cannot be a vacuum in man's soul."

—Norval Geldenhuys

When Paul wrote to Timothy, he encouraged him to "Flee the evil desires of youth, and pursue [follow] righteousness, faith, love, and peace" (2 Tim. 2:22). Withstanding an enticement toward evil must include both *fleeing* and *following*: negative and positive, emptying and filling, external holiness and internal wholeness.

THE SIGN OF JONAH

The **crowds** that gathered when Jesus taught **increased** (Luke 11:29) in numbers, but this was not because Jesus always told them what they wanted to hear. On this occasion, **Jesus said, "This is a wicked generation"** (11:29). This is not the kind of thing you say when you want to draw a crowd. Evidence of its wickedness that caused Jesus to speak harshly to them was that **it asks for a miraculous sign** (11:29). They wanted Jesus to do something spectacular to excite them and to prove He was worth listening to and

WHAT OTHERS SAY

MIRACLES

"To the true disciple a miracle only manifests the power and love which are silently at work everywhere as divinely in the gift of daily bread as in the miraculous multiplication of the loaves."

—Frederick William Robertson

following. Jesus told them there would be no sign **except the sign of Jonah** (11:29). Matthew's gospel explains this by adding, "For as Jonah was three days and three nights in the belly of a huge fish, so the Son of Man will be three days and three nights in the heart of the earth" (Matt. 12:40). The proof of His divinity would be found in the Resurrection. He was God's sign, just as **Jonah was a sign to the Ninevites**. (Luke 11:30). **One greater than Jonah** (11:32) was present, who like the prophet, brought a word from God to a wicked generation.

LIGHT AND DARKNESS

The inability to accept God's messenger and to comprehend God's message was not for lack of light on the subject. Nothing was hidden to those who searched for it. Jesus said that you do not light a lamp and hide it so you do not benefit from it. Instead, you put **it on its stand, so that those who come in may see the light** (11:33). God did not hide His light, but the problem of seeing or not seeing the light exists in the human eye. If **your eyes are good, your whole body also is full of light. But when they are bad, your body also is full of darkness** (11:34).

Many of us grew up singing, "This little light of mine, I'm going to let it shine." The foundation of that song is that Jesus and His truth is light. When He is in you, it makes a difference in your life—a difference that is witnessed by others and draws them to the Light. Jesus took this further to say that our bodies can be "full of light" or "full of darkness." If Jesus, the Light of the World, is within you, you can be **completely lighted, as when the light of a lamp shines on you** (11:36). May the Light shine on you, and may your whole body be full of the Light!

CLEAN ON THE OUTSIDE, DIRTY ON THE INSIDE

The Pharisees were Jesus' primary audience as He talked about prayer, casting out demons, repentance, and seeing the Light. They believed they were the most spiritual of the spiritual. The words of Jesus about their spiritual blindness were a bit more pointed, which would lead toward an unavoidable confrontation. The Pharisees had accused Jesus of eating with publicans and sinners (5:30; 15:2), and on this occasion, it was a Pharisee who invited Jesus to eat with him. **The Pharisee . . . was surprised** to notice **that Jesus did not first wash before the meal** (11:38). Washing before the meal was a matter of both cleanliness and ceremony. In this case, most likely the Pharisee was concerned about a ceremonial cleansing practiced by the religious elders, and Jesus probably intentionally did not wash just so He could have this teaching moment.

Pharisees were obsessed with their ceremonial cleansing, with all of their man-made rules and regulations. They had an elaborate system of religious rites and practices that focused on external compliance. Their spirituality was made up of external practices, not internal purity. Jesus cut through the façade of religiosity when He said, **"You Pharisees clean the outside of the cup and dish, but inside you are full of greed and wickedness"** (11:39). True spirituality and godliness requires an inner cleansing and empowering by the Holy Spirit, which will then affect the external life. There is no life in a religion of external compliance without an internal cleansing.

The Pharisees practiced rigid adherence to the law, which included giving **God a tenth** (11:42) of all of their produce. This practice was not bad, but Jesus used it to show their spirituality was all external and, while they faithfully gave their tithe, they also neglected **justice and the love of God** (11:42).

Jesus was not finished condemning the spiritual deficiencies of the Pharisees. He pointed out that they loved **the most important seats in the synagogues and greetings in the marketplaces** (11:43). They were proud and arrogant. Jesus said they were **like unmarked graves, which men walk over without knowing it** (11:44). Under the law, walking over a grave would defile a person, so the unmarked graves (the Pharisees) would cause others to unintentionally become defiled. The Pharisees poisoned the spirit of all those who came in contact with them. We need to be aware of the power of influence, both by whom we allow to influence us and how we affect those under our influence.

Jesus will not leave us in our sinfulness without confronting the sin in us. One of the experts in the law voiced his opposition to these confronting accusations by the Lord. Closely aligned with the Pharisees were those identified as scribes or teachers of the law, they wrote down the many regulations added to the law of Moses, taught the people regarding them, and were considered the experts in the law. The "expert" said, **"Teacher, when you say these things, you insult us also"** (11:45). Jesus was scorching the Pharisees, but the teachers of the law felt the heat too. So Jesus shifted His attention to them, accusing them of loading **people down with burdens they** could **hardly carry** (11:46). External religion is a heavy burden, and the Pharisees, along with the experts in the law, increased the burden by adding demands far beyond the law of God.

The teachers of the law were condemned by Jesus for making religion a burden, building monuments for prophets whose messages they rejected, and for taking **away the key to knowledge** (11:52). They controlled the interpretation and application of the Scriptures, wielding it as a cruel club rather than a means toward spiritual enlightenment. Not only did they fail to enter into God's truth, but they hindered those who were seeking to enter into it. It is a most serious charge for people who are to help others connect meaningfully with God to actually hinder rather than help them.

After this confrontation, **the Pharisees and the teachers of the law began to oppose him fiercely** (11:53). When sin is confronted, either godly conviction will lead to repentance or hardened consciences will lead to anger and greater resistance. The religious leaders sought to silence the voice of the One who would attempt to awaken their conscience. If they didn't like the message, they would kill the messenger.

ENDNOTES

1. Charles Ryrie, *Ryrie Study Bible: Expository Thoughts on the Gospels, Luke 11–24* (Chicago: Moody Press, 1978), p. 8.

2. Ralph Earle, *The Wesleyan Bible Commentary: The Gospel of Matthew* (Grand Rapids, Mich.: Eerdmans, 1964), p. 37.

3. Adam Clarke, *Clarke's Commentary* (New York: Abingdon, 1977), p. 437.

13

YOUR HEART AND YOUR TREASURE

Luke 12:1–59

The prophet Isaiah wrote, "You will keep in perfect peace him whose mind is steadfast [stayed, fixed], because he trusts in you" (Isa. 26:3). What we fix our minds or hearts on has direct relationship to the level of peace we possess. In these verses, Jesus addressed a series of issues related to what occupies the attention of our hearts, since what we have decided will be the treasures of our lives. Our treasure becomes the focus of our trust. Misplaced trust can lead to various intensities of disturbance in our peace, including pesky worries, problematic phobias, and paralyzing fears. The things that cause us concern usually reveal the priorities and orientations of our lives.

1. FEAR, FORGIVENESS, AND FOOLS (12:1–21)

HYPOCRISY EXPOSED

Whenever Jesus taught, crowds gathered: up to **many thousands, so that they were trampling on one another** (Luke 12:1). Crowds can contain a variety of people with a variety of motives for being there. Some would be in the crowd purely as spectators—curiosity seekers—just because there was a crowd. Some would be there as hecklers, ridiculing the teaching of Jesus that contradicted their tradition. Some would be there as spies, listening for some teaching that could be used against Jesus. Some would be there because they had committed themselves to Jesus and were faithful followers. Some would be there as honest seekers, listening to the teaching and weighing their response. Most church services are made up of a similar mixture of people and motives, except we usually do not have the crowd-control problem of people trampling on one another to get to a front row seat.

Before speaking to the crowd, Jesus turned privately to His disciples and warned, **"Be on your guard against the yeast of the Pharisees, which is hypocrisy"** (12:1). Jesus had some tough things to say against the Pharisees. He had called them a "brood of vipers" (Matt. 3:7), "whitewashed tombs" (Matt. 23:27), "snakes" (Matt. 23:33), and "hypocrites" (Matt. 23:13, 15, 23). His disciples would have seen enough of the empty, false religion of the Pharisees that they would not be in danger of becoming a Pharisee. But Jesus said they should be on their guard against the *yeast* of the Pharisees, which is hypocrisy. It is in the nature of yeast to interact with its surroundings. Jesus used the activity of yeast in a positive way when He said, "What shall I compare the kingdom of God to? It is like yeast that a woman took and mixed into a large amount of flour until it worked all through the dough" (Luke 13:20–21). Paul wrote of yeast as well: "Don't you know that a little yeast works through the whole batch of dough? Get rid of the old yeast that you may be a new batch without yeast—as you really are. For Christ, our Passover Lamb, has been sacrificed. Therefore let us keep the Festival, not with the old yeast, the yeast of malice and wickedness, but with bread without yeast, the bread of sincerity and truth" (1 Cor. 5:7–8). Yeast is an illustration of the power of influence that may be very covert yet effective in its operation.

LIFE CHANGE

INFLUENCE

Influence can be a powerful thing. We can let others influence us to be less than we should be, or with God's help we can influence others to be more than they are. God has called us to be salt and light in the world—influencers for good (Matt. 5:13–14). We are to be transformation agents used by God to change the world, not be changed by it.

Jesus had to warn His disciples to be sure hypocrisy never got started in their hearts. Hypocrisy is playing a part, pretending to be something that you are not. It is outwardly appearing to be something but secretly and inwardly being something else. Since one's spiritual life is an inner condition of the soul that no one can see, hypocrisy is always a spiritual danger. Hypocrites say and do different things in public than they do in private. They are insincere, and they conceal things from others. But Jesus warned that hypocrisy eventually gets exposed. People are not good enough at living a double life to fool everyone all the time. And they never fool God. What is **hidden** will **be made known** and what is **whispered . . . will be proclaimed from the roofs** (Luke 12:2–3).

THE FEAR OF GOD

Jesus taught that we should be persons of integrity who are open and honest. We should not live in fear that someone will pull back the curtain and see inside our souls or lift up the rug and see what we have swept under it. Don't be afraid to live righteously, even if it brings persecution. Evil people may **kill the body and after that can do no more** (12:4). You should be more concerned about being honest and open with God, who **has power to throw you into hell** (12:5). The judgment of God should be feared.

However, our fear of God is balanced with our understanding of His care for us. Jesus said that the insignificant sparrow is not **forgotten by God** (12:6). If His eye is on the sparrow, then you can know He cares for you and will never forget you. **You are worth more than many sparrows** (12:7). There is a fear of God that is healthy, and there is a fear about life that is unhealthy. Jesus said, **"I tell you . . . fear him"** (12:4–5) as well as, **"Don't be afraid"** (12:7). Our fear of God should cause us to live godly and righteous lives, always aware of His holiness. Our relationship with Him should cause us to not be afraid, but to find peace and rest in His care.

ACKNOWLEDGING CHRIST

We should never be afraid to acknowledge Jesus before others. If we are courageous in our identification with Him, He will claim us as His own and will **acknowledge** us **before the angels of God** (12:8). However, if, in our fear of others, we disown Him, He will disown us **before the angels of God** (12:9).

Fear of what other people may think of us leads to hypocrisy and the denial of Christ. Simon Peter would soon taste the result of that fear when a little girl would accuse him of being one of Jesus' disciples. Hypocrisy pretends to be something it is not, because it fears someone will discover the truth. Denial pretends not to be something it is, because it fears someone will discover the truth. Both have their roots in fear, and both are sin.

UNFORGIVABLE SIN

The wonderful message of God's love and grace is that sin is forgivable. Even if you speak **a word against the Son of Man**, it can **be forgiven** (12:10) if you confess your sin and accept Christ by faith. There is hope for the most vile sinner. That is good news! No sinner is beyond God's reach, and no sin is beyond His capacity to forgive.

However, Jesus added a warning: **"anyone who blasphemes against the Holy Spirit will not be forgiven"** (12:10). The unforgivable sin is sin against the Holy Spirit. Matthew's record places this statement immediately following the Pharisees' declaration that Jesus cast out demons by the power of Beelzebub (Matt. 12:31), which suggests that the sin of which Jesus spoke is that of seeing the work of God and declaring it to be the work of the devil. The work of the Holy Spirit is to convict us of sin, convince us of truth, connect us with Christ's atonement, and confirm our relationship with God (John 16:8–13). If we defy the work of the Holy Spirit, we have no access to the source of forgiveness. The only unforgivable sin is the sin that will not respond to the Spirit that would lead to forgiveness.

There is great danger in deadening the voice of the Spirit by constant and consistent denial, in blurring the line between good and evil so that you are no longer sensitive toward either, and in ridiculing the redemptive work of Christ until it is no longer believed to be either necessary or effective. It is possible to push yourself beyond the reach of God and be without Christ and without hope.

ENABLED BY THE HOLY SPIRIT

Jesus encouraged His disciples to live out their faith with boldness, realizing that this could bring them persecution. Their boldness would be met with special enablement by the Holy Spirit. He told them that **when—** not if—they were **brought before synagogues, rulers and authorities,** they should **not worry about** their defense, **"for the Holy Spirit will teach you at that time what you should say"** (Luke 12:11–12). The Holy Spirit is the great enabler, providing the resources necessary to meet the demands of serving Christ. He will always be there to support and enable us when we take our stand for Christ. When we serve in Jesus' name, the Holy Spirit will provide the power and authority.

UNDERSTANDING THE PRIORITIES OF LIFE

On this day, most of the teaching was directed mainly to His disciples, but then a man **in the crowd said to him, "Teacher, tell my brother to divide the inheritance with me"** (12:13). It may have been common to take domestic disputes to respected teachers or rabbis for guidance, but it must have been very disappointing to Jesus to be talking about serious spiritual things and have someone make a selfish demand like this. The issue exposed the materialistic orientation of the man's life and brought another warning from Jesus.

Jesus had instructed His disciples to be on guard against the yeast of the Pharisees, which was hypocrisy. Now He instructed everyone to be on guard against greed. He prefaced His instruction with the extra warning, **"Watch out!"** (12:15). Greed is desire run amuck, an undisciplined desire for more than you have, a willingness to break the rules to get what you want, a mind-set that life is found in the accumulation of "stuff." Jesus said, **"A man's life does not consist in the abundance of his possessions"** (12:15). Try to tell that to the average consumer in North America who has found a way to possess an abundance when he or she doesn't have enough

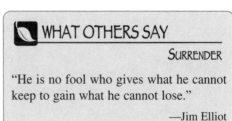

WHAT OTHERS SAY

SURRENDER

"He is no fool who gives what he cannot keep to gain what he cannot lose."

—Jim Elliot

to purchase it—it is called credit. Possessions provide the circumference of many persons' lives, whether those persons are considered wealthy or poor.

Jesus told them a **parable** about a **rich man**'s **ground** that **produced a good crop** (12:16). The fact that he was already a rich man would suggest that he was both a good farmer and a good manager. He had experienced good harvests before, enough that his barns did not have room for the new crop. He already had more than he could consume. Faced with no place to store his new crop, he decided he would **tear down** the **barns** he had **and build** some **bigger ones** (12:18). Then he would have room to **store all** of the excess **grain**. It sounded like the good business plan of a wise businessman. But then he said to himself something that betrayed the basic orientation of his life: **"You have plenty of good things laid up for many years. Take life easy; eat, drink and be merry"** (12:19). The man was greedy, self-centered, incapable of seeing beyond himself, and unmoved to share his good fortune with anyone else. The notion that he was a steward of goods given to him by the good providence of God did not figure into his thinking.

The rich man could not see beyond himself. He could not see any responsibility of sharing with others. He could not see beyond this world. He had enough to take life easy. He could spend his life eating, drinking, and having fun. But God called the man a **fool**. That **very night** the man would die, and **God** asked **him, "Then who will get what you have prepared for yourself?"** (12:20). His abundance could not accompany him into the new world for which he had not prepared. Jesus said, **"This is how it will be with anyone who stores up things for himself but is not rich toward God"** (12:21). We can be rich in this world's goods and be destitute in heavenly possessions.

2. DON'T WORRY—SEEK THE KINGDOM (12:22-34)

DON'T WORRY

While Jesus was speaking about attitudes toward material possessions, He shifted from greed and how to handle abundance to those who are concerned because they do not have enough. This stands in direct contrast to the rich man who alleviated worry about tomorrow by accumulating wealth. If how to handle your wealth is not your worry, you can spend your life worrying about meeting tomorrow's necessities. **Jesus** told **his disciples, ". . . do not worry about your life, what you will eat; or about your body, what you will wear"** (12:22). The rich man's story emphasized that life does not consist in the abundance of a person's possessions. For those who may be poor and who worry about the next meal, Jesus said, **"Life is more than food, and the body more than clothes"** (12:23). Material goods are necessary, but even if we don't have much, they should not be our focus.

The point Jesus made was that your life should not be diminished by anxiety and worry, which cannot **add a single hour to** your **life** (12:28), but in fact can contribute to the shortening of your life. The birds of the air, flowers of the garden, and **grass of the field** are cared for by God, and you are more valuable than they. **"Why do you worry"** (12:26)? Jesus chided those who have the tendency to be anxious, **"O you of little faith!"** (12:28) Faith is the antidote for worry.

Having enough to eat and drink for yourself and your family is a reasonable concern, as long as it occupies a reasonable place in the priorities of your life. Jesus said, **"Do not set your heart on what you will eat or drink"** (12:29). Our priorities are established by that on which we set our hearts. When our priorities are misplaced, life loses its balance and legitimate things become damaging things. The need to work to provide for necessities can become an obsessive drive to move up the ladder of success, dominating a person's time, reshaping a person's value system, and sacrificing a person's family.

SEEK HIS KINGDOM

The pursuit of material possessions is a "rat race," and **the pagan world runs after all such things** (12:30). God's people are to seek the kingdom of God and live in the confidence that necessary things will be given as **your Father knows that you need them** (12:30). The focus of our lives should extend beyond material things to include spiritual treasure and the celebration that our Father has given us a place in His kingdom.

Children of God are to be generous people, motivated to use what they possess to **give to the poor** (12:33). Our possessions are to be used to do the work of God in helping others, and are not to be the means of our trust, because they are temporary. The material things we try to accumulate are subject to wear and tear, attract people who may want to take them from us, and are susceptible to natural deterioration. Spiritual treasure that is stored in heaven is out of reach of thieves and decay. Generosity not only provides help to those who need it, but also provides blessing to the one who gives it.

Our attitude toward material possessions reflects what we have set our heart upon. Our heart is possessed by our possessions, whether material or spiritual, **for where your treasure is, there your heart will be also** (12:34).

3. READY AND WAITING (12:35-59)

READY TO SERVE

Speaking of the kingdom of heaven and the need to plan ahead by having treasure there, Jesus shifted the subject of His teaching to that of being prepared for His second coming. He used the motif of servants **waiting for their master to return from a wedding banquet** (12:36) to illustrate the need to be prepared. The master was expected to return soon, but the exact time was unknown. The delay of the master's return may cause a loss of diligence, but the servants would be expected to **be dressed ready for service** (12:35). The servants would be sure the lamps were burning and ready to **immediately open the door for him** (12:36). Followers of Christ should be prepared and live in anticipation of the return of their Master. Christ wants to find **them watching when he comes** (12:37).

Jesus is presently with His Father, preparing the great marriage supper of the Lamb (Rev. 19:9). The Church, the bride of Christ (Eph. 5:25; Rev. 19:7), composed of every faithful follower of Christ, will gather around heaven's banquet table. Christ **will dress himself to serve, will have them recline at the table and will come and wait on them** (Luke 12:38). Jesus took upon himself the nature of a servant (Phil. 2:7), and His crowning act as a servant will be waiting on His bride in eternity.

EXPECTING HIS RETURN

The Master expects His servants to be ready, **even if he comes in the second or third watch of the night** (Luke 12:38). His return will be **at an hour when you do not expect** (12:40) it, which demands constant readiness. However, this does not mean standing by idly until the sound of the master's arrival is heard. The returning Lord is looking for **faithful and wise manager**s (12:42) whom He will find engaged in their work when He returns. If the master delays his return, there can be the temptation to ease off of assigned duties, anticipating there will be ample time later to get caught up. The unexpected return will catch people unprepared, and Jesus said they will be assigned **a place with the unbelievers** (12:46). Judgment awaits the **servant who knows his master's will and does not get ready or does not do what his master wants** (12:47). *Tomorrow* is a word of hope and opportunity. It can also be a word that can produce procrastination. This moment is all we really have to serve our Lord, and tomorrow is not guaranteed. As Jesus said, "As long as it is day, we must do the work of him who sent me. Night is coming, when no one can work" (John 9:4).

FIRE AND DIVISION

Fire is often connected with divine judgment. Jesus said, **"I have come to bring fire on the earth"** (12:49). There is a tendency to want to make Jesus our friend and benefactor. Jesus came to make abundant life possible (John 10:10), but He also came to bring judgment. The angels sang of peace on earth when He was born, but He said that He also came to bring division.

You cannot remain neutral about Jesus. You must accept or reject Him. Accepting Him brings grace and life, but rejecting Him brings judgment and separation from God. Accepting Christ will bring an inner, personal peace, but it may also bring conflict because you live in relationship with people who have chosen to reject Christ. The fact that you have chosen to follow Christ may bring division between you and family members who do not follow Christ.

INTERPRETING THE TIME

Jesus was facing the crucifixion, which He referred to as **a baptism to undergo** (Luke 12:49). There was growing urgency in His message and increasing distress in His spirit. He spoke to people who could still make choices to enter into the kingdom of God. He could feel the movement of time toward His crucifixion and departure, but the people did not share in His sense of urgency. They could predict the weather by interpreting **the appearance of the earth and the sky**, but they didn't **know how to interpret this present time** (12:56). Some people are adept at explaining the obscure and ignoring the obvious. They can major on minors and minor on majors. They can talk about the weather but never address critical issues of the time.

There was something dramatic in the air, but the people did not sense it. They were caught up in petty disputes rather than seeking quick reconciliation with their **adversary** (12:58) so appropriate attention could be given to matters of the coming Kingdom. A greater judgment awaited them if they continued to ignore the One who came to bring fire on the earth.

We are certainly much nearer the return of Christ than were the people to whom Jesus issued the warning to be ready. However, the delay in His coming may result in less readiness as each generation passes. The apostle Peter warned that we should not consider God's patient desire to give every person opportunity to come to repentance as a failure to follow through with His promise of His Son's return, which will also bring God's judgment (2 Pet. 3:7–10). In light of that, Peter asked, ". . . what kind of people ought you to be? You ought to live holy and godly lives as you look forward to the day of God and speed its coming" (3:11–12).

14

WHO WILL BE SAVED

Luke 13:1-35

It might seem to us that it is easier for some people to be saved than others. On the basis of appearance, some people are so close to the Kingdom that we could easily welcome them in with little hesitancy. There are others who would really have trouble getting past our gatekeepers. What does it mean to be a Christian? Are you a Christian because you believe the right things? Or because you behave the right way? Or because you associate with the right people? How is a person saved? What do you have to do to be saved? Who can be saved? What is salvation? Who sets the standard for salvation? Is it so high that few are able or willing?

We're not the first to ask these critical questions. Luke's gospel records similar inquiries: "What must I do to inherit eternal life?" (10:25; 18:18); "Who then can be saved?" (18:26); "Are only a few people going to be saved?" (13:23). After collecting the questions, Luke recorded the responses of Jesus that provide the answers for seeking souls.

1. REPENTANCE AND A FIG TREE (13:1-9)

THE NEED FOR REPENTANCE

Luke is the only Gospel writer who writes of people who came to Jesus to tell Him **about the Galileans whose blood Pilate had mixed with their sacrifices** (13:1). Though there is no other exact reference to this event in the biblical record, evidently there were Galileans who provoked

Pilate enough that he sent soldiers who killed the Galileans while they were offering their sacrifices in the Temple. The Galileans were known to be political hotheads,[1] and while this barbaric act from the hand of Pilate would be unconscionable, some might say the Galileans got what they deserved. They could say that this cruel outcome was an indication of God's judgment against the sinfulness of the Galileans. In their minds, goodness was always rewarded by God and evil was always punished. Therefore, if you experienced good you were good, and if you experienced bad you were bad. A second illustration of this faulty thinking was mentioned by Jesus—a time when **eighteen** Galileans **died when the tower in Siloam fell on them** (13:4). Again, there is no further record of this event. Sin and suffering were believed to go with each other. This was the hang-up of Job's "friends," who believed his suffering was an obvious result of hidden sin in his life.

Jesus said, **"Do you think that these Galileans were worse sinners than all the other Galileans because they suffered this way?"** (13:2). If suffering is the result of sin, then the greater the sin, the greater the suffering. It should not be too difficult to pick out who the worst sinners are. There are people who tend to categorize people by the degree of sin that is evident in their lives. And, while they get caught up in who has the worst sin, they find it more difficult to spot sin in themselves than in other people.

Lest the reporters of the heinous deed think they were better than the Galileans who were slaughtered, Jesus said, **"But unless you repent, you too will all perish"** (13:3). Sin is a universal condition, of which all persons must repent and seek forgiveness. The judgment against sin is death. Salvation from the judgment against sin must involve repentance, which is acknowledgment of our sin, sorrow that we sinned, and willingness to leave our life of sin.

Sometimes a person rationalizes his or her sin, thinking, *What I did is not nearly as bad as what my neighbor did. His sin was worse than mine, so until he is punished and gets straightened out, there is no pressure on me.* Sin is a violation of the law of God, and repentance is the necessary step in restoring one's relationship with Him.

THE NEED FOR FRUIT

True repentance results in changed behavior. When a person experiences a heart change, it will show up in changed attitudes and actions. In fact, our salvation should be verified by the evidences of transformation. Jesus told a **parable** about **a man** who **planted a fig tree in his vineyard, and he went to look for fruit on it, but did not find any** (13:6). Fruit should be the natural outcome of planting a fruit-bearing tree, and the man's expectations were reasonable. The problem was not that he sought unreasonably but that the tree did not live up to its reason for being planted.

God looks for fruit as natural outcomes in the lives of those to whom He has given life. The fruit of the Spirit is the result of the new life we received when we were regenerated and the work of the Holy Spirit who indwells us. Paul identifies this fruit as "love, joy, peace, patience, kindness, goodness, faithfulness, gentleness and self-control" (Gal. 5:22–23). The fruit of the Spirit may not yet be mature in us, but it should be evident and growing. God has the right to expect, when He comes seeking this fruit in us, that He will find it. The notion that we can say we have accepted Christ yet continue to live the way we always have is not compatible with the word of Christ.

After looking for fruit on his fig tree **for three years** but finding none, the owner of the vineyard instructed the caretaker to **cut it down** (13:7). The caretaker requested that the tree be given another year in which to demonstrate its fruitfulness. He said, **"I'll dig around it and fertilize it. If it bears fruit next year, fine! If not, then cut it down"** (13:8–9). God is willing to extend mercy and opportunity, but if there is no response, opportunity ceases, and even mercy comes to an end. "He is patient with you, not wanting anyone to perish, but everyone to come to repentance" (2 Pet. 3:9). However, we are not to consider God's patience as reason to continue in our sin, thinking He will overlook it.

The lesson of the parable was that Israel was "a planting of the LORD for the display of his splendor" (Isa. 61:3) and His "vineyard on a fertile hillside" (Isa. 5:1), but unless Israel repented and turned back to God, they would be cut down. Israel's history is full of mercy and opportunity, and so is our personal history.

2. HEALING ON THE SABBATH (13:10–17)

Jesus was teaching in a synagogue **on a Sabbath**, and **a crippled woman** (13:10–11) caught His attention. **She was bent over and could not straighten** and had been that way **for eighteen years** (13:11). **Jesus** touched her and **said, "Woman, you are set free from your infirmity"** (13:12), and she was **immediately** healed. While she **praised God**, the **ruler** of the **synagogue** became **indignant**, telling her there were **six days** for her to **come and be healed**, but **not on the Sabbath** (13:13–14). Jesus called him a hypocrite who pretended to be spiritual but used his "spirituality" as a means of denying the work of God. Luke said the woman had been **crippled by a spirit**, and when responding to the ruler of the synagogue, Jesus said she was a woman **Satan** had **kept bound**. Some infirmities may have spiritual origins. All disease and infirmity are the result of sin's infection of our world and the human condition, but not all infirmity is the direct result of the infirm person's sin, or an evidence of demonic attack. In this case, the woman was afflicted by an evil spirit from which she needed to **be set free** (13:16), and Jesus did just that.

Jesus confronted the ruler of the synagogue over the fact that a person could be given allowance on the Sabbath to **untie his ox or donkey from the stall and lead it out to give it water** (13:15), yet He was condemned for freeing the woman from Satan's bondage on the Sabbath. Like the Pharisees, the religious leader wanted to justify himself with his strict adherence to Sabbath laws. But, while doing so, he was ignoring the true work of God, which was the transformation of persons by freeing them from spiritual bondage. The ruler of the synagogue and **all** his cronies **were humiliated, but the people** rejoiced in what Jesus **was doing** among them (13:17).

3. PARABLES ABOUT THE KINGDOM (13:18–30)

WHAT IS THE KINGDOM OF GOD LIKE?

Jesus raised the question as to what the kingdom of God was like and then proceeded to provide an answer to His question. He often used common and readily visible things as illustrations and teaching points. On this occasion, He may have reached out to a nearby plant and pulled some **mustard seed** (13:19) into His hand to use as an illustration. He would use the mustard seed later to emphasize its smallness (17:6). According to Matthew's record, the mustard seed is the smallest of all of the seeds "but when it grows, it is the largest of garden plants and becomes a tree" (Matt. 13: 32). Matthew seems to emphasize that from small beginnings great things can emerge. Luke did not mention the smallness of the seed, but emphasized that the mustard tree became a gathering place for **the birds of the air** (13:19). Luke wrote primarily for Gentiles, so it is appropriate for him to emphasize the universal accessibility of the Kingdom. Anyone, regardless of heritage, nationality, or status, is invited to enter the kingdom of God.[2] The Kingdom is a gathering place where people from various places can find provision and protection in its branches.

Jesus looked for another illustration of the **kingdom of God** and said that it was **like yeast that** is **mixed into a large amount of flour until it worked all through the dough** (13:20–21). Jesus had previously spoken about the "yeast of the Pharisees" of which His disciples should beware (12:2). Several places in the Scripture yeast is used to illustrate the penetrating influence of evil. It interacts with and affects its surroundings, changing what it touches. Jesus makes the point that the kingdom of God works like yeast, too. It powerfully transforms those who enter into it, and through them it infiltrates and influences cultures, organizations, and systems. The kingdom of God has the power to change lives and relationships. Influence can be a powerful thing, and the influence of the kingdom of God can be more powerful than the yeast of evil influence.

Salvation may come to you quietly and through the smallest of events. But you are included in God's gift of grace. When you respond to the work of God in you, it grows and becomes the strength of your life and a place of refuge. Salvation involves transformation. When you accept God's grace, He begins to work in you, transforming you from the inside until you can positively influence the people around you. You are called to be salt, light (Matt. 5:13–14), and yeast in the world. Don't let your salt lose its saltiness, your light be hidden, or your yeast fail to come into transformational contact with the people and systems of your world.

WHO WILL BE SAVED?

Jerusalem always motivated the movements of Jesus. The directional compass of His life pointed toward the Holy City, yet He had ministry to do while on the way. As He **went through the towns . . . teaching** (Luke 13:22) and healing the sick, **someone asked him, "Lord, are only a few people going to be saved?"** (13:23). What prompted the question? Most likely the questioner was a Jew, and he might have picked up on some of the teaching of Jesus that indicated people other than Jews might get into the kingdom of God. Perhaps he was one who was proud of his own spirituality that made him qualified for salvation but would exclude others of lesser spirituality.

Jesus' response tells us that salvation requires a personal choice. Jesus said, **"Make every effort"** (13:24). We are not saved by our effort or by our works, but only by the grace of God. However, God does not save us against our will. We must choose to accept His offer of grace and join our effort in cooperation with His work. We are not unimpassioned participants in salvation, but enthusiastic responders. Salvation is a gift, but it only becomes a gift when it is received by faith. Salvation is synergistic, two efforts coming together, the human will and God's work of grace. Christian effort continues after initial salvation. You do not enter into a relationship with God and then do nothing, but rather the desire to enter becomes an ongoing desire to be transformed into the likeness of Christ. This does not happen automatically or in an instant, but requires desire and discipline on the part of those who seek after God and His holiness.

Salvation is inclusive, any person is eligible and invited to enter in. Any person *can* be saved, however inclusive salvation is not universalism, the belief that everyone *will* be saved. Jesus said that to be saved you must **enter through the narrow door** (13:24). Matthew recorded that as a part of the Sermon on the Mount. Jesus said, "Enter through the narrow gate. For wide is the gate and broad is the road that leads to destruction, and many enter through it. But small is the gate and narrow the road that leads to life, and only a few find it" (Matt. 7:13–14). In both Matthew and Luke, Jesus indicated there is a certain "narrowness" related to entering into the Kingdom. This is certainly not the kind of exclusion caused by the rules and regulations imposed by the Pharisees and teachers of the law that kept people out because of unreasonable burdens and restrictions. The arms of a gracious Father are open wide to welcome lost children home (Luke 15:20). The entrance can be viewed to be restrictive because entering in requires acceptance of the will and way of God. He has expectations of His children that accompany being a part of the family.

Jesus said **many . . . will try to enter and will not be able to** (13:24). This does not mean salvation is by divine selection (or election), that people will be kept out by God who decides who gets in and who doesn't. It does, however, teach that the narrow door will at some point become a closed door. Jesus said that there will be a day when **the owner of the house . . . closes the door** (13:25). This means that the opportunity for entering in through the narrow door will be closed. There will be those who thought they could make their own way into the Kingdom, and they **will stand outside knocking and pleading, "Sir, open the door for us"** (13:25). Jesus was speaking directly to people in the crowd who associated with Him, hung around the edges, ate with Him, and listened to His teaching. They would stand outside the door and watch the door close, before they would seek to enter. Being a part of the crowd hanging around the door does not get you inside. You must enter the Kingdom, not as a part of a crowd, but one person at a time. **The owner of the house** will say, **"I don't know you or where you come from"** (13:25). The door is not open to you because you say you know God. It is only because He knows you. Only He knows your name because you have acknowledged and received His Son, who has acknowledge you to His Father.

Failure to enter into the door to the Kingdom has serious eternal consequences. Jesus taught that there were two ultimate destinations: one was in the kingdom of God, where **people will come from east and west and north and south, and will take their places at the feast** (13:29). The other will be a place where there will be **weeping and gnashing of teeth** (13:28). People there will be experiencing physical and emotional anguish, while people in the kingdom of God will be celebrating. The greatest difference between the two destinations is that for those in the Kingdom, God will say, "Welcome home, good and faithful servant." To the others He will say, **"Away from me"** (13:27). Salvation is eternal life, a quality of spiritual life now and an eternity in the presence of God. Those who are not saved will have an eternity of separation from God. That is the punishment of hell, to have no contact with God.

Salvation is based on our response of faith and obedience to the redemptive work of God in Christ. It is not based on prominence or position, which are often the requirements for entering into many organizations of privilege. The kingdom of God reverses the values that motivate much of earthly life. We might be surprised when we get to heaven and see who is there that we did not expect to see, and who is not there that we thought surely would be. Jesus said, **"There are those who are last who will be first, and first who will be last"** (13:30). Being a Christian may not make you well known or provide you with a front-row seat in the important events of life. But you will be known to the Father, who will welcome you into His house and give you a first-class seat at His banquet table.

Salvation involves making a decision that will determine your eternal destination. God has invited you to enter in, and the choice is now yours.

WHAT OTHERS SAY

SALVATION

Clarence Bence outlines four different views of salvation. People of the Wesleyan tradition see salvation as a gift to be appropriated. Salvation is dependent on our act of faith in the redemptive act of God.

FOUR VIEWS OF SALVATION

Salvation is a potential to be achieved.	Pelagianism	Salvation depends almost completely on what humans do.
Salvation is a miracle to be acknowledged.	Augustinianism	Salvation depends totally on what God does.
Salvation is a reward to be earned.	Semi-Pelagianism	Salvation depends on God's response to what humans do.
Salvation is a gift to be appropriated.	Semi-Augustinianism	Salvation depends on our response to what God has done.

4. JESUS WEEPS FOR JERUSALEM (13:31–35)

Jesus often had a volatile relationship with the Pharisees, since He was quick to expose their hypocrisy and self-righteousness. However, among the bad Pharisees there must have been some good ones who were God-fearing and God-loving. At least Luke puts in a favorable light **some Pharisees** who **came to Jesus** and warned Him that **Herod** wanted to **kill** Him. They **said to him, "Leave this place and go somewhere else"** (13:31). In His response, Jesus called Herod **"that fox"** (13:32), indicating his shrewd and destructive manner as well as Jesus' lack of fear of him. He instructed the concerned Pharisees to tell Herod that He would go on with His ministry of driving out demons and healing people, regardless of the threat: **"I must keep going today and tomorrow and the next day"** (13:33). He had a mission to accomplish and He would persevere—**"I will reach my goal"** (13:32). There is a courage that accompanies a person on a divine mission. We should have more concern that we do not fulfill our God-given purpose in life than we do about those who would try to hinder us.

His immediate goal was to touch the lives of as many people as possible, meeting their spiritual and physical needs. His long-range goal was to be the sacrificial Lamb of God so His redemptive act could touch the lives of people of all ages. So, He was not afraid of what Herod could do to Him. His mission was taking Him to Jerusalem, into the hands of Herod, **for surely no prophet can die outside Jerusalem!** (13:33).

The very mention of the Holy City brought anguish to His spirit, and He cried out, **"O Jerusalem, Jerusalem!"** (13:34). He carried a tremendous burden for the people of Jerusalem, in spite of their historic treatment of God's messengers and their unwillingness to respond to His message. The longing of Christ to embrace them had only been met with rejection. As if He were exposing His inner groaning to anyone who was listening, He said, **"How often I have longed to gather your children together, as a hen gathers her chicks under her wings, but you were not willing!"** (13:34). There is intensity in God's love for us that is often unmatched in our desire for Him. God is more anxious to save us than we

LIFE CHANGE

HOLINESS

Instant maturity or perfection has never been the claim of the Wesleyan message. This message is a declaration of acceptance of the power of grace to accomplish the full work of the Atonement. The optimism of grace runs strong through Wesleyan teaching of sanctification—that God can cleanse the heart from sin and impart a new nature with affections set on loving Him with a whole heart.

are to be saved. Luke does not record any visit to Jerusalem during Jesus' ministry, but John's gospel says Jesus went there to celebrate the Passover (John 2:13). It was then that He had the night visit with Nicodemus and drove the money changers out of the Temple. He had been to Jerusalem, but not many there accepted Him. To offer love and have it rejected brings great pain, and that pain was now being expressed by Jesus.

Salvation is the result of a loving, seeking God, who is not willing to let anyone perish. His heart is broken by our sin and stubbornness. In mercy, He pursues us when we have shown little interest in Him. There is a longing in His heart and a desire to gather lost souls unto himself.

ENDNOTES

1. William Barclay, *The Gospel of Luke* (Philadelphia: Westminster, 1956), p. 177.

2. Ibid., p. 184.

15

CONSIDERING THE INVITATION

Luke 14:1-34

Y ou are invited to participate in the privileges and celebrations of the kingdom of God. Your presence is desired but not demanded. You are free to turn down the invitation. The choice is yours.

We are not members of the kingdom of God by divine decree, arbitrary selection, or genetic predisposition. Relationship with God is based on our response to an invitation offered to us by the One who made forgiveness and spiritual rebirth possible. Salvation involves personal responsibility, and we face moments of opportunity to make decisions of destiny.

God's love welcomes everyone, and the invitation is offered freely to all. In this chapter, however, Jesus emphasized the high cost of discipleship, indicating there are things that will keep people from following Him. His desire that everyone will be drawn to Him is blended with the high cost of commitment to His way and the realization that there will always be those who are unwilling to pay the price. We should celebrate that we were on the invitation list, but we should give careful consideration to the cost before responding to the invitation.

1. KINGDOM ETIQUETTE (14:1-14)

ANOTHER SABBATH HEALING

Lingering around a table often generates valuable conversation. Some of the great teachings of Jesus came as a part of table talk. Jesus was often criticized by the Pharisees and teachers of the law for eating with "publicans and sinners." But on this occasion, **Jesus went to eat in the house of a prominent Pharisee** (14:1) on a Sabbath day. He did not avoid His most vocal critics but was willing to sit down with them and engage their criticism. Offering hospitality was a cultural expectation, and the treatment of guests was governed by cultural rules of etiquette. But even in what was to be a socially polite dinner meeting, Jesus **was being carefully watched** (14:1). His critics were looking for any opportunity to attack and discredit Him. Most likely this is why the Pharisee invited Him to have a meal in his home.

Rather than avoiding their scrutiny, Jesus took the offensive. **A man** who suffered **from dropsy** was there, and knowing what the response of the **Pharisees** would be, **Jesus asked, "Is it lawful to heal on the Sabbath or not?"** (14:2–3). There was no response to His question, so Jesus **healed him and sent him away** (14:4). Before they could condemn His act of healing on the Sabbath as they had done before, He asked them if anyone of them had **a son or an ox that** fell **into a well on the Sabbath day,** would they **not immediately pull him out?"** (14:5). The critical need of the moment to act decisively for the well-being of son or ox was greater than the need to rigidly respond to man-made regulations about the Sabbath. Just as Jesus had put human need above legalism, any one of them would put the rescue of his son above regulations about what constituted breaking the laws of the Sabbath. Jesus skillfully silenced His critics, but it was only a temporary setback for them and would only add to their desire to eliminate Him.

KINGDOM HUMILITY

Other things were happening around the dinner table that did not escape Jesus. **He noticed how the guests picked the places of honor at the table** (14:7). He used the occasion to highlight etiquette in the kingdom of God. Self-centeredness lies at the heart of our sinfulness, and by nature we promote our self-interests; we seek places of honor. But members of the Kingdom are different. Rather than sitting down in the choicest seats and suffering the embarrassment of being asked to give up their seat for someone of greater honor, they choose the lesser seats, antic-ipating people more honored than they will be invited to occupy the choice seats. They are not seekers of position or status. If the host wants them in a place of honor, he can make that determination. There is a vast difference between being honored because you sought it and being honored because someone else wanted to bestow it on you. There are justifiable times when honor is bestowed on people within the Kingdom (Phil. 2:29–30). We applaud and thank God for people who rightfully deserve to be honored by the church. It is right and good that people who serve God and the church be given recognition and shown appreciation. Faithfulness and excellence in service often result in assignment to places of greater responsibility and honor. Moving up is a nice thing when it is not manipulated by you but rather awarded to you.

But, there is something distasteful and unattractive about those who seek position and honor. Ambition can easily become self-serving. Of the seven times the word *ambition* appears in the Scriptures, it is preceded by the word *selfish* five times (Gal. 5:20; Phil. 1:17; Phil. 2:3; James 3:14, 16). In our desire to serve where we can make the greatest contribution and have the greatest influence, it is far better that we allow the Father to assign our place around His table than for us to seek places of promi-nence and discover there are others more worthy. The word of Jesus regarding kingdom etiquette strikes at the heart of our unconverted ego: **"Everyone who exalts himself will be humbled, and he who humbles himself will be exalted"** (Luke 14:11). Humility is a value that is evi-denced within the transformed persons of the kingdom of God. It is a grace that cannot be feigned.

KINGDOM BLESSING

Table talk continued as Jesus turned to His host and challenged him to reconsider his guest list. Normally, **friends, brothers, relatives**, and **rich neighbors** (14:12) are the first to be invited. The reason for gathering people around our tables is to cultivate and enjoy relationship. Sometimes we might invite people so they will reciprocate and invite us and we can benefit from their hospitality, or we can make them indebted to us because they have the capacity to help us. Jesus said the wrong people are too often invited. We should **invite the poor, the crippled, the lame,** and **the blind** (14:13). They have no capacity to **repay** our generous hospitality, so our motivation for inviting them is completely different.

The two guest lists define completely different life views. The first guest list is self-serving. The second seeks to serve others without expectation of return or reward. The first anticipates being **repaid**. The second anticipates being **blessed**. The first results in a repayment that is realized in the present. The second results in blessing that will be realized **at the resurrection of the righteous** (14:14). The first is motivated by the belief that relationships are to be used for personal benefit. The second is motivated by the belief that relationships are opportunities to serve the needs of others.

2. INVITATION TO THE GREAT BANQUET (14:15–24)

Sitting around the table prompted one of the guests to say, **"Blessed is the man who will eat at the feast in the kingdom of God"** (14:15). The Jews believed that when the Messiah appeared He would bring a new age of peace and prosperity, and a great banquet or feast was anticipated as a part of the establishment of His kingdom. Isaiah 27 speaks of a day of God's judgment against sinful people when He will kill the great sea serpent, Leviathan. In Jewish thinking, during the great messianic banquet, they would sit with the conquering Messiah and feast on the slain monster.[1] Of course, the Jews believed that they alone would be invited to this great banquet.

Jesus took this opportunity to tell a story that would teach some of the realities of the kingdom of God. He said that participation in the Kingdom is like a **man** who prepared **a great banquet and invited many guests** (14:16). Contrary to the exclusive thinking of the Jews, the invitation to the banquet goes out to many guests. There are people on the invitation list they would not have considered worthy of attending—Gentiles.

When **time** for **the banquet** arrived, a **servant** was **sent to those who had been invited** with the message, **"Come, for everything is now ready"** (14:17). Jesus is the one who is making things ready, and He is

198

the servant who is personally delivering the invitation. You would think that an invitation to the great banquet would be met with unqualified and excited acceptance. Why would anyone turn down the privilege of sitting down around the Father's table, qualified to be there because of being forgiven and adopted into the family? But this is an *invitation*, not a *summons*, and we are free to choose to ignore or reject the invitation.

Come is a favorite word of God. It invites and suggests there will be welcomed acceptance if you choose to go.

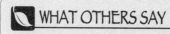

WHAT OTHERS SAY

FREE WILL

"The greatest gift which God in His bounty bestowed in creating, and the most conformed to His own goodness, and that which He prizes the most, was the freedom of the will, with which the creatures that have intelligence, they all and they alone, were and are endowed."

—Dante in *Divine Comedy*

Come is a word that invites a response. When God says, "come," it is more than a courteous option to which you may casually respond if you want. It is an invitation that determines destiny and about which you *must* make a decision.

When the people received their invitations, **they began to make excuses.** One used the excuse that he had **bought a field** (14:18); another **bought five yoke of oxen** (14:19); and another **just got married** (14:20). This is just a story, but still we can be quick to shoot holes through their excuses. Why would someone buy a field before going to **see it**, or purchase several oxen without first trying **them out**? And the generous host would surely have made room for the new bride of the one who just married. These were not legitimate reasons, they were excuses. The people who were invited had other interests, other priorities, and other tables at which they wanted to

LIFE CHANGE

CHOICES

The direction and destiny of our lives are not predetermined. We have the freedom to make choices that determine our future. This great privilege carries a corresponding great responsibility. Our choices should be governed by Kingdom values and principles. We no longer live to please the desires that used to dominate our choices. Now we "find out what pleases the Lord" (Eph. 5:10) and when we make that our choice we find that it is good and pleasing to us as well.

sit, so they exercised their freedom of choice and turned down the invitation. Just because you are free to choose does not mean you are free from the consequences that follow the choice you make.

Rejected by those who were invited first, the host instructed his servant to **bring in the poor, the crippled, the blind and the lame** (14:21). The invitation was expanded to include people considered to be undesirable for most guest lists. The first group invited most likely represented the Jews whom God had chosen to be His people; but many, like the Pharisees and teachers of the law, rejected His new kingdom. So God expanded the invitation to include those who would be considered lesser persons, the religiously underprivileged and those who were marginalized in society.

The servant followed the orders, only to come back to say, **"There is still room"** (14:22). This time the instruction was **"Go out to the roads and country lanes and make them come in, so that my house will be full"** (14:23). The invitation was expanded once again to include any and all Gentiles—you and me. Many undeserving and unlikely people living along a back road of life, far from the kingdom of God, have been surprised by an invitation to come to the table of the King. The country lane along which you live has been visited and an invitation delivered with your name on it. The master's word to **make them come in** should not be construed to support a notion that persons will be dragged into the Kingdom against their will, but rather to communicate the deep desire and urgency of the God who does not desire that anyone perish, but that all come to repentance. He will pursue us with His invitation, short of forcing our will, because sitting at the Father's table remains a matter of personal choice.

There is plenty of hope of salvation in this story for us to celebrate. There is still room, and the master wants His house to be full. There is room for people like you, like your family and friends, like the person next door, and like the person of another ethnic group who may live across town or on the other side of the globe. God is reckless in offering His invitation. He loves to share the blessings of the Kingdom with whomever is willing to come. There is room around His table, and He wants to share the feast of His grace with anyone who will come.

There is plenty of warning in this story for us to consider as well. The master said to those who refused the invitation, **"I tell you, not one of**

those men who were invited will get a taste of my banquet" (14:24). The good things of the Kingdom are reserved for those who respond to the Father's invitation by making the trip to His table. You cannot ignore His invitation and expect to get a taste of the spread He has prepared for those who sit at His table.

Salvation, entering the kingdom of God, is all about His invitation and our response. His grace makes life in the Kingdom possible, and our response of faith makes life in the Kingdom our possession.

3. ESTIMATING THE COST (14:25–34)

Choice suggests that there are alternatives. For us to choose one thing means that we reject another. For us to go down one path means we don't go down another. Choosing worthwhile things means we accept the costs that accompany the choice. Having just spoken of the passion of God to see that everyone gets an invitation to come to His great banquet, Jesus spoke to the passion for the Kingdom that must be demonstrated by those who choose to accept a place at the Father's table.

As many times before, **large crowds were traveling with Jesus** (14:25). He attracted attention, but He was not looking to pack the stadiums. He wanted to impact the world with devoted disciples. He spoke one of His hard sayings to the crowds following Him when **he said: "If anyone comes to me and does not hate his father and mother, his wife and children, his brothers and sisters—yes, even his own life—he cannot be my disciple. And anyone who does not carry his cross and follow me cannot be my disciple"** (14:26–27). Jesus made the marketing of the Kingdom more difficult with these words. In our effort to attract people to Jesus, we can try to interpret these words in ways that soften them a bit. If He

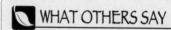

WHAT OTHERS SAY

CONSECRATION

"Where natural affection for one's own family and the blessings of this life compete with or oppose the kingdom's principles and goals, a disciple must make a choice. It is characterized by a deliberate beginning, daily renewal (9:23), and never looking back (9:62)."

—Melvin Shoemaker

wanted people to follow Him, why would He emphasize things that would keep them from being disciples? Three times He said if they did not go along with the demands of the Kingdom, they could not be His disciples.

The term *disciple* appears forty-four times in this Gospel, referring to those who follow and learn from another person. In the Gospels, a wide variety of followers of Christ were referred to as disciples, but in these verses Jesus clearly laid out His expectations for those who He said would be "my" disciples. Three major characteristics must be demonstrated in them: (1) They must love God more than any other relationship; (2) they must be willing to suffer and die for the sake of the kingdom of God; and (3) they must give everything to God. Short of this level of commitment, they cannot be His disciples.

Disciples must be willing to love God more than father, mother, wife, children, brothers, sisters and even their own lives. Jesus used the word *hate* in referring to cherished relationships that a disciple has to be willing to sacrifice. It would be inappropriate to interpret this in any way other than strong insistence that nothing get in the way of your relationship with Christ.

Relationships can compete with the Kingdom and hinder following Jesus. So can an unwillingness to carry a cross. We sometimes say everyone has "their cross to bear." By that we refer to the inconveniences and burdens that come to us as a part of the circumstances of our lives. But this is not what Jesus meant. Though He had not yet endured His cross, He was looking ahead to the instrument of His suffering and death, which would forever become the symbol of redemption. When He said we must carry our cross, He was calling us to be willing to identify with Him and His redemptive mission. We must not sidestep the cost of following Him, regardless where that path takes us.

Shallow decisions, based only on emotion, can get in the way of following Jesus. He is seeking those who will make decisions that last a lifetime, and those decisions must be made with careful thought. Since it is impossible to know all that tomorrow may demand, our decision to follow Jesus, wherever it might take us, must be a commitment based on strong faith. Some people are flashy starters but poor finishers. Jesus wants followers who are willing to stick with Him regardless of the cost. He used building a **tower** to say that before starting, the builder should

first sit down and estimate the cost to see if he has enough money to complete it (14:28). He used laying a **foundation** to warn that the cause is hurt if the builder **is not able to finish it,** because **everyone who sees it will ridicule him** (14:29). Far too frequently God's work has been left unfinished and ridiculed because of the failure of shallow followers. Not only did they discredit themselves, they discredited the work of God through their inability to finish what they began.

Again, Jesus stressed the need to calculate the cost and determine the willingness to pay it by illustrating it with a **king** who planned **to go to war against another king** (14:31). Before he starts the war, he will **first sit down and consider whether he is able** to win. **If he is not able, he will . . . ask for terms of peace** (14:32) before the first swing of a sword. Jesus pressed the point that being His disciple is a costly venture, and the decision to follow Him should not be made casually or carelessly. Finishing is the goal, not just starting.

Too frequently the church has pushed for "decisions" and celebrated "converts" without providing the kind of support and counsel to see that these persons became fully devoted disciples of Christ. There are times when shallow decisions lead to an inoculation against the real thing, making it hard to get those who start and then fail to ever experience true salvation. Jesus addressed this sad possibility by saying, **"Salt is good, but if it loses its saltiness, how can it be made salty again? It is fit neither for the soil nor for the manure pile; it is thrown out"** (14:34–35). The church is not called to count decisions but to create disciples.

Disciples are those who have considered the cost, have determined that with God's help they can finish what they have started, have shouldered their cross, and have decided to **give up everything** (14:33) to follow Jesus. Grace that saves is offered freely, but following Jesus will cost you everything. No, God usually does not ask us to divest ourselves of all we have and leave our occupations and homes. But being a disciple means that we are willing to let God be the owner of everything, including our very lives. What we give without reservation to God, He usually sanctifies and places back in our open hands as tools to be used for His glory and our good. It is what we cling to with clenched fists that keeps us from following Jesus.

Salvation is an invitation from God to come to His banquet to sit at the King's table in a brand-new Kingdom. Salvation is conditioned by our response of faith as we accept the invitation and commit ourselves to make the journey, regardless of the cost. The invitation is His to offer. The response is ours to make.

ENDNOTES

1. William Barclay, *The Gospel of Luke* (Philadelphia: Westminster, 1956), p. 199.

16

THE LOST IS FOUND

Luke 15:1–32

The critics of Jesus said, "This man welcomes sinners" (15:2). What was meant as an accusation to discredit Jesus was really an affirmation of His mission and winsomeness. We can be thankful the accusation is true. If Jesus did not welcome sinners, there would be no salvation possible for us and no place for us with Him.

This chapter exposes Jesus' gracious acceptance of people who are "sinners." The stories Jesus told are filled with optimism: that God cares enough about sinners to go to them, to seek after them, to allow them freedom of choice, and to celebrate when they come home.

Those who perceived themselves to be religiously superior had trouble seeing themselves as sinners. So Jesus told three stories, each with a common plot and point, but each with a different motif. They were three stories of things lost, searched for, found, and celebrated. The last story carries an additional twist that spoke to those who did not spot themselves in the first three scenarios. Jesus wanted the Pharisees to get the message that it is possible to be lost even though you never leave home.

We'll also discover that each parable illustrates the work of a member of the Trinity.

1. RECOGNIZING A SINNER WHEN YOU SEE ONE (15:1–2)

Can you recognize a sinner when you see one? The **Pharisees and the teachers of the law** (15:2) could. The Pharisees were quick to spot **tax collectors and "sinners"** (15:1) in the crowd that gathered around Jesus. Both designations—tax collectors and sinners—rolled easily off their tongues with no distinction between the two terms. Both were considered undesirable and unfit for holy people to associate with. Many tax collectors were unjust individuals, appointed by the Romans to collect taxes from their own people. Their association with the Romans, besides their inclination to extract more in taxes than was due in order to line their own pockets, caused the people to dislike them. It was not difficult to identify them as sinners.

The religious leaders did not mingle with these people, and they thought if Jesus was really interested in maintaining respectability, He would not associate with them either. They were overheard muttering, **"This man welcomes sinners and eats with them"** (15:2). The Pharisees were a religious sect within Judaism who prided themselves as being holy people because they observed the minutest implications and applications of Judaism. Teachers of the law were experts in the law of Moses and could point out the smallest of violations. Another group, the Sadducees, were more political in their orientation and often clashed with the Pharisees. These three groups comprised the religious leaders of the day. They lived in a closed system that offered little grace. Their relationship toward sinners was not designed to convert them, but to condemn and disassociate from them, while Jesus sought to draw them to himself and redeem them.

Jesus knew the hearts of the Pharisees and the teachers of the law and knew they were as lost as those they pointed out as sinners. However, the most difficult people to save are those who do not believe they need saving, and these religious leaders did not see themselves as sinners in need of a Savior.

2. A SINNER BY NATURE (15:3-7)

The parables of Jesus usually used things familiar to the listeners, which led to ready recognition of the point He wanted to teach. These stories are short, simple, and illustrate a moral or spiritual lesson. Shepherds and sheep were common images on the landscape of their lives. His hearers could immediately identify with the desire of a shepherd to find a **lost sheep** (15:5).

Most often, sheep get lost because of their nature. With head downs, they search for a clump of grass, wander off from the rest of the flock, and soon are out of sight. A lost sheep is vulnerable and defenseless and can fall prey to animals or get trapped in a crevasse. When we allow our fallen nature to determine our direction, we can be led toward the promise of fun and good fortune, only to find that danger lurks around the turn in the path.

The parable teaches us that God takes the initiative in saving the lost. The shepherd leaves **the ninety-nine in the open country and** goes **after the lost sheep until he finds it** (15:4). When the shepherd discovers a sheep is missing, he will be motivated by a sense of urgency because he cares for each of his sheep and knows they are dependent on him. No shepherd could love his sheep more than God loves a sinner. The point should not be taken that the ninety-nine "safe" sheep the shepherd leaves are not important to him, but rather that the one lost is so important that he will do everything to find it.

Grace always pursues the object of its love. God will not stand by and allow us to wander away from Him without making every effort to stop us. We can resist His voice and try to hide from His overtures, but He initiates the search and will never give it up. Without His search, we could not be saved. Unlike the sheep, we will not be saved unless we want to be found. We may speak of finding Christ or of inviting Christ into our lives. But we are the ones lost and, in actual fact, *He* finds us and invites us to go home with Him. He initiates the search before we even realize we are lost. We call this *prevenient grace*—grace that

 GREAT THEMES

PREVENIENT GRACE

Because of Adam's sin, all of humanity is born into a sinful state of moral corruption. Augustine emphasized that because of the total depravity of the human soul humanity cannot make any advances toward God. "Even from birth the wicked go astray; from the womb they are wayward and speak lies" (Ps. 58:3). Our only hope is for God to intervene and save us from our original sin and our actual sin. While John Wesley agreed with Augustine and Calvin regarding total depravity, he taught that God has intervened and provided "prevenient grace" that enables us to respond to God's offer of saving grace. We still bear the effects of original sin, but this prevenient grace that is given to every person allows us to cry out for God's help and saving grace. This grace is also adequate for salvation for those who are incapable of making moral choice, whether because of being young of age or mentally incompetent.

is at work in our lives before we are aware of it that makes it possible for us to move toward saving grace.

The compassion of God is suggested as the shepherd **puts** the sheep **on his shoulders and goes home** (15:5–6). The shepherd does not use his staff to drive the sheep back to the fold. He does not lecture the sheep on where it went wrong. He picks the sheep up onto his shoulders and carries it home. What a beautiful picture of Jesus, the Good Shepherd. He comes to where we are and lifts us out of our dangerous plight. We don't know the way home, but that is not a problem, He does. We have been injured in our fall and wounded in our wandering, but that is not a problem, He carries us. His shoulders are broad enough to carry the sins of the whole world, so He can surely carry us. Our fleece is not exactly white as snow, but dirty, tangled, and filled with thorns. The thorns dig into His shoulders; the dirt rubs off on Him; and our wounds soil His garments. But He carries us home. He is the fulfillment of Isaiah's prophecy:

> Surely he took up our infirmities and carried our sorrows . . . he was pierced for our transgressions, he was crushed for our iniquities; the punishment that brought us peace was upon him, and by his wounds we are healed. We all, like sheep, have gone astray, each of us has turned to his own way; and the LORD has laid on him the iniquity of us all (Isa. 53:4–6).

The recovery of the lost sheep is cause for rejoicing. The shepherd **calls his friends and neighbors together and says, "Rejoice with me; I have found my lost sheep"** (Luke 15:6). The mission of Jesus is to "seek and save" those who are lost (Luke 19:10), and each time a lost one is saved, all of heaven rejoices. We are *His* sheep. We were His by creation before we went astray, and we became His again by redemption when He paid the price for our salvation. We may never become aware of all we have been saved from, in terms of potential consequences, but God knows, and He leads heaven in rejoicing that we have been spared from future pain and eternal punishment.

Verse 7 is a veiled word addressed to the Pharisees, similar to when Jesus spoke of the physician who comes to heal those who are sick rather than those who are well. The **ninety-nine righteous persons who do not need to repent** (15:7), like those who need no physician, are those who, because of their trust in orthodox religiosity, become self-righteous and do not see themselves as lost or as needing to repent. Repentance requires recognition of sin, sorrow over it, and a desire to leave it. Failure to recognize your sinfulness means that you will remain in it, like the Pharisees did.

3. A SINNER BY NEGLECT (15:8–10)

The second story of lost things is about **a woman** who **has ten silver coins and loses one** (15:8). It has been suggested that the coins of this story refer to the ten silver coins Palestinian women received as a wedding gift. The loss of the coin would be a sentimental, as well as a real loss of something valued. Sin always degrades and devalues. We only have to look at the evening news to see how devalued life has become and how cheaply people are treated. But to God, each person is worth the whole world, and one lost person is enough to set the wheels of redemptive grace into motion.

Most often, coins are lost by carelessness, neglect, and accumulation of stuff that covers them. We can get lost through our preoccupation with things other than relationship with God and through neglect of spiritual matters. The accumulation of things can occupy such a prominent place in our lives that spiritual things are pushed further and further back on the shelf until they are not visible or valued. Something once valued and of primary importance can become disregarded and secondary. We may not intentionally discard our relationship with God, but we can disregard it until connection with Him is lost.

The parable of the lost sheep illustrates the salvation work of the Son. The parable of the lost coin illustrates the salvation work of the Spirit. To find the lost coin, Jesus said, **"Does she not light a lamp, sweep the house and search carefully until she finds it?"** (15:8). The work of the Holy Spirit in salvation is to illuminate and cleanse. To find the lost coin, the woman lights a lamp. The Holy Spirit turns on the light, convicting persons of sin and convincing them of truth and righteousness (John 16:8). He is the pursuing agent in our salvation, diligently calling our name, carefully pulling back the layers of things that separate us from God, illuminating the condition of our hearts, and revealing the grace of God. The Holy Spirit is also the agent of cleansing, applying the purifying and transformational benefits of the Atonement.

Like the previous parable, discovery of the lost coins results in a celebration: **there is rejoicing in the presence of the angels of God over one sinner who repents** (Luke 15:10). The rejoicing in the first story was that "my sheep has been found." The rejoicing in this story is over a coin that is found. Salvation is impossible without the initiative of God that finds the sinner and becomes complete only with the repentance of the sinner. Repentance is a major theme in Luke's gospel as the necessary human response to the divine initiative of illuminating sin and offering grace.

4. A SINNER BY CHOICE (15:11–24)

The story shifts from lost sheep and lost silver coins to lost sons. The agent of salvation in this story is God the Father. This story is called the parable of the *prodigal son*—"prodigal" meaning reckless, wasteful, and extravagant. The word may also be applied to a kind of generous recklessness in giving to one who might misuse what has been given. This suggests that the story could well be the parable of the *prodigal father* as it reveals a generous father who extends freedom and grace that may be abused. Yet, he is generous in his welcome of the son who returns home.

Sheep may get lost by nature, and coins may get lost by neglect. Sons, unless they are too young to know better, get lost by choice. This parable is about **a man who had two sons** (15:11). There are two parts to the story and two points to make, with each of the sons being the focus of each of the two parts. Both sons had choices to make that caused them to be lost: one in **a distant country** (15:13) and one while remaining at home. The first part of the story is about **the younger one, who said to his father, "Father, give me my share of the estate"** (15:12). Estates are usually divided after the owner has died. In effect, the younger son could, in a spirit of rebellion, be saying to his father, "I wish you were dead." At least he was prepared to sever his relationship with his father and treat him as if he were dead. The relationships of home were secondary to *my* **share**. Self-centeredness lies at the heart of sinfulness and leads to being lost.

Surprisingly, the father **divided his property between them** (15:12)—both the younger and older sons received a portion of the estate. The younger son chose to take his newfound wealth and leave home, believing life would be more fun somewhere else, free from the restraints of home, and the father allowed the son the freedom to leave. God the Father gives us freedom of choice and, as much as it breaks His heart, He allows us to leave if that is what we choose to do. Sin is first of all relational, and it begins when we choose to leave life with the Father.

Anxious to get out from under the controls of home, the younger son packed up and **set off for a distant country and there squandered his wealth in wild living** (15:13). Our sinful nature can cause us to believe that life in the home of the Father is hard and restrictive. If we can get far enough away, we will find freedom and fun. Wild living can have a certain appeal, however wild living can be costly. The word *squandered* suggests wasting something valuable and having nothing left to show for it, which is the result of wild living that leaves emptiness and moral bankruptcy in its wake. **After he had spent everything, there was a severe famine in that whole country, and he began to be in need** (15:14). What started as fun ended in famine. His pocketbook was as empty as his stomach, and a greater emptiness was felt in his soul. His need became acute enough that he **hired himself out to a citizen of that country, who sent him to his fields to feed pigs** (15:15). His hunger was so intense that he wanted to get down with the pigs and eat their food, but in all of his hunger and despair, **no one gave him anything** (15:16). Where were all the "friends" who had partied with him when he was able to pick up the tab? Did no one care about the depth of his need?

When he came to his senses (15:17), he realized he was a noncitizen in a distant country. He did not belong there. He had a greater destiny than seeing his life end in this forsaken, lonely, needy place. Funds and fun were gone. In his desperation, he thought of home and realized that under his father's care even the **hired men** had **food to spare**, while he was **starving to death** (15:17). Lost people often have to reach the bottom before they come to their senses. They can live in denial of the severity of their situation until there is no hope for rescue or recovery, and it is then that thoughts can turn toward home. The son came to realize how much better life was with his father and what a big mistake he had made. He had made choices that led to his ruin, and he had no one to blame but himself. His only hope was to go back to his father, so that's what he decided to do. The Father who gives us the freedom to choose to leave, graciously gives us the freedom to choose to return.

The remorseful son rehearsed what he would tell his father when he saw him: **"Father, I have sinned against heaven and against you. I am no longer worthy to be called your son; make me like one of your hired men"** (15:18–19). He now saw his self-centeredness, disrespect, and wild living as sin. He saw no other hope but to throw himself on the mercy of his father. He admitted that he deserved nothing and was willing to take the least place in his father's household.

 LIFE CHANGE

UNWORTHY

We are unworthy of the Father's embrace, but we are never worthless to Him. Guilt can make us feel worthless, but the Holy Spirit's conviction never makes us feel worthless, only unworthy. The desire to return to the Father is motivated by the hope the Spirit brings to us that we are of great worth to the Father and we will be met by His embrace of grace. Grace means you are unworthy, but it also means you are worth everything to God.

So he got up and went to his father (15:20). Having wallowed around with the pigs, there should be no pride left in him, but if there was, he threw it aside to humbly make his way back to his father. It was his father that he wanted to return to, not just his home. It was the goodness of his father that drew him back home, along with an intuitive belief that regardless of what he had done, his father would be just and fair with him.

Now the story becomes all about the father. Others may have said "Good riddance" to an ungrateful young man, and some more compassionate may have given up any hope they would ever see the runaway again. But the father must have been waiting and watching, because **while the son was still a long way off, his father saw him** (15:20). What kind of emotion would you expect from a father whose son wished him dead and who had thrown away an estate the father had worked hard to provide? When the **father saw** his son, he **was filled with compassion for him; he ran to his son, threw his arms around him and kissed him** (15:20).

His first response was that of compassion, not punishment or revenge. The father ran to his wayward son and, not waiting for words, threw his arms around him in a welcoming embrace. Sin is relational and so is grace. Grace is greater than all our sin. The way home begins with a step toward God, and He will help close the distance quickly.

The son began the speech he had previously rehearsed. He faced his father, confessed his sin, and accepted responsibility by saying, **"I have sinned"** (15:21). He did not try to shift blame, but recognized that it was his wrong actions that led to a broken relationship, the sin was against the father. He declared personal unworthiness and dependence on the mercy of the father. Confession is an admission of sin that is to be followed with repentance, which includes remorse for the sin and a desire to change.

The father cut short what the son had planned to say. The father was not ready to take him back as a slave but as a son, with the full rights and privileges of a son.

Like the two previous stories, finding what is lost calls for a celebration. **The father** called for **his servants** to **kill** a **calf** so they could **have a feast and celebrate** (15:22–23). Relationship was restored, but the son still carried the consequences of his wayward life, and before the party could begin, some changes had to be made. Salvation is transformation. You can no longer live and eat with the pigs. If you are going to sit at the Father's table you need a change of clothes and you need to deal with the smelly residue from your pig-pen days. The father instructed his servants, **"Bring the best robe and put it on him. Put a ring on his finger and sandals on his feet"** (15:22). The Father doesn't expect you to clean up before you come home, nor does He wait until you smell good before He will embrace you. But He wants to clean you up and put some new clothes on you that reflect your status of being His child. It is not acceptable to live like a pig in the Father's house. Salvation that does not include transformation is not God's salvation.

The father gave this analysis of the son's condition while he was away from home: **"This son of mine was dead and is alive again; he was lost and is found"** (15:24). Not only was he lost, as were the sheep and coin, but he was dead. Sin is a relational problem. To be out of relationship with the Father is to be lost and dead (Eph. 2:1). Salvation involves rebirth. "Because of his great love for us, God, who is rich in mercy, *made us alive with Christ* even when we were dead in transgressions" (Eph. 2:4–5, italics added). The son who wanted to treat his father as if he were dead by severing relationships and getting out from under his leadership, was himself dead.

So they began to celebrate (Luke 15:24). The celebration of salvation is not just a celebration in heaven involving the angels, it is a celebration of the family on earth. There is reason to party in the church when a sinner comes home. Celebration should often characterize life in the church, and nothing lights the fire of spiritual enthusiasm like a new convert. We need to see more celebrations, not in the form of hype to try to get something started, but in the form of gratitude for what has already happened as we witness sinners coming home to the Father.

5. A SINNER BY LIFELESS ORTHODOXY (15:25–32)

The celebration over the return of the younger son became the setting for exposing the son who was lost but had never left home. It is this second part of the story that points a finger at those who do not see themselves as being lost. They did not choose to leave home or squander their lives in wild living, but they made other choices that severed relationship with their Father.

The story says that **the older son was in the field** (15:25). Since the father had many servants who could do the field work, it would appear that the older son made a choice to work the fields rather than be with the father. This could appear to be a noble gesture, except when we place work in the field up against worship of the Father. This is the situation that existed in Mary and Martha's home when Jesus said that Mary chose the better thing (Luke 10:42). It is possible to be preoccupied with matters of *doing* and neglect matters of *being*. We can focus on doing all the right things without connecting relationally with the Father. Perhaps the older brother is the saddest person in the parable. He stayed at home but did not have fellowship with the father or participate in the privileges of being a son. Salvation is relationship with the Heavenly Father and enjoying His benefits. There certainly is a time and place for field work, but not as a substitute for relationship with the Father.

What happened next further exposed attitudes of the older son that were not compatible with those of his father. Overjoyed by the return of his son, the father threw a party. The older son left his work in the field, and **when he came near the house, he heard music and dancing** (15:25). When he discovered that the celebration was in honor of his brother who had dishonored the family, he **became angry and refused to go in** (15:28). Contrast the attitude of the father with that of the older son. The father embraced the son and celebrated his return. To the older son, the record of past behavior was more important than the present. Work was more important than relationship. Always being right was more important than confessing wrongdoing. Rather than welcoming his brother home, he became angry and refused to go in to the party. It is hard for those who have never left home to accept all of the celebration over the return of those who did leave. There is something unfair about grace and forgiveness in that it is undeserved and doesn't make the offender pay enough. Elder sons would like to see some real justice and punishment for the wrongdoing of younger, wilder sons.

His father went out and pleaded with him (15:28), but the older brother demonstrated he was a son with a slave mind-set. Rather than enjoying and appreciating the benefits of family life, he exposed his resentment toward his father when he said, **"All these years I've been slaving for you and never disobeyed your orders. Yet you never gave me even a young goat so I could celebrate with my friends"** (15:29). Why would a son, who enjoyed the benefits of a loving father, refer to his work around the father's estate as "slaving"? The younger son realized that in his lostness his father had slaves who were better off than he, while the older son saw his father as no better than a slave master, and he as one of the slaves. Rather than say "my brother," he referred to his younger brother as **this son of yours** (15:30). His pent-up hostility toward his father probably reached back to the day the father gave his brother the freedom to leave home. The older son saw that choice as being irreversible.

The older brother had access and opportunity that went unclaimed. **The father said, "You are always with me, and everything I have is yours"** (15:31). He did not have to wait for the father to give him a young goat so he could have a party with his friends, the goat was already his.

Extending the story of the prodigal son to include his older brother was no accidental, last-minute addition. Jesus was intentionally sending word to the Pharisees and teachers of the law that they could, in their preoccupation with orthodoxy, lose touch with the Father and substitute rule keeping for relationship.

The three stories inform us that to be a sinner is to be lost. We can be lost by following the leading of our fallen nature, by neglect, by rebellious choice, and by dead orthodoxy that is indifferent to relationship with the Father.

The three stories reveal the three persons of the Trinity and their participation in the salvation of the lost. The shepherd illustrates the mission of Jesus, who seeks the lost sheep and carries it back to the fold. The Holy Spirit's ministry is to illuminate, expose, convict, and cleanse. God the Father is represented in the father who grants freedom, waits, welcomes, forgives, enriches, and celebrates the return of His lost children.

The three stories tell us that finding the lost involves God taking the initiative to go into the world of the lost, and the lost making the decision to repent and go home. Being found involves recognizing that you are lost, which the Pharisees had difficulty doing. Spotting sinners can be a pretty easy thing for us to do, but looking in the mirror may be more difficult.

17

THE PROBLEM OF RICHES

Luke 16:1–31

According to Luke, the Pharisees loved money (16:14). We might not want to go so far as to say we *love* money, but we might agree that we *like* it a lot. Even if we denied that we like it a lot, our behavior might demonstrate that we put a whole lot of value in it. We give our priority time to its pursuit and believe many of our problems would be solved if we had more of it. However, money has a way of creating as many problems for us as it solves.

The desire to get rich can be addictive and destructive. Many in our culture tend to live for the moment, squeezing all they can out of the time they have with little thought of the future. They refuse to delay gratification because they live with a short view of life.

This section of Scripture teaches us that we will be held accountable for how we live, what we live for, and what we do with what we have. The work of God in our lives exposes the values that motivate our choices and behaviors. There is a direct connection between temporal matters and our eternal destiny.

1. MONEY AND THE KINGDOM (16:1–18)

A SHREWD AND DISHONEST MANAGER

Jesus told a story about **a rich man whose manager was accused of wasting his possessions** (16:1). The problem Jesus exposed was not with the rich man, but with the way the manager handled the wealth of his employer. Jesus does not condemn wealth, but He has a lot to say about what we do with it, whether it belongs to us or if we are stewards of it on behalf of someone else.

There can be a tendency to handle the money or property of others with less diligence than if it were our own, and waste what is entrusted to us with less concern than if it were ours. As long as our bottom line is not affected, we may not worry about profit or loss, until those whose resources we have wasted check their bottom line. Then we can learn that managers are held accountable for what they have been asked to manage.

The rich man called in his manager and said, **"Give an account of your management"** (16:2). Sooner or later we must answer for what we have done with what has been trusted to our care. Accountability is a good thing and accountability is inescapable. Carelessness and laziness follows those who think they will never have to open the books and show what they have done. In this story, the rich man had heard of the manager's indiscretion and told him **"you cannot be manager any longer"** (16:2). Trust that is broken often leads to the loss of privilege, and that privilege may never be recovered.

Because the dishonest manager lived off of the work of others and had not exercised his work muscles, he admitted that he was **not strong enough to dig** (16:3) and he was too proud to beg. Faced with unemployment, the shrewd manager considered what he could do so that people would welcome him into their homes without his having to beg. **He called in each one of his master's debtors** and **asked, "How much do you owe my master?"** (16:5) and then substantially discounted what was owed by each of the debtors. **The master commended the dishonest manager because he had acted shrewdly** (16:8). Shrewdness is not normally viewed as a positive trait. The word used in the original language can be translated *wise, intelligent,* or *prudent.* The manager was given credit for using what was under his responsibility in an intelligent way as it applied to ensuring his own future by "buying" the favor of those whose debts he had forgiven.

Jesus inserted this bit of interesting insight: **"The people of this world are more shrewd in dealing with their own kind than are the**

people of the light" (16:8). Paul referred to God's people as "children of light" (Eph. 5:8), but nowhere else does the phrase "people of the light" appear in the Scripture. Light is often used in relationship with insight, or knowledge. People who have come to the knowledge of God may not have the insight into how to use the things of this world to their own benefit. The Scripture does not encourage the use of money for self-serving ends, but rather to meet the needs of others. However, in applying the truth behind the story, Jesus said, **"I tell you, use worldly wealth to gain friends for yourselves, so that when it is gone, you will be welcomed into eternal dwellings"** (16:9). Jesus seems to be teaching two things regarding the use of wealth. First, use wealth in ways that benefit others and make them your friends, rather than in ways that disassociate you from others and make them your enemies. Unfortunately, the possession of wealth can actually increase a sense of selfishness, and the desire to protect what you have can isolate you from others. Second, use wealth in ways that not only welcome you into the homes of those with whom you have made friends, but that will welcome you into the eternal dwellings of God. Money cannot buy your way into heaven, but neither does the possession of wealth keep you out of heaven. Appropriate use of wealth brings God's pleasure, and at times, increased blessing. We are managers of resources that belong to God. We should use them in ways that benefit His mission in the world.

The point of the story is not to encourage dishonesty, but rather to urge the wise use of wealth to make friends on earth and investments in eternity. The problem with money is that it is too often selfishly consumed and leads to a present not an eternal mind-set. It is easier to adopt a consumer rather than a manager (steward) mind-set.

TRUSTWORTHINESS

Trust that is lost can be very difficult to regain. Trust that is earned has tremendous benefit, and earning it begins with attention to little things. Jesus said, **"Whoever can be trusted with very little can also be trusted with much, and whoever is dishonest with very little will also be dishonest with much"** (16:10). Trust is built or lost in the little things of life that may be considered insignificant. If someone will steal a dollar from you, will you trust that person with ten dollars? Don't wait until you have more before you demonstrate that you can be trusted as a steward.

Jesus made a connection between material and spiritual things when He said, **"If you have not been trustworthy in handling worldly wealth, who will trust you with true riches?"** (16:11). There are things of greater value than worldly wealth that Jesus called "true riches." He indicated that some people will never have true riches because they have violated the trust of others in matters of worldly wealth. How you handle money becomes an indicator of whether you can be trusted with valuable nonmonetary things. The love and respect of family can be lost because of improper handling of money. Misappropriation of a few dollars can disqualify you from a position of responsibility and influence, both inside and outside the church. If people trust you with the handling of their money, they will usually trust you with many other things in their lives. More importantly, if true riches are things of the spirit, Jesus indicated that God will not open up spiritual treasures to you if He cannot trust you with a little money.

Jesus said, **"If you have not been trustworthy with someone else's property, who will give you property of your own?"** (16:12). Poverty is not proof that you can't be trusted, but some people have few possessions because they have not been faithful in handling the little they have. God can trust some people with more because they have proven themselves to be trustworthy with little. Be sure that if you cheat, misuse, or steal, you will be the loser in your relationships with others and with God.

WHEN MONEY GETS IN THE WAY OF GOD

Money has the potential of becoming your master. It can govern your choices, control your emotions, and dictate your behavior. Jesus said, **"No servant can serve two masters. Either he will hate the one and love the other, or he will be devoted to the one and despise the other. You cannot serve both God and Money"** (16:13). People are to be loved and possessions are to be used. God's design for life is prostituted when money is loved and people are used. Worse, Jesus indicated that we may love money more than we love God. If money becomes your master, it will demand that you live with values that are contrary to God's values.

You cannot live with money as your master and at the same time declare that God is your master.

It is easy to lose your way in life when you become the servant of money. Personal integrity can be compromised and spiritual focus can be lost.

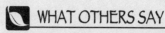

WHAT OTHERS SAY

STEWARDSHIP

"Many of us are concerned that if we commit ourselves as fully devoted followers, Christ will threaten the treasury. He probably will."

—Joseph Stowell

Relationships can be destroyed and decision making can be held hostage. Money can promise peace, contentment, and happiness, but the truth is that money is a cruel master that can produce worry, greed, and heartbreak.

The Pharisees, who loved money, heard all this and were sneering at Jesus (16:14). Throughout the ministry of Jesus, He pointed out a variety of problems with the Pharisees. Now He notes that they are lovers of money, not lovers of God. Seeking to be rich, they became poor in spirit.

The problems of the Pharisees were of the heart. They were religious leaders, but they were bankrupt in their souls. They trusted in their orthodoxy, tradition, and standing in the community. They cared more about what others thought of them than what God thought of them. Jesus **said to them, "You are the ones who justify yourselves in the eyes of men, but God knows your hearts. What is highly valued among men is detestable in God's sight"** (16:15). The word *justify* means "to declare something to be righteous." Righteousness is a quality of being—a matter of the heart. We cannot make ourselves

LIFE CHANGE

RICHES

The love of money is the root of all kind of evil. If you love money:

- no matter how much you have, it is not enough.
- you will trade away a lot of more valuable things in order to get it.
- it becomes addictive.
- being sure you don't lose it will keep you awake at night.
- people become tools to be used to help you get more.

righteous. The fact that we declare ourselves to be righteous, or others think we are righteous, does not make us so. Only God can declare us to actually be righteous, and He knows our hearts. The Pharisees constructed a facade of religiosity that caused people to think they were righteous people, but behind the facade their lives were detestable to God.

It is important that we live above reproach among others. But beyond what others think of us, we need to live without reproach before a God who knows our hearts. He sees the motives behind our actions. He hears the thoughts never heard by others. He judges with values different from those of anyone else. If He is our Master, we must live to please Him as we trust in His grace to truly justify us. The world's value system is completely opposed to what God holds to be valuable. We are in deep trouble if we love what God despises.

SOME THINGS NEVER CHANGE

Change was in the air, and Jesus said to the religious leaders, **"The Law and the Prophets were proclaimed until John. Since that time, the good news of the kingdom of God is being preached"** (16:16). John came preaching that the kingdom of God was at hand and that everyone should repent. The Law was not replaced, but fulfilled in the good news of the kingdom of God. No one should think that the good news of the kingdom of God brought an end to the moral and ethical law of Moses. Jesus cautioned any who might think God's law had been done away with that the laws of marriage and divorce were still in effect. The ceremonial and civil laws of the Old Testament were fulfilled in Christ. If contemporary Christians believe they are exempt from the moral and ethical requirements of the law because they live under grace, they misunderstand the eternal nature of God's law.

2. TWO DESTINATIONS (16:19-31)

RICH AND POOR

Jesus again used riches and poverty to teach a spiritual truth by telling a story about **a rich man** who **lived in luxury** (16:19) and **a beggar named Lazarus** who lay at the **gate** (16:20) of the rich man's house.

Lazarus was **covered with sores and** (16:20) **the dogs came and licked his sores** (16:21). His life was so pathetic and destitute that he longed **to eat what fell from the rich man's table** (16:21). The scene Jesus painted was one that could have illustrated any number of places in Israel, since the divide between the rich and the poor was sharp, clear, and repeated often. This was perhaps more than a fictional story, since a name is given to the beggar who sat at the gate of the rich man's house. Parables were stories used to teach a particular truth and usually did not include named persons, so there is reason to believe this is a real story of a real man. Lazarus was covered with sores, and his stomach cried out for food. He didn't ask for or expect much, just leftover crumbs that would be swept up and thrown away. The only companions he had were the dogs who came by and licked his sores. At least the dogs didn't ignore him like the people who passed by. The picture was of a rich man consuming his wealth on himself and a poor man consumed by his suffering and poverty. The differences between the two could not have been greater.

Riches have the capacity of creating a great chasm between the poor and the rich, when the rich no longer are moved with compassion toward those in misery outside their gates. The rich man had the capacity to make a tremendous difference in a poor man's life, but he did not. It was not as if a charity was soliciting a contribution for some mythical, unnamed poor person whom the rich man would never see. This was Lazarus, a real person who could be seen every day when the rich man looked out his window. This was a real opportunity—one for which he had capacity to take advantage of and one for which he would be held responsible. How could anyone close his eyes or his heart to such an obvious need? Perhaps the rich man lived with the curtains pulled shut so he could insulate himself from the sight outside.

Death is the ultimate statistic—one out of every one dies. Death is no respecter of persons, young or old, rich or poor, prepared or unprepared. We enter with nothing, and we exit with nothing. **The time came when the beggar died, and the angels carried him to Abraham's side. The rich man also died and was buried** (16:22). The chasm that had been created by the rich man's lack of response to Lazarus would now begin to widen. Before, he was the one who lived with advantage, but now his riches could not buy him any advantage. It was the beggar man who would gain true riches. When the beggar died, he was carried by angels to the presence of Abraham. When the rich man died, he was carried by mourners to the cemetery and was buried. The rich man lived for what was temporal, and when his time came there was nothing more to say than he was buried. It was the end. The poor man, however, had lived in the spiritual dimension, and when his time came he was carried into heaven. No doubt he was also buried but it was not viewed as the end, just a change.

HEAVEN AND HELL

The great divide between the two men suddenly took on a more serious reality. It was not just a difference of financial or social standing that separated them. The rich man found himself **in hell, where he was in torment** (16:23). Three different words are generally translated *hell* in the New Testament: *hades*, *gehenna*, and *tartaroo*. The word *hades*, appears twice in Luke's gospel (12:5; 16:23). Hades was generally used to speak of the realm of the dead. Another word translated *hell* is *gehenna*. This originally referred to the Valley of Ben Hinnom, south of Jerusalem, where the filth and dead animals of the city were cast out and burned. It came to be used for the place of the future punishment of the wicked. Close in meaning to *gehenna* is the word *tartaroo*, which appears only in 2 Peter 2:4 and refers to the abode of the wicked dead where they suffer punishment for their evil deeds. In this reference, Luke uses hell as the spiritual realm of the dead and includes the fact that the rich man was in a present state of torment.

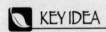
KEY IDEA
HELL

Early in the ministry of evangelist Vance Havner, he pastored a country church where he preached a sermon on hell. A member didn't like the subject and told the Rev. Havner that he should "Preach about the meek and lowly Jesus." Havner replied, "That's where I got my information about hell."

The distance between the two men was great, but the rich man **looked up and saw Abraham far away, with Lazarus by his side** (16:23). By whatever means, the rich man knew Abraham and he recognized Lazarus.

Abraham was an icon of the Jewish faith. The rich man had entertained many notable persons in his home, but to be in the presence of Abraham would have surpassed being with any of the prominent persons he had known in life. And there, next to Abraham, was the beggar he had tried to shut out of his sight. Lazarus, who had been ignored by the masses, was talking things over with Abraham.

The rich man called for **Abraham** to **have pity** on him and **"send Lazarus to dip the tip of his finger in water and cool my tongue, because I am in agony in this fire"** (16:24). The person of privilege now cried for pity. Hell had a fire that caused agony but did not consume. It added real pain to the torment of separation from God, regret, and the awareness of lost opportunity. The man who denied the beggar even a

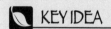

KEY IDEA

HEAVEN

In *Pilgrim's Progress*, John Bunyan wrote, "Drawing near to the city, they had yet a more perfect view thereof. It was built of pearls and precious stones, also the streets thereof were paved with gold; so that, by reason of the natural glory of the city, and the reflection of the sunbeams upon it, Christian with desire fell sick; Hopeful also had a fit or two of the same disease." The deepest desire of a Christian is not for the glory of the city, but for the glory of the Son who reigns there.

crumb from his table was now denied even a drop of water from the beggar's finger. Abraham's word to the rich man was **"Son, remember that in your lifetime you received your good things, while Lazarus received bad things, but now he is comforted here and you are in agony"** (16:25). Life after death will bring justice, and the inequities of life will be corrected. Comfort in this life does not guarantee comfort in the next life, and bad things experienced in this life can melt into oblivion in the celebration of good things in the next life.

Abraham said, **"Between us and you a great chasm has been fixed, so that those who want to go from here to you cannot, nor can anyone cross over from there to us"** (16:26). **A great chasm has been** *fixed*. The chasm between Lazarus and the rich man could have been bridged so easily in the previous life. All it would have taken was for a person who had plenty to share it with someone who had nothing—for a man to shift his focus from himself to someone else. But now, based on where they had placed their faith, they were on either side of a fixed chasm that could not be bridged. No travel will take place between heaven and hell. Even if some were to be moved with compassion to want to ease the suffering of those in hell, they could not. Now is the time for bridging the divides between people and for deciding on which side of the chasm you will spend eternity.

Personal torment led the rich man to think of family who were living just like he had and who would end up in the same place of torment he was now experiencing. He begged Abraham to **send Lazarus** to **warn them, so that they will not also come to this place of torment** (16:27–28). His concern for the spiritual well-being of his family was noble but too late for him to affect. Abraham responded that his family had every opportunity to listen to the word of **Moses and the Prophets** (16:29), but the rich man was convinced that if something spectacular happened, **if someone from the dead goes to them, they will repent** (16:30). To this, Abraham replied, **"If they do not listen to Moses and the Prophets, they will not be convinced even if someone rises from the dead"** (16:31). Each of us has adequate opportunity to respond to the call of God in our lives. Whatever our response to God's grace may be, a time will come when it will be sealed for eternity. The time for responding in faith is now.

This story, whether real or a parable, teaches us several things about death and life after death. It teaches us that the soul is immortal. Death does not end our existence, but it does change the nature of our existence. It teaches us that upon death, we move into a spiritual realm of peace or torment, based on our relationship with God. It teaches us that people are recognizable in the afterlife by the identities known to us in this life. It teaches us that hell is a real place of torment for those who reside there. It teaches us that eternal destiny is set forever after death. There are no second chances or opportunities to cross the chasm between heaven and hell. It teaches us that there is a conscious state in the realm of the dead where emotions are felt and where pain is experienced, even in the absence of a physical body as we know it.

It is terribly sad to see people live for things in this life that will keep them apart from God in the next life. He cannot be purchased and neither can His gift of eternal life.

18

WATCH YOURSELF

Luke 17:1–37

Paul wrote, "Be very careful, then, how you live—not as unwise but as wise" (Eph. 5:15). Followers of Christ are to be careful how they live. They know they need to cultivate holiness in their lives. They know little things can creep into their spirit and damage their spiritual sensitivities. Careful living is a mark of wisdom, not of timidity or lack of confidence. They are aware of the power of their influence. The roadsides of life are strewn with the wreckage of those who started well but later got careless.

Children of God do not live without assurance of their relationship with their Heavenly Father or with fear of inadvertently losing their salvation. Rather, they give careful attention to how they live because they want to please God in every act and attitude, and live in a way that attracts people to God. So, as wise children of God, we watch how we live.

1. FORGIVENESS AND FAITH (17:1–10)

WATCH YOUR INFLUENCE

John Wesley defined sin as "a voluntary transgression of a known law."[1] People are free to make choices, and sin results from willful choices that violate God's purpose. Jesus said, **"Things that cause people to sin are bound to come"** (17:1). The NIV's use of the word *cause* should not be used in a determinative sense or construed to mean individuals have no choice when certain "things" come to them. Sin results from personal choice, and there will always be opportunities to make wrong choices. Christians are not immune to temptation and the lure of sin. The image of the words used in this phrase is that of a trap that is set to draw a person into sin. We do not need to sin, but the possibility of sinning is never removed from us. We need to understand that temptations are "common to man" (1 Cor. 10:13), and things that can cause us to sin are bound to come. The Word of God is full of promise that He can deliver us from the power sin has over us. He is "able to keep you from falling and . . . present you before his glorious presence without fault" (Jude 24).

Temptation is the precursor of sin, though its presence is not sin and its power is not irresistible. The book of James indicates that sin is the end of a sequence that begins with an enticement (temptation) directed at an "evil desire" within us, that is followed by a decision to gratify that desire. After the decision is made to inappropriately gratify the evil desire, sin is given birth (James 1:14–15). Undisciplined desires, unresolved emotional stresses, weakened will due to exhaustion, pressure of others, influence of friends, or unwise continued subjection to tempting opportunities may give temptation more power that it should have, making the birth of sin a greater possibility.

Christians have a responsibility to be careful that they are not easily overtaken by temptation and sin, and they should be careful that they do not live in a way that may cause someone else to sin. Jesus said, **"Woe to that person through whom they** [the causes to sin] **come"** (Luke 17:1). Opportunities to violate the law of God can come through the actions and influence of other people. Parents can create a home environment that leads their children into sinful practice, intentionally or unintentionally. Friends can influence each other to participate in things that can damn their souls. Lovers can cross the line of appropriate behavior and cause each other to sin. Jesus sounded a warning to His followers by pronouncing a "woe" on those who cause others to sin.

Influence is a powerful thing, and we need to be careful that ours is always focused in positive directions. We should influence one another toward "love and good deeds" (Heb. 10:24). We should live so that we make the teaching about God our Savior attractive (Titus 2:10), drawing people toward God rather than driving them away from Him. The Bible speaks about the reputation of Samuel that should be a model for us: "In this town there is a man of God; he is highly respected, and everything he says comes true. Let's go there now. Perhaps he will tell us what way to take" (1 Sam. 9:6). The influence of a life of integrity is powerful. If people in your town wanted to find a man or woman of God, would they think of you?

Sounds of regret will be heard from those who lose their eternal soul because of foolish choices they made that gave birth to sin. The sound of regret will be amplified when joined with the accusing voices of those they caused to sin with them. While sin is a personal choice, sinners enjoy the company of other sinners and often alleviate their guilt by causing others to join them in their sin.

Jesus often expressed compassion toward those who were weak, needy, the least, and the little ones. These are persons who can be easily manipulated, persuaded, and abused. He had a special word of caution to anyone who would **cause one of these little ones to sin** (Luke 17:2). Little ones are not just children, though there certainly must be extra venting of God's wrath directed toward those who damage the lives and souls of children. A *little one* is anyone who comes under the influence of someone stronger. To those who wrongly influ-

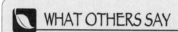

WHAT OTHERS SAY

HOLINESS

G. Campbell Morgan was once asked to define "holiness." He said "Holiness is . . .

1. Not the inability to sin, but ability not to sin.

2. Not freedom from temptation, but power to overcome temptation.

3. Not infallible judgment, but earnest and honest endeavor to follow the higher wisdom.

4. Not deliverance from infirmities of the flesh, but triumph over all bodily affliction.

5. Not exemption from conflict, but victory through conflict.

6. Not freedom from liability and falling, but gracious ability to prevent falling.

7. Not the end of progress, but the deliverance from standing still.

Every child of God can know and experience daily this superb way of living."

ence any of these, Jesus said, **"It would be better for him to be thrown into the sea with a millstone tied around his neck"** (17:2). Physical death, regardless of how traumatic, cannot be compared to the eternal judgment of God against those who sin and cause others to sin.

We need to watch how we influence other people. We are not only responsible for our salvation, but we have a responsibility to move others toward Christ, not toward sin.

WATCH YOUR SPIRIT

In the face of sin's serious consequences, Jesus said, **"Watch yourselves"** (17:3). We need to watch ourselves so we do not fall into sin, and watch that we do not influence others to sin. We also need to watch how we respond toward a brother or sister if he or she falls into sin. We do not live in isolation, and Christians carry a certain responsibility for the spiritual well-being of other Christians.

Jesus said, **"If your brother sins, rebuke him, and if he repents, forgive him"** (17:3). There are two responses you should have toward a believer's sin—rebuke and forgiveness. Some may find the responsibility of rebuking sinning believers easier to fulfill than the responsibility of forgiving them. They may act as if rebuking has been raised to the level of a spiritual gift, and they enjoy confronting the wrongs they see in others. It was to such people that Jesus said, before they made any attempt to take the speck of sawdust out of the eye of an offender, they should first take the plank out of their own (Matt. 7:3–5). However, there are other people who avoid confronting the sin in another disciple's life lest that person turn the table and point out something in them that is less than perfect. People can be driven away from the church because of inappropriate rebuking. On the other hand, people with sin in their lives can be allowed to contaminate a local congregation without anyone rebuking their inappropriate actions or ungodly attitudes. The rebuke of sin, offered in love and with a spirit of humility, should be a function of a healthy Christian community.

The goal of rebuking sin should be to lead the sinner toward repentance, and sin that is repented should become sin that is forgiven. Forgiveness should be as freely offered as the rebuke is. Rebuking sin is not the act of self-righteous people who declare themselves to be better than the sinner, but the act of caring people who want the sinner to experience forgiveness and return to fellowship with God and righteous living.

Repentance by the offender is always necessary for *receiving* forgiveness, but repentance by the offender should not be necessary for *offering* forgiveness by the offended. We need to be able to forgive people who have wronged us before they even ask for it. And we tend to be far slower to freely and fully forgive others than God is. Paul wrote, "Bear with each other and forgive whatever grievances you may have against one another. Forgive as the Lord forgave you" (Col. 3:13). We are to forgive others *because* we have been forgiven, and we are to forgive others *as* we have been forgiven. Jesus tied our need to forgive repentant sinners to our need to watch ourselves. Our spirits can quickly become poisoned if we fail to be forgiving. We may need to walk over the same bridge of grace and forgiveness that we build for others, so we must build one that will carry our weight.

Forgiving the inadvertent, single offense may come fairly easy for us, but it is harder when a person persists in offending us after knowing how much we were hurt, and knowing how freely we forgave their first offense. Repeated responses of forgiveness can appear to us to minimize the wrong or to enable the person to continue offensive behavior. We can quickly reach a point of saying, "Enough is enough." Jesus, however, would say, "Your enough is never enough." Even **"if he sins against you seven times in a day, and seven times comes back to you and says, 'I repent,' forgive him"** (Luke 17:4). True repentance includes deep sorrow for having committed the sin, along with a commitment to forsake that sin. Jesus says we should forgive those who even seem to us to be insincere in their repentance because they keep repeating their sin. This insincere confession may come from an effort to take the pressure off, or from the embarrassment of being caught. No one knows the pain of insincere repentance more than God himself.

Forgiveness is a powerful thing in both the life of the offender and the offended. Forgiveness means you no longer hold the offender responsible, and you are not going to make him or her continue to pay for the sin. Forgiveness is necessary for both the offended and the offender to be able to move on with their lives. Without it, an anchor is set in the past that will forever hold both from emotional growth and spiritual victory.

Watch yourself. The spirit of bitterness and revenge poisons those who harbor it. To be unforgiving is to be unforgiven (Matt. 6:14–15).

WATCH YOUR FAITH

The writer to the Hebrews said, "Without faith it is impossible to please God, because anyone who comes to him must believe that he exists and that he rewards those who earnestly seek him" (Heb. 11:6). Faith is the essential requirement for relationship with God.

The apostles said to the Lord, "Increase our faith!" (Luke 17:5). The word *faith* is used in a number of ways: the collection of doctrines, our belief in Jesus Christ that leads to our salvation, a stabilizing factor in life's tough circumstances, and a belief that a certain thing will happen that releases the power of God. It is this last meaning of faith that can at times cause us difficulty. There are those who maintain that if you believe strongly enough that God will do something, He absolutely will do it. And if He doesn't, your faith was faulty.

Sometimes it would sound as if faith is measured by size or volume. We can have a measure of it, but we can and should have more, just as Jesus seems to have indicated in Matthew 17:20. Sometimes, like in these verses in Luke 17, Jesus seems to have contradicted himself when He said the "volume" of one's faith is not the issue. The disciples wanted the Lord to increase their faith. They viewed faith as a power that would make things happen, and the more they had the more they could make happen. It is not faith but the object of faith that makes things happen. God is the one who makes things happen within His will, in His way, and at His time.

To remove their obsession with faith itself, Jesus told them that the size of their faith was not the issue. He said, **"If you have faith as small as a mustard seed, you can say to this mulberry tree, 'Be uprooted and planted in the sea,' and it will obey you"** (Luke 17:6). Faith is our belief in, commitment to, and trust of Almighty God. The bigness of our faith is not the issue—the bigness of our God is. Faith is our belief in the ability of God to do the impossible and our commitment to trust Him to do the impossible if, when, and how He chooses. We are misguided if we want more faith

232

so we can get the results we want. We need a deeper faith so we can have a more intimate relationship with God and experience the results He wants. Nothing is as exhilarating as experiencing "God things" that can be explained in no other way but that He made them happen—after we surrendered the situations to Him and trusted Him. Our concern should not be that we can talk to trees and get them to move, but that we can talk to God and He will move heaven and earth to accomplish His purpose through us.

WATCH YOUR ATTITUDE

Our motives for doing things and our attitude while doing them is as important as accomplishing those things. Too often we do things for credit, recognition, and praise. But there are things that should be done because there is a duty to do them whether or not anyone knows or applauds us. Jesus reached into the social structures and expectations of His day to give His followers a word about attitude.

Jesus spoke about reasonable and customary interchange between a servant and his master. A servant, coming in from doing his assigned tasks, would not expect the master to wait upon him by providing a meal and inviting him to sit down and enjoy it. Rather, the servant would expect to continue his service by preparing the meal for the master before resting and enjoying his own meal. The servant would not expect the master to **thank** him for doing **what he was told to do** (17:9). He was a servant and it was his duty to serve. No praise or recognition was expected, so no bad attitude resulted when no praise or recognition was given. Unrealistic expectations lead to bent-out-of-shape attitudes.

Our feelings about what we deserve can get us into trouble. We can struggle with issues of position, honor, recognition, and entitlement because we think we have it coming to us. When we do not receive the treatment we feel we deserve, out attitudes turn sour. Jesus said that our obligation as servants is to do everything asked of us and then say, **"We are unworthy servants; we have only done our duty"** (17:10). The sense of unworthiness is not the same as a sense of worthlessness. A person with healthy self-worth can have a healthy sense of unworthiness. Developing the attitude of unworthiness requires a work of God's grace in our hearts and following the example of Jesus, who is our model. The apostle Paul wrote, "Your attitude should be the same as that of Christ Jesus: Who, being in very nature God, did not consider equality with God something to be grasped, but made himself nothing, taking the very nature of a servant" (Phil 2:5–7). This attitude runs contrary to our human nature, which seeks to make us *something* rather than *nothing*. We cling to those things that will define our significance and resist those things that would demonstrate our insignificance and servanthood.

Jesus lifts up a model of servanthood that seeks the advancement of the Master, not of ourselves. It performs duty without expectation of praise or reward and obediently serves with humility and love.

2. WATCH YOUR GRATITUDE (17:11–19)

Jesus was **on his way to Jerusalem** and **traveled along the border between Samaria and Galilee** (17:11). Tensions sometimes ran strong between Jews and Samaritans. Samaritans were considered "half-breeds" because they were descendants of other nationalities who mixed with the Jews who remained in the region during the captivity. The Jews largely did not associate with the Samaritans (John 4:9). The Jewish community was the primary mission of Jesus, but there were Samaritans who responded quickly and openly to His ministry, so He often used them to prod the Jews for their lack of response to His message.

Ten men who had leprosy met Jesus **as he was going into a village** (17:12). Leprosy was a dreaded disease that had social as well as physical consequences. People afflicted with leprosy were declared to be unclean and were not to have direct contact with others, which caused these men to stand **at a distance and** call **out in a loud voice, "Jesus, Master, have pity on us!"** (17:12–13).

No disease was beyond the ability of Jesus to heal, and His means of healing varied from case to case. Luke recorded another healing of leprosy in chapter 5 in which Jesus healed the leprous man with a touch and a word. In this case, Jesus instructed the ten men, saying, **"Go show yourselves to the priests"** (17:14). When Jesus healed the single leper, He also sent him to the priest, saying, "Don't tell anyone, but go, show yourself to the priest and offer the sacrifices that Moses commanded for your cleansing, as a testimony to them" (Luke 5:14). The ceremonial law of the Jews placed the responsibility with the priests for pronouncing lepers clean or unclean. Jesus sent them there to fulfill the law and to provide a credible witness to the healing.

As they went, they were cleansed (17:14). Their obedience to the instruction of Jesus became their means of healing. The priests did not heal them, nor did a ceremony of cleansing or application of ointment. A level of faith was exercised in their coming to Jesus and in their obedience, which was sufficient enough to receive God's gift of healing. However, it seems that one of the ten moved to a higher level of faith who, **when he saw he was healed, came back, praising God in a loud voice** (17:15).

Verse 14 indicates that all ten of the lepers "were cleansed" of their leprosy—they were healed. Verse 19 indicates that the one leper who came back and **threw himself at Jesus' feet and thanked him** (17:16) was "made well." While all were physically healed, the one who came back to Jesus experienced a deeper work of being "made well," a word most often translated "saved" or "made whole." It is possible to be free from disease but not be whole. It is possible to be whole and yet have a physical disability. Wholeness involves well-being, spiritual and emotional, not just physical health. Physical healing should never be our primary goal, but rather wholeness. The leper's return to Jesus to recognize Him as Lord and thank Him demonstrated a deeper level of faith and led to a greater level of personal wholeness. Jesus said to him, **"Rise and go; your faith has made you well"** (17:19). Obedience brought healing to the others; faith brought wellness to the one.

Evidently some or all of the other lepers were Jews, since Jesus emphasized that the one who returned was a Samaritan. He said, **"Where are the other nine? Was no one found to return and give praise to God except this foreigner?"** (17:17–18). While Jesus rejoiced in the "foreigners" who welcomed Him into their country and lives, the rejection or avoidance by the Jews brought Him great pain. He expressed this agony of His soul when He cried, "O Jerusalem, Jerusalem, you who kill the prophets and stone those sent to you, how often I have longed to gather your children together, as a hen gathers her chicks under her wings, but you were not willing!" (Luke 13:34).

Living with gratitude, regardless of life's circumstances, releases God to bring greater levels of wholeness to our broken lives.

3. THE DAY OF THE LORD (17:20–37)

WATCH YOUR KING

Oppressed people often look for institutions or powers that will deliver them. In the minds of many Jews, the kingdom of God would be an earthly system of government that would vindicate them as the chosen people of God and deliver them from foreign rule and occupation. **The Pharisees** asked Jesus **when the kingdom of God would come,** and He **replied, "The kingdom of God does not come with your careful observation, nor will people say, 'Here it is,' or 'There it is,' because the kingdom of God is within you"** (17:20–21). Some translations have Jesus saying "the kingdom of God is *among* you," which might infer that Jesus was speaking of himself, as the King among those who accept His lordship. Whether *within* or *among*, the kingdom of God consists of the presence of Jesus and acceptance of His work in the human heart. His kingdom can be seen, not in governments, institutions, or programs but in the lives of people who have yielded themselves to the lordship of Christ. Many have missed the kingdom of God because they looked for it in the wrong places.

Not only did many miss the coming of the kingdom of God, many more will miss the return of Christ when He will establish His eternal reign. It would seem that when Jesus referred to "the days of the Son of Man," He moved from speaking of the present existence and nature of the Kingdom to that of the future day of the Lord and His return. The day of the Lord occupied much of the writing of the prophets (Isa. 13:6; Ezek. 13:5; Joel 1:15; Amos 5:18; Obad. 1:15; Zeph. 1:7; Zech. 14:1) and was spoken of several times by Paul, such as when he wrote, "Now, brothers, about times and dates we do not need to write to you, for you know very well that the day of the Lord will come like a thief in the night" (1 Thess. 5:1–2).

Generally, the day of the Lord speaks of a day of divine intervention that will signal the end of time and the ushering in of a new order. It will be a day of judgment and justice. For the oppressed, it is longed for as a time of liberation and vindication. For the wicked, it is dreaded as a time of God's wrath.

There will be those who insist Jesus has already returned and is "over here" or "over there." Jesus said, **"Do not go running off after them"** (Luke 17:23). He will return at a time when He is unexpected. There will always be speculations and claims, but no human knows the time of His coming. His return will not be in secret, however. Everyone will know, because **his day will be like the lightning, which flashes and lights up the sky from one end to the other** (17:24). To His followers, who must have had difficulty understanding what He was talking about, Jesus said that **he must suffer many things and be rejected by this generation** (17:25). Suffering and rejection are not usually assigned to kings, and in the Jewish mind would certainly not be the case with God's Chosen One. But before the Son of Man could return as the King of Kings, He must first become the Suffering Servant.

WATCH YOUR PRIORITIES

The day when Jesus returns will be much like **the days of Noah** (17:26). People were going about life as usual with no particular concern about impending calamity or judgment. **People were eating, drinking, marrying and being given in marriage up to the day Noah entered the ark. Then the flood came and destroyed them all** (17:27). Whether because of disbelief of the judgment of God or belief in their own invincibility that led to an "it will never happen to us" mentality, people ignored issues of righteousness clear up to the time the door shut on the ark. But then they were on the outside and judgment came to them. God's grace is like Noah's ark—a place of refuge from the storm and a means of salvation. You don't want to be outside when the door is closed.

People in Noah's day were not unique. People acted the same **in the days of Lot** (17:28), the days of Jesus, and in our day. Those in Lot's day **were eating and drinking, buying and selling, planting and**

building (17:28). There is nothing wrong with any of these activities. This is the stuff that occupies life on our planet. In fact, Paul condemned those who were so certain Jesus was coming soon that they quit working and doing those things necessary for sustaining life. The problem comes when we live with total disregard for God and His purpose. It is a matter of priority. Eating, drinking, buying, selling, planting, building, and marrying should fall into their appropriate place under the recognition of God as Lord of all of our life. We only function well when Christ is preeminent, and we begin to unravel when other things take priority. Paul said, when Christ has supremacy in everything, "all things hold together" (Col. 1:17–18).

Jesus used graphic language to speak of God's judgment: **fire and sulfur rained down from heaven and destroyed them all** (Luke 17:29). Some have difficulty equating the God of love as also a God of judgment. Love and judgment meet perfectly in the nature of God. His gracious love is wonderful to experience, and His wrath should be fearfully avoided. Sadly, the destruction experienced by those in the days of Noah and Lot will be experienced **on the day the Son of Man is revealed** (17:30) by those who have ignored God for other pursuits.

We can become so mesmerized by other pursuits and priorities that even when God in mercy provides a way of escape, we can look back with lustful eyes and perish. Jesus warned that we should not **go back for anything** (17:31). His simple warning echoes through the years: **"Remember Lot's wife!"** (17:32). Nothing more needs to be said.

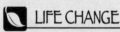

LIFE CHANGE

OPEN HANDS

God cannot fill our hands with His good gifts when they are clenched around lesser things. We are defined by the things that we cling to. Only hands that have released their grip on things of earthly value can be open to receive things of heavenly value. It is in letting go that we free to receive things worth hanging on to.

Jesus shared a great paradox about priorities: **"Whoever tries to keep his life will lose it, and whoever loses his life will preserve it"** (17:33). He is not encouraging reckless living, but rather calculated abandonment to the things of God. Those who really live are those who are willing to give their life for something bigger than they are.

When the little things of life become the priorities we cling to, we miss the big purpose of life.

The people of God live carefully. They watch themselves so they do not injure the faith of others; they retain a forgiving spirit; they keep their confidence and trust in God; they have grateful hearts; they keep first things first; and they acknowledge God's will as their motivating purpose.

ENDNOTES

1. John Wesley, *Works, XI.* Kansas City, MO: Nazarene Publishing House, reprint of authorized edition published by the Wesleyan Conference office in London, 1872. p. 396.

19

SEIZING THE MOMENT

Luke 18:1–19:27

G od was so pleased with Solomon that He told him He would give him anything he wanted (1 Kings 3:5–9). What an opportunity! If God told you that, what would you ask for? Moments of opportunity come to us that reveal our values, desires, and spiritual motivations. These opportunities must be seized and acted upon, or the moment will pass and the opportunities may never come to us again.

Jesus asked a man, "What do you want me to do for you?" His response would demonstrate what He desired most in that moment. A young man asked Jesus what he needed to do to have eternal life. The response of Jesus would reveal the values and motivation of the man's heart, providing a moment of decision that would have eternal impact. A man who was small in stature heard that Jesus was passing by. This was his one opportunity to intersect the life and ministry of Jesus, so he demonstrated his desire by taking extraordinary means to see Him. His action brought salvation to his entire family.

This is a chapter about seizing the moment. What is it that you want? How badly do you want it? What are you willing to do to get it? If the opportunity to do what was necessary to get it were to come to you right now, what would you do? God provides the moments of opportunity, and it is our responsibility to make the most of every one them (Eph. 5:16).

1. PRAYER TO WHICH GOD RESPONDS (18:1–14)

PERSISTENT PRAYER

Our wants and desires often find their way into our prayers. Prayer is often viewed as a means of getting God to do something for us—something He is reluctant to do. It is probably a blessing that God does not always answer our prayers by giving us what we ask for. James said we may want something but not get it because we don't ask God for it. But then he said that we may ask God for something and not get it because we ask with the wrong motives (James 4:2–3).

Too often, when faced with adversity or reverses in life, we give up. After enduring great hardships for the gospel, Paul said, "We do not lose heart. Though outwardly we are wasting away, yet inwardly we are being renewed day by day" (2 Cor. 4:16). Rather than giving up, losing heart, and abandoning hope, we are encouraged to pray. Prayer renews us inwardly as we spend time in the presence of God, and prayer has the potential to change our circumstances as we declare dependence on the power and provision of God.

Jesus wanted His disciples to know **they should always pray and not give up** (Luke 18:1), so He told them a parable about a widow who took an issue to **a judge who neither feared God nor cared about men** (18:2). The widow did not receive any action from the judge, but she **kept coming to him with the plea, "Grant me justice against my adversary"** (18:3). The woman had experienced the traumatic experience of losing her husband. While she was dealing with the tough stuff of life without a husband, someone took advantage of her, whom she describes as an adversary, someone who was against her. She didn't want special treatment or favors. She just wanted justice. But the judge was unjust, and it is not likely that justice will be granted through an unjust judge.

The only way the widow knew to get justice from an unjust system was to be persistent. **Finally** the judge **said, "Because this widow keeps bothering me, I will see that she gets justice, so that she won't eventually wear me out with her coming!"** (18:4–5).

Jesus wanted His disciples to know that rather than give up when faced with injustice and adversity, they were to go to the just **God** who will **bring about justice for his chosen ones, who cry out to him day and night . . . he will see that they get justice, and quickly** (18:7–8). We may suffer injustice in this world. Others may treat us unfairly. But we are God's chosen ones, and He will always treat us fairly and justly. He may not straighten out all of the kinks in our fallen world, but we can rest in His faithful and just care of us.

The emphasis of the parable should be placed on not giving up. The opposite of giving up is holding on, keeping hope alive, trusting God, who is just. We are to pray in faith, believing God is just. When He acts on our behalf, it is not because He wants to get rid of our pestering requests, but because He knows what is best for us. The importance of persevering faith is emphasized when Jesus asked, **"When the Son of Man comes, will he find faith on the earth?"** (18:8). When motivated by the Holy Spirit to pray for certain things, our prayer should be characterized by faith and persistence.

We persist and do not give up because we are children of a just God. We pray in faith, believing "he exists and that he rewards those who earnestly seek him" (Heb. 12:6). Perhaps our emphasis should be on persistent faith rather than persistent prayer, if we interpret persistence to mean we can eventually wear God down by pestering Him.

THE PRAYER OF A RIGHTEOUS MAN

Prayer is our opportunity to address our Heavenly Father. Any confidence or boldness we may have in approaching the presence of God is not because of personal merit, but because of His mercy and the fact that the way into His presence was opened to us through the sacrificed body of Jesus Christ (Heb. 10:19–22). There were those around Jesus who were **confident of their own righteousness and looked down on everybody else** (Luke 18:9). A couple of problems existed in these persons. First, they considered themselves to be superior to others. Second, they viewed themselves to be so inherently good that they did not need any righteousness but that which they generated out of their own goodness.

Jesus addressed the issue of self-righteousness by contrasting the prayers of two men who **went up to the temple to pray** (Luke 18:10), one a Pharisee and the other a tax collector. **The Pharisee stood up and prayed** (18:11). Going to the Temple and praying were good things. In fact the Pharisee looks like the kind of person we would like to have in our church. He was not like those who were **robbers, evildoers, adulterers** (18:11). But then his self-righteous superiority pops out as he tells God he is not like the nearby **tax collector** who was also there to worship and pray. The tax collector was a Jewish agent of the Roman government, and many of them were known to cheat their fellow Jews. The Pharisee was known to **fast twice a week and give a tenth of all** (18:12) he got. However, he **prayed about himself** (18:11), making himself and his goodness the focus of his prayer. He thanked God that he was **not like other men** (18:11). Righteousness is doing right things, but it is more than that. It is being made right and receiving the merits of Jesus' righteousness. The Scripture says that our righteousness is nothing better than "filthy rags" (Isa. 64:6), so we are in trouble when we start telling God how good we are. Righteousness is not a matter of comparison with others, believing we are okay as long as other people are worse than we are.

If given a chance, the Pharisee would have held the tax collector off at a distance, but the tax collector did not give him that chance. He **stood at a distance,** not seeing himself as worthy of associating with the other worshippers. **He would not even look up to heaven but beat his breast and said, "God have mercy on me, a sinner"** (Luke 18:13). The tax collector assumed the proper position. **"I tell you that this man, rather than the other, went home justified before God"** (18:14). Justification is a judicial term, a legal declaration of "not guilty." We can rationalize and excuse our sinfulness. We can declare ourselves not guilty because we are victims of circumstances or the pressures of others. But we do not have the authority to say we are not guilty. Only God can do that, and failure to acknowledge we are sinners and plead for mercy will leave us unjustified before God.

Self-centeredness is at the heart of unrighteousness and exhibits itself in spiritual arrogance. Jesus said, **"Everyone who exalts himself will be humbled, and he who humbles himself will be exalted"** (18:14). The only choice is whether we want God to be the one to humble us or we take that posture ourselves. His plan is to exalt us is a much better plan than ours could ever be.

2. ENTERING THE KINGDOM OF GOD (18:15–30)

RECEIVING THE KINGDOM LIKE A CHILD

People brought **babies to Jesus to have him touch them. When the disciples saw this, they rebuked them** (18:15). Why would people want Jesus to touch their babies? Maybe they believed He was a famous person, and they could brag to people about this. Maybe they believed Jesus was close to God, and by touching Him something spiritual could rub off on their child. Maybe they saw a kindness in Jesus, and they just wanted Him to hold their child for awhile. Regardless of their motivation, the disciples saw it to be an imposition on the Master's time. He had more important and pressing things to do. However, children were a priority to Jesus, and He called them to Him and said, **"Let the little children come to me, and do not hinder them, for the kingdom of God belongs to such as these"** (18:16).

Everyone is important to Jesus, especially children, who have a special place in the kingdom of God. So, Jesus said that **"anyone who will not receive the kingdom of God like a little child will never enter it"** (18:17). How can a little child, who does not understand the values demonstrated in making a choice or the consequences that accompany a choice, receive the kingdom of God? Generally children demonstrate simple faith, trust, and great capacity for believing in God. This childlike faith needs to be nurtured toward mature faith, but too often people can become cynical, less trusting, and more difficult to bring to salvation as they grow older. Secular culture can persuade

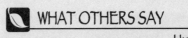

WHAT OTHERS SAY

HUMILITY

"The gates of heaven are so easily found when we are little, and they are always standing open to let children wander in."

—James Matthew Barrie

some that they are too sophisticated and too smart to believe in God. Life can become too complicated to simply "trust and obey." Those who would try to insulate children from the claims of the gospel do them a great injustice. Those who delay their confession of faith in Christ until a later time do themselves a great injustice. Jesus loves the little children, and the kingdom of God belongs to them.

THINGS CAN KEEP YOU FROM THE KINGDOM

A certain ruler asked him, "Good teacher, what must I do to inherit eternal life?" (18:18). The fact that he was referred to as a ruler would imply that this man was a person of position with access to wealth. His question could imply that he was aware that wealth and position did not qualify a person for inheriting eternal life. Eternal life is more than unending life. Jesus promised eternal life as a present possession of His followers, a present quality of life that spanned time and eternity (John 3:16, 32; 5:24). In His high-priestly prayer, Jesus said, "Now this is eternal life: that they may know you, the only true God, and Jesus Christ, whom you have sent" (John 17:3). Eternal life is the product of a saving relationship with God that enriches us and matures in us from now through eternity. The ruler knew he did not possess it, but he desired it. If it required him doing something, he wanted to know what it was so he could do it.

The response of Jesus exposed the inability of human effort, apart from following Him, to give birth to eternal life in the human heart. He answered: **"You know the commandments: 'Do not commit adultery, do not murder, do not steal, do not give false testimony, honor your father and mother'"** (Luke 18:20). The commandments cited by Jesus were issues related to other persons. The Ten Commandments also include issues related to God. Jesus knew that the ruler's righteousness was defined in terms of keeping himself above reproach in relationship with others. Jesus wanted to show him how even in his best efforts he would fall short. The ruler's response, **"All these I have kept since I was a boy"** (18:21) was admirable. All of his life he had been careful in his relationships with others. He had kept himself morally and ethically clean.

To some, such a man would be a worthy candidate for admission into church fellowship. He had money, influence, and a clean record. The only problem was that he did not have eternal life, and Jesus was about to expose a flaw in what the ruler would consider to be his best quality. Jesus said to him, **"You still lack one thing. Sell everything you have and give to the poor, and you will have treasure in heaven. Then come, follow me"** (18:22). The man's righteousness was based on horizontal relationships, not a vertical relationship with God. So Jesus told him to demonstrate how committed he was to his horizontal righteousness by giving everything he had to the poor. He could then come and follow Him in developing the vertical relationship. The one thing that the ruler lacked was relationship with God, not compassionate ministry to the poor. Giving everything to the poor was the one thing that stood in the way of the one thing he lacked. **When he heard this, he became very sad, because he was a man of great wealth** (18:23). Jesus put His finger on the area of the man's life that would keep him from following Him. His love for the things he had accumulated would be greater than his love for Christ. His gain would become his loss and he knew it. The wealth he thought had made him happy was now the cause of his sadness. His horizontal righteousness was flawed, and he had no vertical righteousness. He came face to face with eternal life and walked away empty. An opportunity not seized became lost forever.

Jesus said, **"How hard it is for the rich to enter the kingdom of God!"** (18:24). Luke has a lot to say about rich people, and most of it is uncomplimentary because of their treatment of the poor. In this case, Jesus pushed the issue beyond the compassionate care of others to say that riches can be a hindrance to entering the kingdom of God. In the Old Testament, if a person was wealthy it was often an indication of God's blessing and a sign to others that God had a special relationship with that person. But there is an inherent danger in wealth that can turn this blessing into a curse. The Bible does not condemn the accumulation of wealth, but it gives plenty of warning to the rich about what they are to do with it. Paul warned, "the love of money is a root of all kinds of evil. Some people, eager for money, have wandered from the faith and pierced themselves with many griefs" (2 Tim. 6:10).

Jesus stressed the difficulties of being rich by saying, **"It is easier for a camel to go through the eye of a needle than for a rich man to enter the kingdom of God"** (Luke 18:25). It is not impossible for the rich to enter the kingdom of God, it is just difficult, because a person's riches cannot go along with him or her into the Kingdom. Jesus is not saying that the only way to get eternal life is to sell everything you have and give it away. Rather, He is saying wealth will not grant you entrance into the Kingdom and you might find it difficult to enter the Kingdom because of your wealth. The image of a camel going through the eye of a needle is a grammatical structure called hyperbole, which is an obvious exaggeration used for effect. Jesus often used hyperboles to get a point across, such as mustard seed faith that moves mulberry trees (Luke 17:6). A hyperbole is not intended to be taken in a literal sense, but to make a strong point.

THE IMPOSSIBILITY OF SALVATION

Those who witnessed a rich, moral, law-keeping man denied eternal life by his own choices, **asked, "Who then can be saved?"** (18:26). If this man, who had everything going for him could not be saved, then what hope is there for anyone else? Again, Jesus exposed the inability of human righteousness to gain eternal life by replying, **"What is impossible with men is possible with God"** (18:27). Salvation cannot be gained by human effort, even if it involves selling everything you have and giving it to the poor (1 Cor. 13:3). Salvation is only possible through God, given as a gift of His grace.

Whether it was an attempt by Peter to impress Jesus that he and the other disciples were different from the rich ruler, or if it was intended to be an affirmation of their devotion, **Peter said to him, "We have left all we had to follow you!"** (Luke 18:28). Indeed they had left everything, and they had modeled a response to accumulated things opposite that of the rich ruler. The willingness to leave everything was only one dimension of following Christ, howbeit an important one. Jesus said that those who are willing to leave everything **for the sake of the kingdom,** including relationships with family, will **receive many times as much in this age and, in the age to come, eternal life** (18:29–30). You cannot give up more for the sake of Christ than you will gain in return. The enemy will make you think that the cost of following Jesus is too much, but if you are unwilling to leave everything to follow Christ, like the rich ruler you will walk away with your hands full and your heart empty. Empty your hands and you can gain a full heart.

3. JESUS PREDICTS HIS DEATH (18:31–34)

Jesus had resolutely set out for Jerusalem (Luke 9:51), and He affirmed that resolve when He **took the Twelve aside and** said, **"We are going up to Jerusalem"** (18:31). It was not just a statement of information, but one of determination. He added, **"Everything that is written by the prophets about the Son of Man will be fulfilled"** (18:31). Jerusalem and the events that would be faced there would not be avoided. All of God's plan of salvation would be fulfilled there, along with everything that had been promised and prophesied about it.

Jesus used the title for himself that Luke highlights throughout his gospel: the Son of Man. As He moved toward His suffering and death, Jesus identified with humankind. He is God in human flesh, ready to bear the sins of humanity. Jesus gave the Twelve advance warning of what would happen to Him in Jerusalem: **"He will be handed over to the Gentiles. They will mock him, insult him, spit on him, flog him and kill him"** (18:31–32). Jesus had full knowledge of the treatment He would endure from the very creation of the earth (Rev. 13:8), yet He did not walk away from it, but toward it. In these verses, the Gentiles were credited with participating in the insult and suffering that He would endure. The Jews are usually pointed to as the ones who killed Jesus, but all peoples caused His death.

Though the future was dark, Jesus gave them reason for hope: **"On the third day he will rise again"** (Luke 18:33). It would soon become obvious that **the disciples did not understand any of this** (18:34). The crucifixion would turn the world of the disciples upside down, and they would not remember these words of hope. Beyond trauma-induced forgetfulness, **its meaning was hidden from them, and they did not know what he was talking about** (18:34). Sometimes the meaning of things is hidden from people because of an act of God, an individual's hardness of heart, spiritual things that must be spiritually perceived, or because of an inability to connect the dots. For whatever reason, the disciples did not understand what Jesus was talking about and were unprepared for what lay ahead.

Often God speaks through His Word, His voice within us, or a message delivered to us by another; but if we do not listen with understanding, the moment slips by, leaving us without vital spiritual knowledge.

4. BLIND MAN HEALED (18:35–43)

The road to Jerusalem took Jesus through **Jericho**, and as He **approached** the town He came upon **a blind man sitting by the roadside begging** (18:35). The man **heard** the commotion of **the crowd**, discovered that it was **Jesus** who was **passing by**, and **called out, "Jesus, Son of David, have mercy on me!"** (18:36–38). An opportunity was passing near him and would pass him by unless he seized the moment. He had knowledge of Jesus and called out to Him using the title Son of David, which is, beyond this encounter, used only one other time in Luke's gospel (Luke 20:41). Matthew, who emphasized the messianic, kingly role of Jesus, used the title ten times. The blind man called out for mercy, which was not often offered by others who simply walked on by him.

Those around him **told him to be quiet, but he shouted all the more** (18:39). Jesus heard his cry for mercy and asked him, **"What do you want me to do for you?"** (18:41). It would seem to be a strange question to ask a blind man. Wouldn't it be obvious that a blind man would want to be able to see? Our greatest wants do not always correlate with our greatest needs. Besides, we do not always believe Jesus is able to do what we need. So Jesus gave him opportunity to articulate what his want really was.

What do you want Jesus to do for you? Is it what you really need? If given the opportunity to tell Jesus one thing you want Him to do for you, what would you say? Your response will say something about your priorities.

The man knew what he wanted Jesus to do, and he believed Jesus was able to do it. So **he replied, "Lord, I want to see"** (18:41). He was a beggar, and he could have asked Jesus for money, as he did everyone else who passed by. Blindness was a root problem, and begging was a surface manifestation of the deeper need. We often want God to help us with surface issues rather than root problems. **Jesus said to him, "Receive your**

sight; your faith has healed you" (18:42). The blind man's cry for mercy was based on the belief that Jesus *could* do something to help him, and He *would* do something to help him. Jesus saw faith in the man, which became the means for his healing.

Immediately he received his sight and followed Jesus, praising God (18:43). A miracle of immediate healing occurred. This is the kind of miracle most people would like to receive when they ask God to help them. This is the only kind of miracle most people recognize as being a miracle—one that is immediate. However, some miracles are gradual and should result in praising God as well as those that happen immediately. Three things resulted from this man's encounter with Jesus: He received his sight, he followed Jesus, and he praised God. He was transformed from blind to seeing, from sitting alongside the road to walking the road alongside Jesus, and from being the victim of human disability to joyfully praising God. He seized the moment, and his life was changed forever.

Miracles come in all shapes and sizes. The timing of some is immediate, but others may be delayed. Jesus healed with a word, by touching the person, by being touched by the person, and through instructing the person to take particular action. Sometimes Jesus healed simply out of compassion, but other times because of faith expressed by the person or the faith of others expressed on behalf of that person. Usually Jesus healed people up close and personal, but there were times when He healed from a distance, never seeing the person but only hearing of the need. Jesus had the authority and power to intervene in any situation in any way He chose.

God can use the human touch, medical intervention, prayer, or the natural processes built into our bodies to do the unexplained. We are most likely to recognize a miracle, and give God credit for it, when it happens immediately and without human explanation. This may cause us to fail to recognize God at work on our behalf as He brings wholeness to us in His time and way. There are enough things inside us and in our physical environment to attack and kill us almost any day. Any time we are protected from disease and returned to wellness after being infected is a miracle. And that is not intended to diminish the meaning of a miracle but rather to expand our recognition of a miracle and our gratitude to God for it.

Any problem too big for us to solve is an opportunity for God to demonstrate His power. We should not let the opportunity pass by without telling Him what we want Him to do for us. Maybe He is waiting for us to identify our need and ask Him to intervene.

5. ZACCHAEUS: SMALL MAN, BIG OPPORTUNITY (19:1–10)

The miracle of healing the blind man outside Jericho was not the end of the noteworthy events of that day. **Jesus entered Jericho and was passing through** (19:1). Jericho was not His destination, but He was passing through; and if anyone in Jericho wanted to see and talk with Him, they would have to seize the moment or He would soon be gone. In Jericho lived **a man** named **Zacchaeus** who **was a chief tax collector and was wealthy** (19:2). There could be good reason to believe there was a direct connection between being a tax collector and being wealthy. Like Levi, Zacchaeus would have been a Jewish agent of the Roman Empire employed to extract taxes from his fellow countrymen. As mentioned, most tax collectors collected a little extra for their own benefit and were disliked by their communities because of it.

Zacchaeus **wanted to see who Jesus was, but being a short man he could not, because of the crowd** (19:3). Whether motivated by curiosity or by honest inquiry for spiritual reasons, we can certainly say that the Holy Spirit was at work drawing Zacchaeus toward a moment of decision with Jesus. Because he was too small to see over the heads of those who got there first, **he ran ahead and climbed a sycamore-fig tree** (19:4). His motivation was strong enough that he took unusual means just to get a look at Jesus. **When Jesus reached the spot, he looked up and said to him, "Zacchaeus, come down immediately. I must stay at your house today"** (19:5). We may talk about "finding the Lord," but who finds whom in the matter of salvation? Do we invite Him into our lives, or does He invite us to come to Him? Certainly our soul longs for and searches for a Savior, but the Savior, like a shepherd, is looking for His lost sheep. When we take a step toward Jesus, He reaches the rest of the way toward us. Zacchaeus acted on his spirit's motivation to see who Jesus was, but it was Jesus who saw the little man in the tree and understood his spiritual need. Jesus invited himself to the house of Zacchaeus, who **welcomed him gladly** (19:6). Middle Eastern culture was hospitality based, and without hesitation Zacchaeus welcomed Jesus into his home.

The interchange between Jesus and Zacchaeus happened openly in a crowd. That crowd included **people** who **began to mutter, "He has gone to be the guest of a 'sinner'"** (19:7). Once again the label "sinner" was easily applied to a tax collector. Zacchaeus did not need anyone else to proclaim him to be a sinner. He already knew he was, and, in the presence of the Holy One, he knew he could not remain the way he was. So he **said to the Lord, "Look, Lord! Here and now I give half of my possessions to the poor, and if I have cheated anybody out of anything, I will pay back four times the amount"** (19:8). Zacchaeus was willing to do the only thing he knew to do—make restitution for the wrongs he had done. Too often people are in search of cheap grace and easy confession that overlooks matters of restitution. Restitution is confessing to those you have wronged and taking the necessary steps to repay what can be repaid and repair what can be repaired. Confession should be as public as the sin and restitution as extensive as the damage. Without pressure, Zacchaeus committed himself to do what he could do.

Jesus said, **"Today salvation has come to this house ... For the Son of Man came to seek and to save what was lost"** (19:9–10). No person, regardless of size, position, or apparent obstacle is beyond the reach of salvation. It is a

LIFE CHANGE

RESTITUTION

Restitution is humbling and can be costly, but it frees the spirit and takes great steps in healing relationships that sin has damaged. Confession and repentance are first given to God because it is His law we have violated and relationship with Him that has been severed. We gain great freedom when we then turn to others we have wronged and add restitution to our confession and repentance.

wonderful thing when salvation comes to a household. It is particularly wonderful when the head of the house takes the initiative to bring Jesus home with him or her. A whole family was touched by the grace of Jesus because a man seized the moment, responded to an invitation to meet with Jesus, and welcomed Him into his home. We can all rejoice that Jesus had a firm grip on His mission. He knew exactly why He had come into our world, and it was to seek and save the lost. The salvation that came to the house of Zacchaeus comes to our home too, if we seize the moment when Christ passes by us.

6. PARABLE OF TEN MINAS (19:11–27)

THE OPPORTUNITIES OF STEWARDSHIP

Jesus was getting close to Jerusalem, and there were **people** in His entourage who **thought that the kingdom of God was going to appear at once** (19:11). Jesus told them a story about seizing the opportunity to accept His lordship and invest the resources that have been given to us. **A man** left his servants in charge of a portion of his wealth while he **went to a distant country to** be **appointed king, and then** he would **return. He called ten of his servants and gave them ten minas. "Put this money to work," he said, "until I come back"** (19:12–13). It is not difficult for us to draw clear parallels between the story Jesus told them of the would-be king and His story. Jesus was the one who would leave in order to become a king. We are the servants in the story who are vested with what belongs to Him and for which we have responsibility and accountability. Until He returns, we have the responsibility to put to use the resources entrusted to us. The amount or nature of those resources may vary among us, but when He returns, we will be held accountable for what we have done with what we have had, regardless of amount or type of resource. In this parable, ten minas were divided among ten servants. A mina (pound) was a Greek weight of exchange and represented about three months' wages at that time.

The amount given to each servant was not the important part of the story, but what was done with what was received was the point. Everything we have, including life itself, is a gift from God that is given to us to be used for godly purposes and not to be squandered or squirreled away. Nothing really belongs to us; it is loaned to us. It is called *stewardship,* taking care of something that belongs to another. It is the recognition that we are not *owners*, but *caretakers*.

There were those in the story who did not like the idea of the man returning to be their king, but when he did return as king, he called in **the**

servants . . . in order to find out what they had gained (19:15) with the minas that had been given to them. One had gained **ten more** (19:16), and another had gained **five more** (19:18). To each of them, the king gave a corresponding number of cities for them to **take charge of**. A third servant returned the mina, saying he had **kept it laid away in a piece of cloth** (19:20). He had done nothing with it, and his reasoning was, **"I was afraid of you, because you are a hard man"** (19:21). The response of the king was to take the mina from him and give it to the servant who had gained ten minas. He said, **"I tell you that to everyone who has, more will be given, but as for the one who has nothing, even what he has will be taken away"** (19:26). Jesus reinforced the principle expressed earlier that if you are trustworthy with few things, you will be considered trustworthy with more. Further, to do nothing with what you have is unacceptable.

The story ended with a greater bite to it when the king said, **"Those enemies of mine who did not want me to be king over them—bring them here and kill them in front of me"** (19:27). How you choose to use what you have been given will result in a judgment of accountability and reward. Your relationship toward the King, however, will result in a judgment of destiny. The Bible teaches that there will be two judgments following the return of Christ. One is when all will stand before God at the great white throne judgment to see if our names are in the Book of Life (Rev. 20:12). The second is for followers of Christ to be held accountable and will result in degrees of reward, based on the quality of our life labors (1 Cor. 3:12–15).

God has placed things in our hands, and we have opportunity to invest them in ways that will increase to His benefit and our blessing. Whether we think we are gifted with much or little, we are to put what we have to use. The opportunity to do something with what we have been given must be seized, or it will be taken away from us.

Part Four

In Jerusalem

LUKE 19:28–24:53

J erusalem held a significant place in the heart of Jesus. The journeys of His ministry were always with Jerusalem in mind, and His steps were measured in their relationship to the Holy City. Luke records in nine places Jesus journeying to Jerusalem (9:31, 51, 53; 13:22; 17:11; 18:31; 19:11, 28, 41).

Jesus was born in Bethlehem and was raised in Nazareth. He began His ministry in Galilee. But throughout His ministry there was an obvious progression toward the Holy City. Beginning in chapter 9, and continuing through most of chapter 19, Jesus was moving toward Jerusalem, the city of His destiny.

20

HOME AGAIN

Luke 19:28-21:4

J ews lived with the city of Jerusalem in their hearts, making the trek to Jerusalem for the major Jewish festivals every chance they got. The Temple, their spiritual and social center, was their spiritual home regardless of where they lived.

Jesus always had His face turned toward Jerusalem. He told the disciples, "We are going up to Jerusalem, and everything that is written by the prophets about the Son of Man will be fulfilled" (Luke 18:31). Bethlehem was His birthplace. Nazareth was where He was raised. But He had said, "I must be about my Father's business." This brought Him back to Jerusalem, where His earthly ministry would find its fulfillment. Everything He had done was with Jerusalem in mind. It was the one city over which He cried. He came to this city when He was twelve to fulfill the law, now He returned to fulfill God's redemptive plan. It was as if He were coming home. This was His destiny, and He was home—again.

1. JESUS RIDES INTO JERUSALEM (19:28-48)

ARRIVING AT THE DESTINATION

After completing the parable about stewardship and the return of the King, Jesus **went on ahead, going up to Jerusalem** (19:28). The entourage **approached Bethphage and Bethany at the hill called the Mount of Olives** (19:29). Bethany was about two miles east of Jerusalem on the road to Jericho. Lazarus, Mary, and Martha, special friends of Jesus, lived there, and He often visited in their home. Between Bethany and Jerusalem was the Mount of Olives with a special garden that He frequented for prayer and renewal. It was a place to which He would be drawn a couple more times before going home to His Father.

Jesus **sent two of his disciples** on **to the village ahead** of the group with the instruction to **find a colt tied** up **there, which no one** had **ever ridden.** They were to **untie it and bring it** (19:29–30) to Jesus. If questioned about taking the colt, their reply was to be **"The Lord needs it"** (19:31). If you saw someone taking an animal that belonged to you, you might be inclined to get physical with him or at least ask him what he was up to. The owner of the colt asked before he defended his property, and they responded as they had been told: "The Lord needs it." Nothing more is indicated. No persuasive speech. No arguments. No overcoming reluctance. No lectures from the owner about getting the colt back in reasonable time without damage. The Lord needed it, and the owner gave it. Such simple obedience and willing response should characterize our relationship with the Lord. If we have it and the Lord needs it, we should let Him have it.

The two disciples **brought** the colt **to Jesus, threw their cloaks on the colt and put Jesus on it** (19:35). Another prophecy was fulfilled that was spoken by the prophet Zechariah: "Rejoice greatly, O Daughter of Zion! Shout, Daughter of Jerusalem! See, your king comes to you, righteous and having salvation, gentle and riding on a donkey, on a colt, the foal of a donkey" (Zech. 9:9). The humble colt carried the King. Word of Jesus' arrival at Jerusalem gathered a crowd, and **as he went along, people spread their cloaks on the road** (19:36). They descended the Mount of Olives and approached the entrance into the city. The **crowd . . . began joyfully to praise God in loud voices for all the miracles they had seen: "Blessed is the king who comes in the name of the Lord! Peace in heaven and glory in the highest!"** (19:37–38). The other Gospels add that the people cried, "Hosanna," which means "save us now." Many in the crowd were looking for a popular king, a political figure, who would liberate them and bring the kingdom of Israel to prominence again. The King was indeed coming into His kingdom, but not as they expected.

We call this the triumphal entry of Jesus into Jerusalem, but it is probably misnamed. The proclamation of Jesus being king was loud and enthusiastic, but it lacked understanding and long-lasting meaning. The cheering crowds would, within days, abandon Him. There was probably more travesty than triumph surrounding Jesus' entry into Jerusalem that day.

BROKENHEARTED OVER THE CITY

Jesus was a man who was in touch with His emotions and who felt things deeply. He was often "moved with compassion" as He witnessed the needs of people. **As he approached Jerusalem and saw the city, he wept over it** (19:41). Twice the Scriptures tell us that He wept: once as He shared in the grief of Mary and Martha upon the death of their brother, Lazarus, and at this time as He grieved over the spiritual darkness that gripped the people of the Holy City. Jesus sympathizes with our weaknesses (Heb. 4:15), but He cares most about our spiritual condition. If you have wandered far from God, you can be sure He has wept over you.

As He wept, Jesus said, **"If you . . . had only known on this day what would bring you peace—but now it is hidden from your eyes"** (Luke 19:42). Peace was within their grasp, but in all of the noise and excitement of the moment, the people were missing an opportunity to experience it. We may never know how close we have been to a great blessing, only to miss it because we were not looking for it. Truth can be hidden from us for a lot of reasons, including misplaced focus.

Rejecting God and His Son would have serious consequences to this great city. The tears Jesus shed were because His heart was broken over the judgment that would come upon Jerusalem and its people. God's righteousness and justice require judgment against sin and sinners, but it breaks God's heart to do it. Through His tears, Jesus was heard to say, **"The days will come upon you when your enemies will build an embankment against you and encircle you and hem you in on every side. They will dash you to the ground, you and the children within your walls. They will not leave one stone on another, because you did not recognize the time of God's coming to you"** (19:43–44). In A.D. 66 the Jews had endured enough of Roman occupation and revolted against it. Titus, a general in the Roman army (later to become emperor), was sent to squelch the uprising and laid siege to Jerusalem, breaching its walls and burning the city in A.D. 70. Josephus, historian of the time, said

1.1 million people perished and 97 thousand were carried away into captivity.[1] God's Word is true, and His judgment is sure. As unfair as it may seem, children often pay a price for the sins of their parents.

AT HIS FATHER'S HOUSE AGAIN

One of the first accounts of Jesus' early years was of His visit to the Temple at age twelve. He was later led by the devil to the Temple area during His temptation, and John's gospel says He returned to celebrate the Passover on one occasion during His ministry (John 2:13), but there are no other references in Luke of Jesus going to the Temple. When He returned to Jerusalem, the Temple was the first place He went. His first visit involved entering into discussion with the religious leaders, but on this occasion **he entered the temple area and began driving out those who were selling** (Luke 19:45). After His first visit to the Temple, He called it "my Father's house" (Luke 2:49). This time He quoted Isaiah 56:7: **"My house will be a house of prayer"** (Luke 19:46). The Temple was to be a sacred place, where people came to pray, worship, and learn the ways of God. Jesus said the people had **made it a den of robbers** (19:46). Matthew's record adds, "He overturned the tables of the money changers and the benches of those selling doves" (Matt. 21:12). The people came to the Temple to offer their sacrifices, and those who had enough means would bring animals from their flocks for sacrifice. The poor would buy doves in the Temple courts for their sacrifice, and there were those who sought to benefit from this religious activity by taking advantage of the poor.

The Temple was the center of Jesus' activity in Jerusalem, and He spent **every day . . . teaching at the temple** (19:47). Not everything that went on around the Temple was focused on worshipping God. Jesus went about teaching, **but the chief priests, the teachers of the law and the leaders among the people were trying to kill him** (19:47). The religious leaders, who said they worshipped God, were so twisted in their thinking that they wanted to kill His Son. It is possible even for religious people to compartmentalize their lives until they can say they believe something but behave in ways contradictory to that belief. Priests were the connecting link between God and the people. They offered sacrifices to God on behalf of the people, but they were now preparing to sacrifice the Lamb of God on the altars of their own twisted self-interest.

The religious leaders were thwarted in their murderous intent **because all the people hung on his words** (19:48). People come to faith in Christ one person at a time, and that faith involves more than hanging on His words. Though the crowds hung on His words, soon they would step back and let the religious leaders have their way. There can be a fickleness that accompanies group mentality. Decisions made with crowds often do not stand up when people are alone and must live out the word of Christ in their lives. Words that challenge the mind must become words that capture the heart.

2. QUESTIONS OF AUTHORITY, TAXES, AND THE RESURRECTION (20:1–47)

WHO GAVE YOU AUTHORITY?

During a time of teaching in the Temple, the religious leaders asked Jesus, **"Tell us by what authority you are doing these things. Who gave you this authority?"** (20:2). Jesus "taught as one who had authority, and not as their teachers of the law" (Matt. 7:29). He spoke with an authority that captured the minds of people, and He acted with an assurance that captured the imagination of the people. The religious leaders could not match the authority of His words or the power of His influence, so they challenged the source of His authority.

Jesus answered their question with a question: **"John's baptism— was it from heaven, or from men?"** (Luke 20:4). For all of his strange appearance and behavior, John was greatly respected by the people. The religious leaders knew that if they said God commissioned the ministry of John, Jesus would ask them why they did not accept it. However, if they said John's ministry was humanly contrived, they would face an uprising at the hands of the people. **So they answered, "We don't know where it was from." Jesus said, "Neither will I tell you by what authority I am doing these things"** (20:7–8). Not every evil-intentioned question needs to be answered, and you do not have to engage in every argument that is an attempt to trap you. Jesus could have told them the source of His authority, but they were not interested in receiving truth, only in trapping Him. He didn't give them that satisfaction.

Earlier Jesus spoke about the truthfulness and authority of His words when He said, ". . . the one whom God has sent speaks the words of God" (John 3:34). He was sent by God, and He spoke the words of God. This is the only effective authority of any minister of God in the church today. Preachers can only speak with authority as they are sent by God and speak the Word of God.

MISTREATING THE HEIR

The theme of the previous chapter reappears as Jesus told of an owner who entrusted the care of his property to others while he went away. The story in Luke 19:19–27 focuses on how the stewards handled the property given them, but in this story, the focus is on how the stewards handled the owner's son, who was sent to get some fruit from the vineyard.

The story began when **a man planted a vineyard, rented it to some farmers and went away for a long time** (20:9). In the previous story, the owner who went away and returned later to see what had been done with his property could be interpreted to be Jesus. In this story, the owner could be interpreted to be God the Father. In both cases, it is underscored that God is the true owner of everything, and we are the renters or stewards. We are God's by creation, as is everything in our universe. He created everything and chooses to loan it to us to care for—including life itself.

Harvest time is built into the cycle of living things. A time comes when fruit is anticipated from the investment that was made at the time of planting. The vineyard belonged to the man who had planted the vines and had trusted their care to the tenants. **At harvest time he sent a servant to the tenants so they would give him some of the fruit of the vineyard** (20:10). It was a reasonable expectation. The theme of reasonable expectation of return on investment appears on numerous occasions throughout the Scripture. In Luke 13:6–9, it was about a fig tree planted in a vineyard. The expectation was for fruit, but none appeared, even after extra care and attention was given to the tree. In Isaiah 5:1–7, the Lord planted a vineyard from which fruit was anticipated, but again, none appeared. That story concludes with this statement: "The vineyard of the LORD Almighty is the house of Israel, and the men of Judah are the garden of his delight" (Isa. 5:7). Israel was God's special planting, from which He anticipated a harvest.

But when the servant came to get some fruit, **the tenants beat him and sent him away empty-handed** (Luke 20:10). Three times the owner of the vineyard sent servants for fruit, and each time they were beaten, **treated shamefully**, and **wounded** (20:11). Throughout history, God has sent His servants into His vineyard as His representatives, to speak on His behalf, and to seek fruit in return for the investment made by the Owner. Often, Israel mistreated God's representatives and ignored His right to expect something from them for the blessings He gave them.

The owner of the vineyard said, "I will send my son, whom I love; perhaps they will respect him" (20:13). But, rather than respecting the son, **the tenants** said, **"This is the heir. Let's kill him, and the inheritance will be ours"** (20:14). The Letter to the Hebrews begins with a parallel to this story. "In the past God spoke to our forefathers through the prophets at many times and in various ways, but in these last days he has spoken to us by his Son, whom he appointed heir of all things, and through whom he made the universe" (Heb. 1:1–2). God so loved the world that He sent His Son to save everyone who would receive Him. But sadly, Jesus "was in the world, and though the world was made through him, the world did not recognize him. He came to that which was his own, but his own did not receive him" (John 1:10–11).

The evil tenants **killed** the owner's son. Jesus asked the logical follow-up question: **"What then will the owner of the vineyard do to them?"** (Luke 20:15). He provided the response to the question: **"He will come and kill those tenants and give the vineyard to others"** (20:16). No one would argue with the owner's right to avenge the death of his son. The response of the listeners to the story was **"May this never be!"** (20:16). Such inhuman, unwarranted, and selfish treatment of a vineyard owner's servants and son should not be tolerated. They did not make the connection between the story and their own disassociation from God and mistreatment of His messengers. Jesus asked the listeners the meaning of Psalm 118:22, where it is written: **"The stone the builders rejected has become the capstone?"** (Luke 20:17). Jesus went on to say, **"Everyone who falls on that stone will be broken to pieces, but he on whom it falls will be crushed"** (20:18). The apostle Peter quoted from this Psalm as well and made direct connection with Jesus.

> I lay a stone in Zion, a chosen and precious cornerstone, and the one who trusts in him will never be put to shame. Now to you who believe, this stone is precious. But to those who do not believe, "The stone the builders rejected has become the capstone," and, "A stone that causes men to stumble and a rock that makes them fall." They stumble because they disobey the message (1 Pet. 2:6–8).

HOPING TO CATCH HIM

The teachers of the law and the chief priests were angered because they perceived that Jesus told the **parable** about rejecting the vineyard owner's representatives and killing his son as being **against them** (Luke 20:10). He dared to quote their own Scripture and use it against them. So they began to look for a way to have Him arrested. **They hoped to catch Jesus in something he said so that they might hand him over to the power and authority of the governor** (20:20). If the Romans would arrest Him, the teachers of the law and chief priests could escape criticism from the Jews who were friends of Jesus. They asked Jesus, **"Is it right for us to pay taxes to Caesar or not?"** (20:22). Jesus knew what they were up to, so He told them to show Him a coin, asking, **"Whose portrait and inscription are on it?"** (20:24). The coin was a **denarius,** which was the principal silver coin of the Roman commonwealth. From the parable of the laborers in the vineyard it would seem that a denarius was the ordinary pay for a day's labor at that time (Matt. 20:2–13).

Jews were required to use this currency to pay the tax assessed them by the Romans, so even handling the coin would anger the Jews, as it reminded them of the burden of taxation and the occupation of their land by the Romans.[2] The religious leaders thought Jesus would surely have to identify with His people in their animosity toward the rule of the Romans, which would set Him up for speaking evil against Roman rule and get Him arrested.

The questioners replied that the portrait on the coin was that of Caesar, to which Jesus responded, **"Then give to Caesar what is Caesar's, and to God what is God's"** (Luke 20:25). They had hoped they would catch Jesus in a "separation of church and state" statement that would either discredit Him with the Jews or bring the wrath of the Romans upon Him. However, Jesus established a principle for God's people who live in a world that is ruled by non-Christian governments. There are responsibilities that need to be met toward God and toward the state. That is not to say that giving to God what is due Him will never cause problems with Caesar, but what is due God should never be avoided by bowing to the demands of the secular state. Spiritual wisdom certainly is needed in discerning the issues for which a person is willing to suffer the consequences of civil disobedience. Christians are called upon to "fear God and honor the king" (1 Pet. 2:17), and spiritual conscience must guide each of us in how we can honor civil laws and leaders without violating our commitment to God's law.

The response of Jesus **astonished** those who had tried to **trap him**, and **they became silent** (Luke 20:26).

QUESTIONS ABOUT THE RESURRECTION

Matthew identified the religious leaders in the preceding paragraph as Pharisees and Herodians (Matt. 22:15–16). The Herodians were Jews who were supporters of the family of Herod, who had been appointed by the Roman emperor to rule over Israel.[3]

Another group, the **Sadducees** (Luke 20:27), came to Jesus with a question. This is the only reference to the Sadducees in Luke's gospel. The Pharisees were a religious sect of Judaism, and the Sadducees were more politically oriented, consisting of more of the wealthy upper class of people who tended to collaborate with the Romans so as to not jeopardize their wealth.[4] Sadducees did not believe in the resurrection of the dead, so they posed a complicated question that was intended to bring ridicule upon Jesus. They based their question on the law of Moses that said **if a man's brother dies and leaves a wife but no children, the man must marry the widow and have children for his brother** (20:28). They took that principle of the law and posed a situation in which there was a family of seven brothers. One of them died, and a brother took the childless widow to be his wife. He died, and another brother married her. This happened seven times until finally the woman died. The Sadducees then posed the question to Jesus, **"At the resurrection whose wife will she be, since the seven were married to her?"** (20:33).

The essence of Jesus' response was that life in this age cannot be compared to life in the age to come. People **marry** in **this age**, but in the next age they **will neither marry nor be given in marriage** (20:34–35). Social relationships common to this life will not exist in the next. In the next life, people will **no longer die; for they** will be **like the angels** (20:36). Scripture indicates that angels are immortal beings who once had a period of freedom of choice for which they were accountable, and now that choice is eternally sealed. The faithful angels will spend eternity serving and worshipping God. As **children of the resurrection** (20:36), we will be like the godly angels.

How do you prove to someone that there is life after death if there is nothing to give as evidence? Jesus said that when God met Moses at the burning bush, He identified himself as **"the God of Abraham, and the God of Isaac, and the God of Jacob"** (20:37). If these men were not alive in another realm, God would not have used their names, because **He is not the God of the dead, but of the living, for to him all are alive** (20:38).

A WORD AGAINST THE TEACHERS OF THE LAW

The questions by the Sadducees ended, and the teachers of the law were pleased with Jesus' answer, since they believed in the resurrection. But Jesus shifted His focus to the teachers of the law and asked them, **"How is it that they say the Christ is the Son of David?"** (20:41). The Messiah was to be a descendent of David and was sometimes referred to as being the Son of David, which was the name by which the blind man addressed Jesus in Luke 18:38–39. Jesus quoted David's words **in the Book of Psalms** (20:42) in which he spoke of the Messiah as Lord, and then Jesus asked, **"How then can he be his son?"** (20:44). How could He be both David's son and also be his Lord? The point Jesus was making was that a greater person than David was present, One whom David would call "Lord."

The teachers of the law accepted David and revered his words, but did not accept the One who came to fulfill those words. **Jesus said to his disciples, "Beware of the teachers of the law"** (20:46). They performed their religious acts for a show. They sought **places of honor** and loved to be seen in their **flowing robes** (20:46). They preyed on helpless and weak people. Jesus said, **"Such men will be punished most severely"** (20:47). The judgment of God will come upon those who do not accept His Son but who use their religious standing for personal benefit and develop religious practices that are contrary to the principles of the kingdom of God.

3. THE WIDOW'S OFFERING 21:1–4

As Jesus moved around the Temple area, He **saw the rich putting their gifts into the temple treasury** (21:1). There were thirteen collection boxes in the Temple courtyard where Temple taxes and freewill offerings could be placed.[5] Since many of the people loved to be seen when doing their religious acts, it can be imagined that the rich made a show of giving their gifts. While Jesus watched the rich giving their gifts, **he also saw a poor widow put in two very small copper coins** (21:2). She had no husband to provide for her, which would contribute to her poverty. The word used for *coins* suggests that they were the smallest of coin currency existing at the time. She could not have given

LIFE CHANGE

LITTLE IS MUCH

A song of long ago said, "Little is much, when God is in it." We should never keep from offering to the Lord whatever we have, thinking it to be too small and insignificant. God looks at the size of our heart, not the size of our offering. He can take a little boy's lunch and feed a multitude. He can take a widow's mite and enrich her life as well as someone else's.

an offering any smaller, but as Jesus compared her offering with those of the rich, he said, **"This poor widow has put in more than all the others"** (21:3). Her gift was huge because it was **all she had to live on** (21:4). She did not give out of excess revenue; she gave everything and had nothing left. In giving to God, it is not a matter of how much you give but how much you have left. Others gave **out of their wealth; but she out of her poverty** (21:4). Her gift was not measured by amount, but by abandonment and attitude. She did not give out of a desire to be seen, but out of a desire to worship God. She held nothing back from God, trusting her livelihood to the gracious hands of God.

ENDNOTES

1. William Barclay, The Gospel of Luke (Philadelphia: Westminster, 1956), p. 269.

2. Ralph Earle, *The Wesleyan Bible Commentary: The Gospel of Luke* (Grand Rapids, Mich.: Eerdmans, 1964), p. 322.

3. William Smith, *Smith's Bible Dictionary*, s.v. "Herodians."

4. William Barclay, *The Gospel of Luke* (Philadelphia: Westminster, 1956), p. 260.

5. Ibid., p. 265.

21

THE BEGINNING OF THE END

Luke 21:5-38

Whether by nuclear bombs, global warming, or the return of Christ, there is a general sense that this planet—and our life on it—will someday come to an end. It is natural that people would like to know when and how the end will come. Particularly when times are troubled, people tend to be fascinated with talk of the end times.

The Jews had developed an understanding of a future day, the day of the Lord, when their enemies would be consumed and a new day of God's promised blessing would come to His people. The prospects of the day of the Lord are both grim and blessed. It is a day of judgment and of reward. Even though we know things will sometime come to an end, we tend to live as if they won't. We seem to be more at home here when times are good.

1. THE END TIMES (21:5-36)

DESTRUCTION OF THE TEMPLE

The Temple was not one building but a complex of several beautiful parts. One day, **some of** Jesus' **disciples were** talking **about how the Temple was adorned with beautiful stones and with gifts dedicated to God** (21:5). The Temple was at the center of Jewish life. It was the house of God, constructed first by Solomon, destroyed by the Babylonians, rebuilt by returning exiles in the late sixth century B.C., and then remodeled extensively by Herod. The people contributed gifts that adorned the Temple with the best of precious stone and metals. It was unthinkable that anything would ever destroy this permanent structure in their lives. But while they stood in its shadow admiring its beauty, Jesus said, **"The time will come when not one stone will be left on another; every one of them will be thrown down"** (21:6). The stones would not *fall down*, as with gradual decay or natural disaster. They would be *thrown down*—destroyed by human hand and evil intent. The very idea would seem like the end of the world to a Jew.

SIGNS OF THE END

Word that the Temple would be destroyed grabbed their attention, and they asked, **"When will these things happen?"** (21:7). It is only natural that something as dramatic as the destruction of the Temple and the collateral events would cause people to want to know *when* it would happen. They would want to know if it was imminent enough to worry about it or if there was something that could be done to prevent it. *When* is a reasonable question, along with wanting to know indications that the time is near.

It would appear that Jesus moved from speaking about the destruction of the Temple, which was fairly imminent and would occur in A.D. 70, to speaking about end-time events that would be further out in the future. These two events seem to blend together in this discussion, which may be more obvious when reading this discourse in Matthew 24–25. Prophetic discourses do not always outline things in progressive sequence or provide all the information to neatly tie together the details that are given.

Jesus provided a list of things to look for as the end times approach:

Many will come in my name, claiming "I am he," and, "The time is near" (Luke 21:8).

There will be **wars and revolutions** (21:9).

Nation will rise against nation (21:10).

There will be great earthquakes, famines and pestilences in various places (21:11).

There will be **fearful events and great signs from heaven** (21:11).

Almost every generation experiences enough that could fit into this list for them to believe the end is near. Certainly Paul believed it would happen in his day, and many Christians of that time did as well. Most of us have lived past a number of dates that were declared by someone to be the absolute date for the return of Christ.

The list would seem to indicate that the last days will include false prophets and antichrists. Jesus said, **"Watch out that you are not deceived,"** and **"Do not follow them"** (21:8). Deception has always been a tactic of Satan, "the father of lies" (John 8:44). The last days will be marked with political unrest as well as conflict between countries and uprisings within countries. The last days will include an increase in natural disasters and cataclysmic events in the universe. As this age comes to a close, things will look pretty grim. Juxtaposed against the events of that day are the words of Jesus: **"Do not be frightened"** (Luke 21:9). Deception and fear are the greatest enemies the follower of Christ will face as the last days approach. We must be informed students of the truth and grounded in it. We must be confident people of faith not in circumstances, but in God's provision and care of His children. Fear is our enemy. Faith is our ally.

The apostle Paul spoke quite often of the last days, indicating that there will be terrible times in the last days. "People will be lovers of themselves, lovers of money, boastful, proud, abusive, disobedient to their parents, ungrateful, unholy, without love, unforgiving, slanderous, without self-control, brutal, not lovers of the good, treacherous, rash, conceited, lovers of pleasure rather than lovers of God—having a form of godliness but denying its power" (2 Tim. 3:1–5). He said the day of the Lord would come as "a thief in the night" (1 Thess. 5:1–3), and that it would not come until "the rebellion occurs and the man of lawlessness is revealed, the man doomed to destruction. He will oppose and will exalt himself over everything that is called God or is worshiped, so that he sets himself up in God's temple, proclaiming himself to be God" (2 Thess. 2:4). The apostle Peter added that "in the last days scoffers will come, scoffing and following their own evil desires" (2 Pet. 3:3); and "The heavens will disappear with a roar; the elements will be destroyed by fire, and the earth and everything in it will be laid bare" (3:10). Luke also recorded these cataclysmic events in the book of Acts. There will be "wonders in the heaven above and signs on the earth below, blood and fire and billows of smoke. The sun will be turned to darkness and the moon to blood before the coming of the great and glorious day of the Lord" (Acts 2:19–20).

The nature of the signs of the end should bring fear to the hearts of those who are unprepared, but Jesus told His followers not to be deceived or afraid.

PERSECUTION

Things will get worse before they get better; and when you think it can't get worse, it will. It is one thing to witness havoc and destruction happening in the world, but it is quite another thing when you experience persecution and betrayal happening to you, particularly if it is caused because of your faith in Christ. Jesus told His disciples that before all of these other things happen, they would be persecuted and have charges brought against them **"all on account of my name"** (Luke 21:12). This may not have been in their minds when they signed on to follow Him. It certainly is not a part of our marketing strategy to bring people into our churches. If persecution is going to happen, we would prefer that it happen to someone else in some faraway country. We accept Christ into our lives for all the good things it means for us. When bad things happen to us on account of Him, we may question if it is worth being identified with Him. That is why there were those He said could not be His disciples and that anyone who wanted to follow Him should be sure to first count the cost (Luke 14:25–34).

It may seem strange, but over the years the Church has thrived most in times and places of persecution. You would think that if identifying with Christ means being harassed, beaten, and killed, the voice of the Church would be silenced in times of persecution, but the opposite has been true. Jesus said to the disciples, **"This will result in your being witnesses to them"** (21:13), and they soon discovered the reality of these words. The powers that opposed Christ tried to crush the witness of His Church, but like stomping on a campfire, burning embers were scattered across the face of the earth, igniting fires wherever they landed. When faced with pressure and persecution, people of the Church have prayed like Peter: "Now, Lord, consider their threats and enable your servants to speak your word with great boldness" (Acts 4:29). God has answered their prayers.

Jesus promised them that when they stood before those who would accuse and discredit them, He would give them **"words and wisdom that none of your adversaries will be able to resist or contradict"** (Luke 21:15). Followers of Jesus must rely completely on Him and trust Him even for the words to say when things get really tough.

No one would know betrayal as deeply as Jesus. For a bit of pocket change, one of His disciples would soon betray Him with a kiss. Though the Twelve may not have been overtly hindered in following Jesus by their family and friends, Jesus said they should expect to be betrayed by family and friends, **"and they will put some of you to death"** (21:16). Perhaps the most difficult thing is to be faithful to Christ in spite of opposition and persecution by family and friends.

Jesus was always honest with His followers regarding the costs of following Him. He told them, **"All men will hate you because of me"** (21:17). He always gave them reason to keep their faith in Him regardless of how tough things got. It would seem that in the context of persecution, betrayal, and death, Jesus contradicted himself when He said, **"But not a hair of your head will perish"** (21:18). Only a follower of Christ could understand what He meant when He said, **"By standing firm you will gain life"** (21:19). Persecutors may bring death to the body, but they cannot kill the soul. You only truly live when you find something worth dying for, and dying for it will gain you life in a greater dimension than could ever be experienced in this world.

THE DESOLATION OF JERUSALEM

Discussion about the Temple provided opportunity for Jesus to answer questions about the end times. Then He shifted back to speak to His disciples about the more imminent destruction of the Temple. He told them that they would know Jerusalem's **desolation** was **near** when they would see **armies** (21:20) surrounding the city. The word *desolation* is a very strong word, indicating that Jerusalem would not just be captured by an invading army, but that the city and Temple would be laid waste and stripped of their grandeur. Jesus said the siege of Jerusalem would be a **time of punishment** (21:22). Not all cataclysmic events are acts of divine judgment, though there certainly have been times when that has been true. Israel's history had consisted of times of blessing, of drifting away from God, of judgment and punishment by Him, and repentance and return to Him. His punishment was intended to lead them back to Him. Jesus said there would be **great distress in the land** (21:23) as people **fall by the sword** (21:24) and are taken prisoner. **Jerusalem will be trampled on by the Gentiles until the times of the Gentiles are fulfilled** (21:24). As mentioned earlier, Jerusalem fell to Roman siege and the Temple was desecrated and destroyed in A.D. 70. More than one million people perished and nearly a hundred thousand were carried away into captivity.[1] Gentiles have both trampled and controlled the Holy City for hundreds of years. Today the city stands without its Temple and with rival religious factions still vying for its control.

Jesus seems to weave back and forth between the imminent destruction of Jerusalem and the end of the age. In verse 25, He seems to shift back to signs of the last days, indicating **signs** in the solar system and upheaval on **earth** (21:25). **The heavenly bodies will be shaken**, and people **will faint from terror** (21:26). When things reach their worst, and hope for civilization is gone, the **Son of Man** will be seen **coming in a cloud with power and great glory** (21:27). It is then that the faithful are to **lift up** their **heads, because** their **redemption is drawing near** (21:28). We are already redeemed from our sin, but we have yet to experience full redemption from the consequences of sin in our lives and in our world. In just a matter of weeks, the disciples would watch as Jesus ascended into the clouds. As they looked up, two angels would say to them, "This same Jesus, who has been taken from you into heaven, will come back in the same way you have seen him go into heaven" (Acts 1:11). He will return with power and great glory to become the Lord of Lords and King of Kings.

LOOK AT THE FIG TREE

No one knows the day of His return, but every follower of Christ is to be vigilant regarding the events of the day and discerning regarding the movements of God. Jesus said to **look at the fig tree** (21:29) that goes through natural stages that relate to the seasons. **When** the **leaves sprout**, you can tell **summer is near** (21:30). God's people should be able to tell that **the kingdom of God is near** (21:31) by looking at what is going on in the world. Difference of opinion remains about Jesus' word that **"this generation will certainly not pass away until all these things have happened"** (21:32). He could be saying the present generation would see the fulfillment of the destruction of Jerusalem. Or, He could have meant that the generation that experiences the events of the last days of which He had just spoken will see the consummation of the ages.

Not many things have eternity built into them, and occasionally we can be reminded of the temporary nature of the things around us. Jesus said that even the heavens and the **earth will pass away** (21:33). There is nothing created that we can put our confidence in, but Jesus said, **"my words will never pass away"** (21:33). You can place your confidence in Christ and His eternal Word of promise to you.

God's people should not live carelessly in troubling days, nor should they be overwhelmed by what consumes others. They are to be careful lest their **hearts will be weighed down** (21:34). They are to be alert lest **that day close on** them **unexpectedly like a trap** (21:34). They are to **watch and pray** (21:36). We are not to be people who isolate ourselves from the world or live with our heads in the sand. We are to pray with our eyes open to what is going on in our world and what God would want us to be doing. Confident in God's faithfulness to us, we remain faithful to Him, knowing that our redemption is drawing near.

2. RETREATING TO THE MOUNT OF OLIVES (21:37–38)

Each day after arriving in Jerusalem, **Jesus** taught **at the temple** (21:37). The outer courts would be filled with worshippers and people who would gather to listen to the teachers who assembled there. From

277

early morning until evening, Jesus taught those who would listen. Then, as evening would come, He would go **out to spend the night on the hill called the Mount of Olives** (21:37). The Mount of Olives, with its Garden of Gethsemane, was a special place of retreat for Jesus, where He would often go for solitude and prayer. During the days preceding His crucifixion, He needed a break from the crowds and additional communion with His Father. The Mount of Olives was a short walk from the eastern gate of Jerusalem through the Kidron Valley. It was close enough to reach quickly, yet far enough away from distractions.

LIFE CHANGE

RETREAT

We should learn from Jesus the necessity of prayer and renewal. As a verb, *retreat* can mean to flee or run away from a battle. As a noun, retreat can mean a place of sanctuary or refuge. We need to learn to find our place of sanctuary so we can be renewed through communion with God and return to the battle with the ability to advance the cause of Christ.

In a few short days, this garden would become the scene of His prayer of submission to the will and plan of God. Its serenity would be shattered by a kiss of betrayal, cursing soldiers, and swinging swords. But for now, it was a place of quiet retreat where Jesus could prepare for the storm that would come.

This was the beginning of the end of Jesus' earthly ministry.

ENDNOTES

1. William Barclay, *The Gospel of Luke* (Philadelphia: Westminster, 1956), p. 269.

22

TABLE TALK

Luke 22:1-38

Some of the most significant conversations take place when families and friends gather around a table. At mealtime, Jesus taught some of His most insightful lessons and developed the deepest relationships. He had many meals with His disciples, but none with the level of significance as the last one, particularly since it was also the Passover meal. It took on even greater significance as it instituted a meal that would be observed throughout the ages and throughout eternity (Luke 22:16). We call it the Lord's Supper or Communion. The Last Supper instituted the Lord's Supper.

The Passover meal, which they had come together to eat, celebrated freedom from the bondage of Egypt. But it

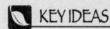 KEY IDEAS

MEMORABLE MEALS

The Gospels capture several significant mealtimes during which Jesus communicated eternal truth:

Matthew's house (Matt. 9)

The home of a leading Pharisee (Luke 7)

Feeding the five thousand (Luke 9)

Simon the leper's house (Mark 14)

Zacchaeus's house (Luke 19)

The Upper Room with His disciples (Luke 22)

became the forum for serious talk about the impending crucifixion. The slaying of the Passover Lamb would find its fulfillment in Christ.

1. THE PASSOVER MEAL (22:1-20)

SATAN ENTERS JUDAS

Crowds began to grow in the city of Jerusalem as **the Feast of Unleavened Bread, called the Passover, was approaching** (22:1). The Passover was one of the most significant events in Jewish history, and every male over the age of twelve was required to go to Jerusalem to observe the festival whenever possible. The Passover commemorated Israel's release from Egyptian captivity when the death angel visited Egypt, bringing death to every Egyptian firstborn male child. The angel passed over the Jewish homes where the blood of a sacrificed lamb was placed on the doorpost. Passover was followed by the Feast of Unleavened Bread, which was a week-long commemoration of Israel's deliverance from Egypt. All leaven was removed from Jewish houses during this time of preparation for the Passover.

 **JEWISH CUSTOMS**

FEASTS AND FESTIVALS

The major postexilic Jewish festivals included Passover, Feast of Unleavened Bread, First Fruits, Pentecost, Trumpets, Day of Atonement, and Feast of Tabernacles.

Jesus' first visit to Jerusalem and observance of the festival is recorded in Luke 2:41. This final visit to Jerusalem would fulfill everything symbolized within the Passover. The sacrificial lamb was fulfilled in Jesus and the unleavened bread—a symbol of removing all sin from the house—was fulfilled through the redemptive work of Christ in human hearts.

At a time when they should have been busy preparing for the Passover, the religious leaders were busy **looking for some way to get rid of Jesus** (22:2). They did not realize they were helping God provide for a new covenant that would replace the old covenant they were to be celebrating (Heb. 8:8–9). The Passover Lamb was being led to the slaughter where His sacrifice would satisfy the penalty of sin and break the stranglehold of sin on the human heart.

Luke records these shocking words: **Then Satan entered Judas, called Iscariot, one of the Twelve** (Luke 22:3). Satan's strategy has always been to cause those close to Jesus to implode through spiritual emptiness or to defect through serious compromise of godly values. Paul warned of the devil's schemes and the need for the people of God to be fully armed and protected (Eph. 6:11). Jesus would soon sit at the Passover table surrounded by those closest to Him, but Satan would be hard at work around that table as well. Wherever God is doing great things, Satan can be found in the shadows. Jesus would soon warn Simon Peter of how much Satan wanted to sift him as wheat (Luke 22:31), and Peter would experience the reality behind the warning. But conditions were different with Judas. Satan did not just *attack* Judas as he would Simon, he *entered* him. Questions have always been raised as to why, if Jesus knew the hearts of people, He would include someone in His inner circle of disciples whom He knew would betray Him. If there were a satisfactory answer, the question would probably not have to be asked again. Whatever the answer, the potential exists for being in the inner circle with Jesus and still having the capacity to allow Satan to enter one to the degree that he dictates the choices one makes.

Influenced by Satan, Judas began his defection. He **went to the chief priests and the officers of the temple guard and discussed with them how he might betray Jesus** (22:4). Judas took the short walk from intimate relationship with Jesus to association with the religious leaders to develop the strategy for betraying the Lord into their hands. Betrayal is such an ugly word. You can anticipate ill treatment by an enemy, but betrayal comes at the hand of a comrade, a friend, which lends an additional sting to it. Judas knew who the enemies of Jesus were, and he chose to join them, though his motivation for doing so cannot be fully known. Judas was a political zealot, and perhaps he wanted to force the hand of Jesus to finally take a stand against the Roman occupation, overthrow it, and establish His new kingdom. Perhaps he was motivated by the prospect of financial gain, since the religious leaders **were delighted and agreed to give him money** (22:5). The Gnostic gospels, written by non-Christians in the second and third centuries and not considered a part of the Christian canon, include the Gospel of Judas. It attempts to make Judas an ally of Jesus who acts at the direction of Jesus so He could be released from the prison of His human form. From whatever view you choose, it is hard to paint a positive face on betrayal. This was the work of Satan through Judas, with his full cooperation.

Judas joined the growing list of cowards as he **watched for an opportunity to hand Jesus over to them when no crowd was present** (22:6). There were still devoted followers who would probably be willing to fight for Jesus, so Judas wanted to do his dastardly deed of betrayal when others would not see. Evil people seek darkness and anonymity to keep their evil deeds secret. Betrayal is usually a cowardly deed carried out with no claim of bravery.

THE UPPER ROOM

Before there could be a celebrative reminder of their liberation from the bondage of Egypt, the Jewish people needed to be reminded of the awfulness and pain of captivity. This was the purpose of **the day of Unleavened Bread on which the Passover lamb had to be sacrificed** (22:7). The focus was on the lamb whose blood, when sprinkled on the doorposts of a home, protected the firstborn son from the angel of death (Ex. 12:21–27).

Jesus sent Peter and John to meet with a man who would allow them to use his guest room, **a large upper room** (Luke 22:12), as a place where He and His disciples could eat the Passover. Families usually celebrated Passover alone in their homes. Jesus and the Twelve had become family, since each had left everything—including family—to be together in ministry. They had no house in which to meet, so they went to a borrowed room for this most important meal. Jesus rode into town on a borrowed colt, ate the Passover in a borrowed room, and would be buried in a borrowed tomb. This world was not His home, and He had few, if any, belongings here. It is hard to lose your focus on mission if a place does not own you and you own nothing or owe anything to it.

THE LAST SUPPER

Jesus and his apostles reclined at the table (22:14), a scene immortalized by Leonardo da Vinci's famous Last Supper painting. However, God did not need a painting to make this a memorable time for His people. Not even da Vinci with all of his artistic ability could capture the significance of the table talk that took place that night.

The celebration of deliverance was muted by words of impending suffering. Jesus expressed His eagerness to have this last meal alone with His disciples, **"before I suffer"** (22:15). He told them He would **not eat** the Passover with them **again until it finds fulfillment in the kingdom of God** (22:16). Jesus could mean that He and His disciples would not share this kind of meal together again until they sit around the table of the marriage supper of the Lamb in heaven. However, for us, the Passover found its fulfillment in the crucifixion, resurrection, and Pentecost; so when we gather around the Lord's Table, we are in the kingdom of God, and the communion we share is a fulfillment of the Passover. He is present as we eat it.[1]

Jesus took some bread and gave it to the disciples with instructions to eat it. In itself, this would not have been unusual, but that all changed when He said, **"This is my body given for you; do this in remembrance of me"** (22:19). The bread Jesus broke and gave to His disciples was common bread, just like we may use for observing the Lord's Supper. However, there are different views regarding the substance of that bread as it relates to Jesus' declaration, "This is my body." Does a change occur in the substance of the bread that literally changes it into the body of Jesus? (See sidebar.)

He also took a cup of wine and gave it to them to drink,

 GREAT THEMES

THE LORD'S SUPPER

There are essentially four positions regarding the bread and the body of Jesus in Communion. One is called *transubstantiation* (the Roman Catholic position)—the belief that the bread, when consecrated by the priest or minister of God, becomes the actual body of Jesus—one substance becomes another. A second position is called *consubstantiation* (the Lutheran position)—the belief that the bread does not change its molecular structure, but the real bodily presence of Jesus accompanies the consecrated bread. The third is the *memorialist* view, which was held by Ulrich Zwingli who insisted the elements remained as they were and are signs that remind partakers of the redemptive act and become a means of public confession of faith. The fourth is the *spiritual presence* position (Reformed or Calvinist), which is somewhat a blend of the position of Luther and Zwingli. John Wesley described the Eucharist as a memorial of Christ's past sufferings, a means of present graces, and a pledge of future glory.[2]

saying, **"This cup is the new covenant in my blood, which is poured out for you"** (22:20). The pouring out of His blood would provide for a *new* covenant. A covenant is a relationship between God and His children, based on mutual commitments and promises. The *old* covenant was based on keeping the law of Moses. The Jewish system of sacrifices was set up to be the means of restoring their covenant relationship by atoning for their inadequacies through the sacrifices, thereby keeping up their part of the covenant. Jesus would give His life once for all time in order to establish a new covenant relationship between humankind and God (Heb. 8:6–13).

Jesus' use of *body* and *blood*, when referring to the bread and wine, are not to be taken literally, but were used symbolically by Him to represent His life that would be given for them (and us) and His nature and presence that should fill them.

This simple part of the last meal—bread and wine—has become a significant part of Christian experience. It is obvious that observing the Lord's Supper quickly became a part of the community life of the Church. Paul particularly captured its significant nature when he wrote to the church in Corinth (1 Cor. 10, 12). The Lord's Supper, often called Holy Communion or the Eucharist, is recognized by most Christians as being a sacrament of the Church. John Wesley defined a sacrament as "an outward sign of inward grace, and a means whereby we receive the same."[3]

We can have several attitudes when we come to the table of the Lord. It can be a memorial time, when we remember the death of Christ and its atoning benefit to us. It can be a time of celebration, when we thank God for our salvation through the cross, which is the meaning of Eucharist (from a Greek word for *thanksgiving*). It can be a time for spiritual reflection and examination as encouraged by Paul. It can be a time of declaring our common life and bond with other believers and with Christ (1 Cor. 10:16–17). It can be a time in which we experience a foretaste of the coming kingdom of heaven, when we will sit at the marriage supper of the Lamb.

2. BETRAYAL, CONTROVERSY, AND DENIAL (22:21–38)

A QUESTION OF GREATNESS

Jesus brought up the matter of His upcoming betrayal. He said, **"The hand of him who is going to betray me is with mine on the table"** (Luke 22:21). Many people would have liked to have had a chance to remove Jesus as a troublemaker, but the disciples did not think one of them would be involved. **They began to question . . . which one of them it might be who would do this** (22:23). Of course, you would expect all of them to insist they would be incapable of such a thing. Amazingly, the guilty one did not appear to be accused by any of them. It would have been interesting, though unproductive, for us to hear of whom they might have been suspicious. The fact is, each person around the table had the capability of betraying Jesus, as does each of us. Pointing fingers of suspicion toward others is never good. Paul said we should examine ourselves before eating from the table of the Lord, lest there be tendencies within us that could lead to sin.

 GREAT THEMES

FALLING FROM GRACE

John Wesley taught that the possibility of turning from grace back into sin always remained in the believer, though the departure from grace should not be considered necessary or easy. He listed the steps of a man who moves from grace to sin:

1. The divine seed of loving, conquering faith, remains in him that is born of God. "He keepeth himself" by the grace of God and "cannot commit sin."

2. A temptation arises.

3. The Spirit of God warns that sin is near and bids to more abundantly watch unto prayer.

4. He gives way, in some degree, to the temptation, which now begins to grow pleasing to him.

5. The Holy Spirit is grieved; his faith is weakened; and his love of God grows cold.

6. The Spirit reproves him more sharply, and says, "This is the way; walk in it."

7. He turns away from the painful voice of God, and listens to the pleasing voice of the tempter.

8. Evil desire begins and spreads in his soul, till faith and love vanish away: He is then capable of committing outward sin, the power of the Lord being departed from him.

The Twelve had just been told that Jesus would suffer and die, and that one of them would betray Him. You would think this revelation would dominate their conversation and solidify their loyalty to Him and to each other, like families do when one of them is threatened. Instead, **a dispute arose among them as to which of them was considered to be greatest** (22:24). It is strange how petty things can rise to great levels of importance at times when far more weighty things should occupy the time and conversation. The table talk turned inward and petty. This is the proverbial discussion of rearranging the deck chairs on the *Titanic*. Their Lord was about to be crucified, and they could only talk about themselves. Their world was about to come crashing down, and they could only— with carnal self-centeredness—talk about personal greatness. Which disciple used what argument to declare he was greater than the others?

Jesus demonstrated unusual restraint and patience with these men. This was their last meal together and the last opportunity He had to speak eternal truth into their lives before His crucifixion. Their insensitivity opened the door for a final bit of teaching from Jesus about the meaning of greatness. It is sad that they were in the presence of greatness and seemed to not recognize it. So with gentleness, not apparent irritation, He told them that greatness is not found in lording it over other people. **Instead, the greatest among you should be like the youngest, and the one who rules like the one who serves** (22:26). In Jewish culture, the oldest son always took prominence and received the family blessing. Greatness is not the result of birth order, blessing, or access to control. Rather, greatness is found in losing oneself in meaningful service.

Jesus elevated servanthood to a higher level of greatness than that of ruling over others. He is Lord by essential being, but He voluntarily took upon himself the "very nature of a servant" (Phil. 2:7). He declared His mission to be one of serving: "The Son of Man did not come to be served, but to serve" (Matt. 20:28). But when given the opportunity, human nature gravitates away from servanthood toward lordship, away from serving to being served, because our culture correlates greatness with authority and being served. In fact, Jesus acknowledged cultural greatness when He asked, **"Who is greater, the one who is at the table or the one who serves? Is it not the one who is at the table?"** (Luke 22:27).

There is appropriate honor and respect that should be shown persons of status and position. But Jesus demonstrated greater greatness through His word and action: **"But I am among you as one who serves"** (22:27). True greatness is not found in one who has legitimate power and position but in one who voluntarily seeks a place of service. If you seek a place, let it be a place to serve,

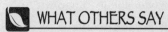

WHAT OTHERS SAY

OBEDIENCE

"In the house of everyone of us there is a drawer full of things which can only be called junk, and yet we will not throw them out; we cannot make ourselves do so, because when we touch and handle, and look at them, they bring back to us this or that person, or this or that occasion. They are common things, but they have a meaning far beyond themselves. That is a sacrament."

—William Barclay

not a place where you can leverage power and control others. The line of those applying to be servants is usually quite a bit shorter than those applying for prominent positions of prestige, power, and authority.

Not all greatness is to be found in the kingdoms of this world. To the Twelve who stood by Him through His ministry Jesus said, **"I confer on you a kingdom, just as my Father conferred one on me"** (22:29). William Barclay wrote, "Those who have shared in the bearing of Christ's cross will some day share in the wearing of Christ's crown."[4] Kingdom seekers have waged wars to *conquer* kingdoms, but Jesus *confers* kingdoms upon His faithful followers. In God's kingdom, positions are granted on the basis of character and conduct, not on the basis of conquering and controlling.

WORDS OF WARNING AND HOPE TO A CLOSE FRIEND

Simon Peter was one of the first to leave everything to follow Christ. He, along with James and John, made up an inner circle of Jesus' close friends. Simon was deeply committed, but he was impetuous and tended to have a bit of brashness in his speech, sometimes talking before he thought and speaking before he knew all the facts. Jesus loved him, so when He spoke to Simon it was not in harsh accusation, but rather in loving warning. **"Simon, Simon, Satan has asked to sift you as wheat"** (22:31). Jesus knew what was about to happen to Simon—Simon did not. Simon was his name when he first came to Jesus, who gave him the name *Peter*, which means "rock." Sensing his vulnerability as he faced the threshing floor, Jesus used his preconversion name *Simon* rather than the name *Peter*. He had the capacity to be more like chaff than a rock.

Sometimes it is good that we do not know what is coming at us in the future or we might give up before we even get there. However, there are times when it can be lifesaving to be put on alert so we can be extra diligent and make extra preparation. Driving through life with no warning or stop signs can be catastrophic, and Simon needed Jesus to warn him about what was around the next bend in the road. Satan had asked to attack him. As active and sinister as Satan may appear, he is not all powerful and cannot act where God prohibits, as the story of Job demonstrates (Job 1–2). He planned to sift Simon as wheat, which would be a clear illustration in that day. The kernels of wheat, still lodged in the heads and attached to the straw, would be beaten on the threshing floor and tossed in the air so the wind could blow away the chaff, leaving the wheat. Satan planned to shake Peter's life and separate him from his faith.

What Simon could look forward to was grim, however Jesus said, **"But."** That is a conjunction that has the capacity of reversing the outcome. Jesus continued: **"I have prayed for you"** (Luke 22:32). It is encouraging to have people tell us they are praying for us. The boost to our spirit is important, but more important is their contact with the Almighty on our behalf. Some things are only possible through prayer, and sometimes we are unable to adequately pray for ourselves. Jesus, God's Son, who has unique knowledge of the Father and access to Him, said to Simon, "I have prayed for you." Satan's attack would be furious, but Jesus was praying. We are assured in John 17 that Jesus prays for us as well. It is a part of His intercessory ministry while He is in heaven and we are on earth.

Jesus told Simon He was praying **"that your faith may not fail"** (22:32). The greatest attack by Satan does not predetermine failure. Jude pointed us to the Lord who has unlimited glory, majesty, power, and authority, and gave us this wonderful benediction: "To him who is able to keep you from falling and to present you before his glorious presence without fault and with great joy" (Jude 24). The apostle John wrote that the children of God overcome every evil spirit that comes against them "because the one who is in you is greater than the one who is in the world" (1 John 4:4).

Jesus knew Simon would suffer a moment of failure, but that he would find his way back to a place of restored relationship and strengthened faith. He told Simon, **"When you have turned back, strengthen your brothers"** (Luke 22:32). Amazingly, God in His great mercy restores those who return to Him, and He has the ability to weave our failures into the fabric of our fully restored lives in such a way that we can help others be strengthened. Often, those who have been through great trial have a capacity for understanding and helping others who go through the same trial. There is a sense in which redeemed persons can "redeem themselves," in terms of accepting forgiveness for their failure, by strengthening others where they themselves were broken.

Peter seems always to have been slow to grasp his weaknesses but quick to speak of his commitment. His quick reply to Jesus was, **"Lord, I am ready to go with you to prison and to death"** (22:33). He was not a surface follower or a person of shallow faith, so you have to believe he meant it. "Peter fell to a temptation which could only

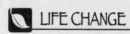

LIFE CHANGE

STRONGER IN THE BROKEN PLACES

God's grace allows Him to restore those who fall and fail in moments of weakness. His restoration power can heal the resulting brokenness and make those who fall strong again—even stronger in their broken places. God can transform our failures into showplaces for His redeeming and restoring power.

have come to a brave man."[5] Paul confessed there were times, while living with a "carnal mind," that the things he said he would never do he ended up doing, and the things that he said he would do he ended up not doing (Rom. 7). Peter's resolve was strong, but his will would prove to be weak. He would be given another opportunity in the garden to pray that he not fall into temptation, and another warning from Jesus that "the spirit is willing but the flesh is weak" (Matt. 26:1). But he would sleep through that opportunity.

In spite of Peter's readiness to die for Christ, Jesus told him that soon, before the rooster crowed, he would **deny three times** (Luke 22:34) that he even knew Him. How could it be that a person so close to Christ, and so committed to the kingdom of God, could feel the need to say he did not even know Jesus? What pressure could be so great to cause him to deny the One for whom he had such love? It may not be the strength of the pressure as much as the weakness of the will that gives Satan his advantage. Peter would soon succumb to the pressure and be forever haunted by the sound of a rooster crowing.

YOU NEED A SWORD

The last words with His disciples were rather strange ones. It was the final time Jesus had to prepare them for what lay ahead, and He asked if they had ever lacked for anything while they were involved in ministry with Him. They replied that they never lacked—He had provided for them, though they went out **without purse, bag or sandals** (22:35). To which Jesus replied that they were going to be facing a different day, and if they had a purse and a bag they needed to take it. Then He added, **"If you don't have a sword, sell your cloak and buy one"** (22:36). He was not advocating a radical departure from all He had taught them about how to respond to enemies. Rather, He was telling them they would be caught up in the conflict that would surround Him, and though the sword was not to be used in aggression, there might be a time they would need it for self-defense. Their swords would need to be more spiritual than literal (Eph. 6:17). The **disciples** took the words literally and told Jesus that they had **two swords**, which He said were **enough** (Luke 22:38).

What had been written about the Lamb of God was being fulfilled. He began His ministry after reading from Isaiah and declaring that the words were fulfilled in Him. Jesus reached back again to the writing of the prophet Isaiah about the suffering Savior being **"numbered with the transgressors"** and said, **"What is written about me is reaching its fulfillment"** (22:37). Within a matter of hours, hundreds of years of prophecy would find their fulfillment in His sacrifice. Abraham, Isaiah, Moses, and Elijah must have caught their breath as they watched from heaven, and all of history held its breath as the Son of God walked out of the Upper Room to complete His earthly destiny.

The time for eating and talking was over. It was now time for the action to begin that would lead to the great event of atonement.

1. Ralph Earle, *The Wesleyan Bible Commentary: The Gospel of Luke* (Grand Rapids, Mich.: Eerdmans, 1964), p. 332.

2. Rob Staples. *Outward Sign and Inward Grace.* (Kansas City: Beacon Hill Press, 1991), pp. 212–225.

3. Ibid.

4. William Barclay, *The Gospel of Luke* (Philadelphia: Westminster, 1956), p. 280.

5. Ibid., p. 282.

23

THE GARDEN REVISITED

Luke 22:39-53

Frequent visits by Jesus to the Mount of Olives and the Garden of Gethsemane made it a sacred place. He went there to pray, to renew himself after days of exhausting ministry, and to talk with His Father about His mission. On this night, this sacred place would be shrouded in a darkness deeper than any other night. The only light that would pierce the darkness would be the light of torches carried by those bent on taking the life of Jesus. And a betraying kiss would be reflected in that flickering torchlight.

1. PRAYER IN THE GARDEN (22:39-46)

After arriving in Jerusalem, Jesus spent each day "teaching at the temple, and each evening He went out to spend the night on the hill called the Mount of Olives" (21:37). On this eventful evening, **Jesus went out as usual to the Mount of Olives, and his disciples followed him** (22:39). According to Acts 1:12, the Mount of Olives was about "a sabbath day's journey" (two thousand cubits or roughly one thousand yards) east across the Kidron Valley from Jerusalem. It is associated with some of the most important events in Jesus' life. It was here that Jesus foretold the destruction of Jerusalem (Matt. 24:3), taught His disciples the Lord's Prayer, wept over Jerusalem on His way to the Holy City (19:37), and ascended to heaven. Matthew (26:36) and Mark (14:32) say it was in a special grove of olive trees, the Garden of Gethsemane (meaning "oil press"), where Jesus went on that Mount.

Both Matthew and Mark record that the meal came to an end in the Upper Room, and "after they had sung a hymn," they went out to the Mount of Olives (Matt. 26:30; Mark 14:26). Was it a joyful song or one of serious reflection? What was the procession like that made its way to the Mount of Olives? Were they quietly reflecting on what the talk around the table meant? Did anything sink into their consciousness about the unfolding drama that would soon surround them?

When they reached the garden, Jesus said to them, **"Pray that you will not fall into temptation"** (Luke 22:40). Jesus knew what was about to happen, they did not. The best help He could be to them was not to protect them from temptation, but to encourage them to pray. Prayer was to prepare them for tomorrow's victory over temptation. We never know what lurks around the corner in our lives. Our road may lead us through places of temptation, but prayer can be one of the means of keeping us from falling.

Jesus left the disciples to pray for their own needs while He walked on alone and **knelt down and prayed** (22:41) for what He was about to face. It is wonderful when others will pray with you and for you, but there are times when you must walk on alone. Prayer was a pattern of His life. He prayed prior to major events, not only after suffering a crisis. The fact that He knew what lay ahead was all the more reason for Him to spend time with His Father. We cannot overhear all of His prayer, but the Gospels tell us the heart of it: **"Father, if you are willing, take this cup from me; yet not my will, but yours be done"** (22:42). This is not a picture of a reluctant Savior, but of a God-man who knew full well the cost of being a Savior. The agony of His soul was reaching its crescendo. The cup from which He would have to drink was not just death or physical suffering or rejection by the masses. He knew that to carry the sin of the world He must endure separation from the Father. There was no other way. He was fully submissive to His Father's will.

While He agonized in prayer, **an angel from heaven appeared to him and strengthened him** (22:43). Heaven came close as Jesus agonized in prayer with His Father. Three years earlier, when the temptation He experienced from Satan came to an end, "the devil left him, and angels came and attended him" (Matt. 4:11). He was strengthened, yet anticipated what would transpire in the next few hours. **Being in anguish, he prayed more**

earnestly, and his sweat was like drops of blood falling to the ground (Luke 22:44). The suffering of Jesus began before He was nailed to the cross. The word *anguish* suggests tremendous emotional wrestling, which was so intense that even His sweat was like drops of blood falling from His brow. Whether by angels or the Spirit of God, we also are ministered to in times of personal crisis.

The disciples were oblivious to the agony Jesus was suffering. He returned to them and **found them asleep, exhausted from sorrow** (22:45). There was good reason, physically and emotionally, for them to be sleepy, but in extraordinary times sleep becomes a secondary need, and this was one of those times. They perceived enough of what was happening to be in sorrow, but unlike Jesus they did not fully understand what they would soon be experiencing. He encouraged them again: **"Get up and pray so that you will not fall into temptation"** (22:46). We are particularly susceptible to temptation when physically and emotionally exhausted. Matthew's record says this interaction between Jesus and His disciples was repeated three times. The word

LIFE CHANGE

FACING TEMPTATION

The fact that we are disciples of Christ does not mean we will have protection from the enemy's schemes, but it does mean that we have access to adequate preparation to prevent us from falling.

translated *temptation* is the same word used for Jesus' encounter with Satan in Luke 4:13, and again when Jesus taught His disciples to pray, "Lead us not into temptation, but deliver us from evil" (11:4). The path toward deliverance from evil passes through the practice of prayer. Prayer prepares and strengthens the spirit while it cultivates relationship with the Father, in whose presence the attractiveness of temptation fades.

2. BETRAYED WITH A KISS (22:47–48)

The encouragement to pray while there was time, was interrupted by a **crowd** led by **Judas, one of the Twelve** (22:47). Satan had entered Judas, who by this time had struck his deal with the chief priests for thirty pieces of silver and "watched for an opportunity to hand Jesus over to them when no crowd was present" (22:3–6). Judas left during the meal in the Upper Room (John 13:30) to cut his deal and then anticipated Jesus would go to the garden, as was His practice. He gathered the henchmen and led them to Jesus. Our behavior can often be governed by the crowd with which we run. What Judas would not do when the crowd of Jesus' followers was present, he would do now when in a crowd of Jesus' opponents.

In certain parts of the world, a kiss was and still is a traditional greeting among men.[2] Judas **approached Jesus to kiss him** (Luke 22:47), using this indication of friendship to identify Jesus to His enemies. One of the greatest hurts in life is to have someone pretend to be your friend, only to exploit your friendship and betray you.

3. A LAST HEALING (22:49–53)

THE BEGINNING OF THE REIGN OF DARKNESS

The drowsy disciples snapped out of their sleepiness when the mob showed up. The threat of the crowd brought greater concern to them than the threat of temptation. The protection they failed to seek through prayer, they would now try to accomplish with their swords. **When Jesus' followers saw what was going to happen, they said, "Lord, should we strike with our swords?"** (22:49). This question takes us back to the exchange just prior to going to the garden, when Jesus told them that if they didn't have a sword they should "sell your cloak and buy one." Jesus was not encouraging combat and the use of weapons, but He was informing them that the struggles they would face would intensify, and they would be fighting for their lives. There is no evidence that they were accustomed to carrying swords, but they must have had two in their possession this night. The disciples sensed what was about to happen, and they were prepared to use the swords to defend themselves and their Lord.

One of them struck the servant of the high priest, cutting off his right ear (22:50). John identified this person—not surprisingly—as being Peter (John 18:10). He had said he would be willing to die for

Christ and this just could be his time. Fortunately for the victim, Peter was not skilled in sword-swinging and had poor aim. The servant lost an ear, but he could have lost his head. Peter was a man of action. Sometimes he was impulsive in his action, but no one could say he did not love his Lord as he stood against the crowd.

Jesus was not **leading a rebellion**. The crowd did not have to **come** after Him **with swords and clubs** (Luke 22:52), and He would not defend himself with violence. To His followers He said, **"No more of this!"** (52:51). Jesus had taught His followers to love their enemies and to bless those who despitefully used them. In this moment of personal agony, He thought of others, even His enemies. **He touched the man's ear and healed him** (22:51). The last recorded miracle of Jesus was that of healing the severed ear of one of His enemies.

Fully submissive to the will of God and the unfolding plan of salvation, He said to the mob, **"This is your hour—when darkness reigns"** (22:53). The night was dark, but it was destined to grow darker. There is no darkness greater than that which surrounds sin. Soon even the sun would cease to shine as the deeds of sinful humanity reached their darkest. Satan is the prince of darkness, and at least for the moment, he appeared to be in charge. This was *his* hour, and for but this short time he would have his way with Jesus.

THE LAMB IS LED TO THE SLAUGHTER

Seizing him, they led him away (22:54). Isaiah's prophecy was being fulfilled as Jesus "was led like a lamb to the slaughter" (Isa. 53:7).

If you look at the people in the garden that night, you might find yourself. There were those who slept when they should have prayed. There was Judas, who was willing to sell out his Master for a few coins. There were religious leaders who had lost the meaning of being a child of God. There was Peter, who was committed, but weak under pressure. There was a wounded servant who had experienced a touch of mercy and would not know what to do about it. And there was Jesus, submissive to the will of God though knowing the cost would be tremendous. Do you see yourself somewhere in the garden that night?

ENDNOTES

1. *Life Application Bible: The Living Bible*. Wheaton: Tyndale House Publishers. 1989. p. 220.

24

COURAGE OR COWARDICE

Luke 22:54-71; 23:1-25

Occasions come when we choose whether we will stand courageously for truth and righteousness or cowardly bow before that which is false and unjust. Three people in this section of Luke's record were faced with an opportunity to be courageous, but each caved when pressed to declare their faith or stand up for justice. Simon Peter's bravado turned to mush when challenged by a young girl. Both Pilate and Herod found the power of their positions manipulated by the pressure of the crowd.

1. PETER'S DENIAL (22:54-62)

Luke identified the arresting mob as the "chief priests, the officers of the temple guard, and the elders" (Luke 22:52). Under their control, a late-night trek began from one jurisdiction to another in an attempt to get someone to condemn Jesus. **Seizing him, they led him away and took him into the house of the high priest** (22:54). He was taken to the high priest, the council of the elders, Pilate, Herod, and back to Pilate again. In the middle of the night, the religious leaders dragged Jesus to the highest-ranking religious leader for condemnation, where they hoped they could trip him up in cross-examination as they had tried before.

No disciples walked with Jesus, but **Peter followed at a distance** (22:54). There is little need for us to condemn Peter for following **at a distance.** He demonstrated a bravery at this point that the other disciples did not. He mingled with the mob as it went to the house of the high priest. His problem was not that he followed at a distance, but that he tried to blend in. The mob **kindled a fire in the middle of the courtyard and had sat down together,** and **Peter sat down with them** (22:55). Three times Peter was identified as being a follower of Jesus, and each time he denied it. To **a servant girl** who **said, "This man was with him,"** he replied, **"Woman, I don't know him"** (22:56–57). The third denial had no more than escaped his lips than he heard a rooster crow. At the same time, **the Lord turned and looked straight at Peter** (22:61), and His look awakened Peter's memory of what Jesus had told him earlier in the evening: **"Before the rooster crows today, you will disown me three times"** (22:61, see verse 34). When Peter looked into the eyes of Jesus he must have seen more pain than accusation. William Barclay wrote, "The penalty of sin is to face, not the anger of Jesus, but the heartbreak in His eyes."[1] Once again Peter disappointed himself and demonstrated cowardice in the face of pressure. The tough, self-assured fisherman **went outside and wept bitterly** (22:62). It was time to be courageous, but he had demonstrated cowardice.

Under the pressure of being identified with Jesus, Peter denied that he had any acquaintance with or association with Him. Most likely, rather than verbally denying Jesus, we seek to separate ourselves from Him

---

LIFE CHANGE

CHRISTLIKENESS

Charles Spurgeon once said, "A Christian should be a striking likeness of Jesus Christ." William Secker said, "It would be well if there were as great a similarity between the life of Christ and the life of Chrstians as there is between a just copy and the original. What He was by nature, we should be by grace." Do you live enough like Jesus that you can be accused of being one of His followers?

by quietly blending in with those who oppose Him. Being lost in the comfort of the crowd is preferred to sharing in "the fellowship of his sufferings" (Phil. 3:10). Peter's denial is too often repeated by those who sit with the crowd rather than stand up and stand out for Jesus.

Each morning, as the roosters heralded the beginning of a new day, Peter would be reminded of his failure and the look of pain on the face of Jesus. How often do we bring pain to Jesus when we fail to identify ourselves with Him?

2. JESUS BEFORE THE COUNCIL OF ELDERS (22:63–71)

As the night went on, the crowd turned nasty. They **began mocking and beating** (22:63) Jesus and saying **insulting things to him** (22:65). The physical and emotional abuse had begun. **They blindfolded him and demanded, "Prophesy! Who hit you?"** (22:64). They taunted and insulted him. **At daybreak**, Jesus was taken from the high priest's house to a meeting with **the council of the elders of the people** (22:66). This council included **the chief priests and the teachers of the law** (22:66) and was known as the Sanhedrin, which was the supreme court of the Jews and would have authority over religious disputes. No criminal charges could be made against Jesus, so the accusers went straight to the only place of vulnerability—Jesus' claim of oneness with God the Father. **"If you are the Christ, . . . tell us"** (22:67). The name *Christ* means "Anointed One" and is the English translation of the Hebrew word for *Messiah*. Their question was not posed as a desire to come to the truth, but as a means of catching Jesus in the lie of claiming that He was the Messiah, the one for whom the Jews longed.

Jesus did not answer their question, but responded, **"From now on, the Son of Man will be seated at the right hand of the mighty God"** (22:69). A messianic psalm declares, "The LORD says to my Lord: 'Sit at my right hand until I make your enemies a footstool for your feet.' The LORD will extend your mighty scepter from Zion; you will rule in the midst of your enemies" (Ps. 110:1–2). The place at the right hand of God was reserved for the Chosen One, and even during what would be considered by many to be His defeat and destruction, Jesus knew He was on His journey back to the side of His Father. This world was only His temporary home made necessary by God's redemptive plan, but His rightful place was on the throne with His Father. Whatever they would do, they would not defeat or destroy Him. His destiny was a heavenly throne.

When asked if He was the Son of God, Jesus did not give a direct answer, but rather **replied, "You are right in saying I am"** (22:70). By saying "I am," Jesus used the name God told Moses he should use to identify Him to the Israelites: "I AM WHO I AM. This is what you are to say to the Israelites: 'I AM has sent me to you'" (Ex. 3:14). The religious leaders caught the significance of Jesus' words and found it enough to charge Jesus with blasphemy: claiming to be God, which under Jewish law was punishable by death. His death was what they wanted, but under Roman occupation they had no authority to kill Him. They would have to appeal to Roman authority.

3. TRIAL BEFORE PILATE AND HEROD (23:1–25)

OFF TO PILATE

Armed with the charge of blasphemy that had been witnessed by the Sanhedrin, **the whole assembly rose and led him off to Pilate** (Luke 23:1). Pilate was the Roman procurator, the administrative official with legal power in Judea. He was headquartered in Caesarea but would go to Jerusalem during Jewish feasts to help ensure there would be no uprisings against the Roman occupation. The accusers knew Pilate would not be interested in their religious charges against Jesus, so they had to make up some lies that would charge Him with a political crime. **They began to accuse him, saying, "We have found this man subverting our nation. He opposes payment of taxes to Caesar and claims to be Christ, a king"** (23:2), none of which was true. When He had been asked if it was right to pay taxes to Caesar, He had replied, "Give to Caesar what is Caesar's, and to God what is God's" (Luke 20:25), far from the false change of opposing the payment of taxes.

Pilate would have concern if Jesus were attempting to overthrow the government and establish a new kingdom. So he asked Jesus if He was **the king of the Jews**. Jesus' response, **"It is as you say"** (23:3), was vague enough that Pilate did not see Him as a threat to Rome, and he announced to the crowd, **"I find no basis for a charge against this man"** (23:4). Pilate was brave enough to declare the innocence of Jesus, but not brave enough to release Him and face up to the crowd that insisted Jesus be condemned and crucified.

SENT TO HEROD

Galilee was under the jurisdiction of Herod, and when Pilate learned that Jesus was from Galilee, **he sent him to Herod, who was also in Jerusalem at that time** (23:7), This was a convenient way out for Pilate, who did not want to be responsible for an injustice, but neither did he want to offend the Jewish leaders. Herod had heard about Jesus, and **he had been wanting to see him . . . he hoped to see him perform some miracle** (23:8). He viewed Jesus as a joke, someone who could provide him with some amusement.

Herod got no response from Jesus when he asked Him questions. Herod may have had judicial authority over portions of Israel, but he did not have authority over the Son of God, so Jesus kept silent before him. Meanwhile, **the chief priests and the teachers of the law were standing there, vehemently accusing him** (23:10). Herod was caught between a silent defendant and shouting accusers.

Herod realized he had no grounds for convicting Jesus, so he **sent him back to Pilate** (23:11). But before doing so, he dressed **him in an elegant robe,** and he **and his soldiers ridiculed and mocked him** (23:11). Pilate's cowardice was matched by Herod's uncivilized mockery of an innocent man—two men with political and positional power, but with no moral conscience or commitment to justice.

BACK TO PILATE

Jesus taught His followers to turn enemies into friends through prayer, loving acceptance, and forgiveness. But sin has the power to turn enemies into friends, too, as partners in crime form unlikely alliances to protect themselves. Forced to deal with the mob that was bent on getting false charges against Jesus to stick, Herod and Pilate found themselves forged into an unlikely alliance. **That day Herod and Pilate became friends—before this they had been enemies** (23:12). Jesus was taken from Herod, who found no grounds for conviction, to a second appearance before Pilate, who again announced to the crowd, **"I have examined him in your presence and have found no basis for your charges against him"** (23:14). Though Jesus had **done nothing to deserve death** (23:15), in an effort to appease the crowd's thirst for blood, Pilate said, **"I will punish him and then release him"** (23:16). Without sufficient charge against the defendant, any punishment by Pilate was unjust and unlawful.

In the eye of Roman justice and Jewish law, Jesus had done nothing to deserve death. More importantly, in the eye of God's law, He had done nothing to deserve death. It was that innocence that made His sacrifice effective for the forgiveness of our sin. "God made him who had no sin to be sin for us, so that in him we might become the righteousness of God" (2 Cor. 5:21).

SWAYED BY THE MOB

The mob would not be appeased with some symbolic punishment. They were bent on seeing Jesus permanently eliminated. Their cry for His crucifixion became mixed with their cry for **Barabbas** (23:18) to be released to them. Matthew's gospel adds, "It was the governor's custom at the Feast to release a prisoner chosen by the crowd, and a notorious prisoner, called Barabbas, was held in custody (Matt. 27:15–16). No doubt, Pilate thought that given the choice between an innocent citizen and a notorious prisoner who **had been thrown into prison for an insurrection in the city, and for murder** (Luke 23:19), the crowd would choose to release Jesus. After all, Barabbas was a threat to society, but Jesus had only gone about doing good. Pilate really wanted to **release Jesus,** but rather than exercise his authority in the matter, he repeatedly **appealed** to the noisy crowd. **But they kept shouting, "Crucify him! Crucify him!"** (23:20). Perhaps Pilate did not want to have a riot in Jerusalem on his record, so he **decided to grant their demand** and **surrendered Jesus to their will** (23:25). **Their shouts prevailed** (23:23).

Dark days call for men and women of moral courage. Before we condemn the cowardice of Peter, Pilate, or Herod, we need to check how courageous we are in declaring our faith in Jesus Christ and in standing up for truth and righteousness.

ENDNOTES

1. William Barclay, *The Gospel of Luke* (Philadelphia: Westminster, 1956), p. 282.

25

MISSON ACCOMPLISHED

Luke 23:26–56

E very human inherits the results of Adam's sin and therefore is destined to experience the universal penalty for sin—death. Because Jesus took upon himself the likeness of human flesh (Phil. 2:7), He was born to die not because He had sinned but because we had. His death was a *sacrifice*; it was purposefully offered on our behalf. His death was *substitutionary*; He assumed our punishment. His death was *satisfactory*; it fully met the judicial demands of God and allowed Him to justify humankind. His death was *sufficient*; His one-time sacrifice fully satisfied the penalty for all sin for any repentant sinner for all time. It is called the Atonement.

1. ON THE WAY TO THE CROSS (26:26–31)

With the messy work of getting the conviction of an innocent man completed, the mob **led him away** (Luke 23:26). In reality, the King of Kings *allowed* himself to be led away. Matthew recorded that when He was arrested in the garden, Jesus said, "Do you think I cannot call on my Father, and he will at once put at my disposal more than twelve legions of angels? But how then would the Scriptures be fulfilled that say it must happen in this way?" (Matt. 26:53–54). All power in heaven and earth had been vested in Him, but He submitted himself into the hands of those who would have their will with Him, because He was committed to a redemptive mission that required Him to die.

They led Him through the streets of Jerusalem toward the place of crucifixion outside the city gates. Tradition has identified a street in the Old City of Jerusalem as Via Dolorosa, Latin for "Way of Grief." It was customary for criminals to carry their cross to the place of their execution, enduring the physical demands on their body because of its weight, while also enduring the verbal and physical abuse of the taunting crowds that accompanied them.

The Roman cross traditionally consisted of two pieces: the center timber that was permanently set in the ground at the place of crucifixion, and the crossbar that was carried to the site by the victim. Jesus was weakened by the beatings He had endured, and He struggled under the weight of the cross. **They seized Simon from Cyrene, who was on his way in from the country, and put the cross on him and made him carry it behind Jesus** (23:26). Simon was probably a Jewish pilgrim on his way into Jerusalem to celebrate Passover week. Cyrene was a Greek colony in what is now Libya, in Northern Africa. If Simon was on his way into Jerusalem, he probably had not heard of the events surrounding the trial of Jesus and may not have been aware of the man whose cross he carried. Picked arbitrarily out of a crowd, he had the dubious honor of carrying the instrument of death to the place of crucifixion.

Our ordinary days can quickly be interrupted and transformed into moments that forever change the direction of our lives. Crosses can be thrust upon us that we did not ask for and for which we are unprepared. Sometimes these are divine interruptions when we are brought shoulder to shoulder with Jesus and given opportunity to identify with Him and participate in redemptive activity. Some think that this chance encounter between Simon and Jesus became the means of his salvation. Whether or not this is true, grace provides similar moments for us to come close to Jesus and to join Him in His mission of bringing salvation to everyone.

Mingled with the taunts of the soldiers and the shouts of those who wanted Jesus crucified, were sounds of sorrow from those who loved Jesus. **A large number of people followed him, including women who mourned and wailed for him** (23:27). Hearing them, Jesus told them not to weep for Him, but for themselves and their children. He knew that catastrophic days were ahead when the Romans would destroy the Temple and the city of Jerusalem.

2. HE COULD NOT SAVE HIMSELF (23:32–38)

Jesus was crucified along with **two other men, both criminals,** who **were also led out with him to be executed** (23:32). Jesus was about to carry the sins of the world to the cross, joined by two common criminals, thereby fulfilling the words of the prophet Isaiah that the suffering Savior "was numbered with the transgressors" (Isa. 53:12). The procession ended at Golgotha (Matt. 27:33), **the place called the Skull** (Luke 23:33).

Calvary (Golgotha) is the English name given to the hill outside Jerusalem on which Jesus was crucified. The New Testament describes Calvary as close to Jerusalem (John 19:20) and outside its walls (Heb. 13:12). Tradition has marked the place of crucifixion by the construction of the Church of the Holy Sepulcher, inside the city wall and near the Damascus Gate. In the late 1800's, Charles George Gordon suggested a different site outside the city wall, on top of a hill that carries features that make it look like a skull. Nearby is a beautiful, quiet garden with a tomb carved in the rock, which could be like the burial place of Jesus, though tradition would place it elsewhere.

There they crucified him (23:33). Jesus had already endured a scourging from a whip with pieces of metal or bone attached to several leather strands. He also was struck in the face numerous times, and His head was pierced with the thorns from a makeshift crown. He endured humiliation and pain, but nothing like He would experience through crucifixion. Roman crucifixion was a horrible and painful way to die. (We get our English word *excruciating* from this torturous death.) The victim would be forced to lie upon the wooden crossbeams while long spikes were driven through the wrists and feet. The weight of the body would often dislocate the shoulder and elbow joints, and the position of the body would make it extremely difficult to breathe, usually causing death by suffocation. To breathe, the victim was forced to push up on his feet to allow for inflation of the lungs. As the body weakened and pain in the feet and legs became unbearable, the victim was forced to trade breathing for pain and exhaustion. Roman crucifixion was designed to humiliate and mutilate before killing.

Jesus was crucified **along with the criminals—one on his right, the other on his left** (23:33). Three crosses occupied the hilltop: Jesus in the middle, surrounded by criminals. The cross was used for the worst of criminals, but Jesus transformed this instrument of shameful death into a symbol of hope and life. The cross still rises as a place for salvation from the sin that surrounds it.

 WHAT OTHERS SAY

SALVATION'S PLAN

"Anyone can devise a plan by which good people may go to heaven. Only God can devise a plan whereby sinners, who are His enemies, can go to Heaven."

—Lewis Sperry Chafer

The Gospels record seven "last words of Jesus." The first words from the cross recorded by Luke are **"Father, forgive them, for they do not know what they are doing"** (23:34). These words capture the spirit of Jesus, who, though suffering injustice and cruelty at the hands of evil persons, desired that His Father show them mercy and forgiveness. The apostle Peter captured the reaction of Jesus in the crucible of suffering when he wrote, "Christ suffered for you, leaving you an example, that you should follow in his steps. He committed no sin, and no deceit was found in his mouth. When they hurled their insults at him, he did not retaliate; when he suffered, he made no threats" (1 Pet. 2:21–23).

A circus atmosphere swirled around the cross. **The soldiers mocked him** (Luke 23:36) **. . . and divided up his clothes by casting lots** (23:34).

LAST WORDS OF JESUS ON THE CROSS

Luke 23:34	"Father, forgive them, for they do not know what they are doing."
Luke 23:43	"I tell you the truth, today you will be with me in paradise."
John 19:26–27	"Dear woman, here is your son. . . . Here is your mother."
Matt. 27:46b	"My God, my God, why have you forsaken me?"
John 19:28	"I am thirsty."
John 19:30	"It is finished."
Luke 23:46	"Father, into your hands I commit my spirit."

The rulers sneered at him. People stood around **watching** (23:35). When Jesus got thirsty, **they offered him wine vinegar** (23:36). Then someone started the taunt, **"Save yourself"** (23:35). The soldiers picked up the chant and said, **"If you are the king of the Jews, save yourself"** (23:37). Others shouted, **"He saved others; let him save himself if he is the Christ of God, the Chosen One"** (23:35). The criminal on one side of Jesus **hurled insults at him: "Aren't you the Christ? Save yourself and us!"** (23:39). If they had only known that He could not save them, or anyone, if He were to save himself. His mission held Him there. Saving himself was not on His mind, but saving you and me was. Nails did not hold Him on the cross; love for us did.

Jesus had told His disciples that moments come to us when, if we choose to save ourselves, we lose (9:24; 17:33). Moments come when our salvation, our ultimate purpose, is found in our willingness to lose our lives for something bigger than ourselves. This was one of those moments. Too often God's greater purpose for us is lost in our attempts to save ourselves. Jesus was willing to lose His life so He could save ours.

Above His head a sign was placed **which read: THIS IS THE KING OF THE JEWS** (23:38). John's gospel says, "the sign was written in Aramaic, Latin, and Greek" (John 19:20), since people from many places had come to Jerusalem for the Passover. Matthew and Mark's gospels say that this was "the written charge against him" (Matt. 27:37; Mark 15:26). Pilate had the sign made after questioning Jesus several times if He considered himself to be the king of the Jews. The chief priests wanted Pilate to change the sign to read "This man claimed to be king of the Jews," but he refused (John 19:21). The sign declaring Him to be a king hung there juxtaposed against the awfulness of the cross—divine royalty hanging between common criminals—kingdom authority submitting to earthly injustice.

3. A CRIMINAL IN PARADISE (23:39–43)

Evidently one of the criminals did not have enough of his own sin and shame to occupy his thoughts and cause him to regret his crimes. He felt he had to hurl insults at Jesus. The criminal on the other side of Jesus rebuked the thoughtless criminal: **"We are punished justly, for we are getting**

what our deeds deserve. But this man has done nothing wrong" (23:41). The innocent One was being punished for the guilty ones. If we got what we deserve, we would never see salvation. Mercy is God not giving us what we deserve. Grace is God giving us what we do not deserve. We have little to complain about when we receive just punishment. But justification is the wondrous blessing of salvation, when God looks at the charges against us, proclaims us to be guilty, but then forgives the act, wipes the record clean, and proclaims us to be without condemnation because of Christ's atonement. Our guilt is undeniable, but His innocence is imparted to us and determined by the Judge to adequately meet our need.

 KEY IDEA

What Happens When You Die?

The Scripture basically uses three words to describe the state of the dead: *Sheol*, which refers to a state or place of the dead, sometimes with the element of misery; *Hades*, which refers to the invisible world of departed spirits; and *Paradise*, which refers to a park or garden. The Scriptures teach us that:

At death the souls of the righteous go immediately into the presence of Christ and of God.

At death the souls of the wicked are banished from the presence of the Lord.

The souls of the departed exist in a state of consciousness.

The righteous dead are in a state of blessedness and rest.

The wicked dead are in a state of suffering and unrest.

The intermediate state following death is not the final state of believers.

The second criminal acted on what little he had come to know about the Man on the center cross. He said, **"Jesus, remember me when you come into your kingdom"** (23:42). His knowledge may have been incomplete, but he knew he was in the presence of the King. He knew he was about to die, and he wasn't ready. There must have been enough saving faith in his heart, because **Jesus answered him, "I tell you the truth, today you will be with me in paradise"** (23:43). He didn't have opportunity to "go forward" at an altar call. He didn't have time to be baptized, take Communion, learn the Apostles' Creed, or study the Bible. His was a "deathbed conversion" that was acknowledged by Jesus as being genuine and acceptable. He did nothing to deserve it, but he went from a sinner's cross to the arms of God in a moment.

There is hope for those who are yet outside of the kingdom of God, regardless of age or circumstance. As long as there is ability to turn to Jesus in faith, there is hope of salvation. While this is true, what a waste of life it is to wait so long. And delay is a risk no one should calculate to take. Mercy and grace cannot be casually tried or held off for "a more convenient" time.

The criminal did not have to go to some probationary place such as purgatory. He would go straight to paradise. His soul would not go into a sleep mode to be awakened at some later day of resurrection. That very day he would be with Jesus.

Three crosses dominated the Jerusalem skyline that day. The Man on the center cross died *for* sin. The man on the left died *in* sin. The man on the right died *to* sin. One died to pay the *penalty* for sin. One died, *pardoned* from his sin. One died as a *punishment* for his sins. The cross in the center is the hope and provider of salvation. The crosses on either side represent the only two responses that are possible: to accept and be saved, or to reject and be lost.

4. JESUS' DEATH AND BURIAL (23:44–56)

THE SUN STOPPED SHINING

John recorded the meeting with Pilate as occurring during "early morning" (John 18:28). Mark has Jesus on the cross at "the third hour," or 9:00 A.M. Luke says that three hours later, at **about the sixth hour, darkness came over the whole land until the ninth hour, for the sun stopped shining** (Luke 23:44–45). For three hours, during the midday when the sun should be at its brightest, it stopped shining. The prophet proclaimed that "the sun of righteousness will rise with healing in its wings" (Mal. 4:2), but before the Son could shine, the sun stopped shining. Darkness covered the Calvary scene. Sin was being carried to the cross, and it was as if God himself could not look upon its awfulness.

Something wondrously symbolic occurred in the middle of the darkness—the **curtain of the temple was torn in two** (Luke 23:45). A large curtain separated the Holy of Holies from the rest of the Temple. The ark of the covenant with its mercy seat was in the Holy of Holies where only the high priest, on one day each year, the Day of Atonement, could part the curtain and enter. Mark said it was at the point of Jesus' death that the curtain of the Temple was torn and adds that the tear went "from top to bottom" (Mark 15:38). The Great High Priest had entered into the Holy of Holies and opened it up for access to the presence of God through His torn body. It was not as if the curtain were torn from its bottom by human hands, but as if God reached down and ripped it open from its top. The writer to the Hebrews wrote, "We have confidence to enter the Most Holy Place by the blood of Jesus, by a new and living way opened for us through the curtain, that is, his body, and since we have a great priest over the house of God" (Heb. 10:19–21). We can enter where no unworthy person could ever think of entering, because our Savior is also our High Priest.

The last words of Jesus on the cross were directed upward: **"Father, into your hands I commit my spirit." When he had said this, he breathed his last** (Luke 23:46). The physical suffering and the spiritual agony was over. The dastardly deed of His enemies had accomplished its evil intent, but they did not understand the blessing they had released upon humanity. They would never know that the cruel instrument of death upon which they hung Christ would forever become a cherished symbol for throngs of people who would be redeemed by the blood of the Lamb. His last breath secured new life for those who claim His death as taking the place of their own.

Two people entered paradise that day: Jesus and the criminal who would soon join Him. Perhaps another conversion took place that day, for Luke said that **the centurion, seeing what had happened, praised God and said, "Surely this was a righteous man"** (23:47). At least the events of the day caused him to acknowledge God and to see the righteousness of Christ. At least he was confronted with an opportunity to see, hear, and believe. Others had equal opportunity, but of the crowds it says, **When all the people who had gathered to witness this sight saw what took place, they beat their breasts and went away** (23:48). They went away, turning their backs to the cross and the Savior. It is reminiscent of the rich young man of whom it was written, "he went away sad, because he had great wealth" (Matt. 19:22).

The cross will always stand at the crossroads of life where some are drawn to the love and forgiveness of the Savior who died there, and some go away. Jesus accomplished His mission. He did what only He could do to make salvation possible. Now it is up to us to respond.

JOSEPH OF ARIMATHEA

Often at Roman crucifixions, the dead were left for the birds and animals to feed on the decaying flesh; another indignity that accompanied death on a cross. **A man named Joseph** (Luke 23:50) was sympathetic to Jesus and was moved to go **to Pilate** to ask **for Jesus' body** (23:52). Joseph was **a member of the Council, a good and upright man, who had not consented to their decision and action** (23:51–51). He was a man of influence and evident wealth. **He came from the Judean town of Arimathea and he was waiting for the kingdom of God** (23:51). Joseph was a

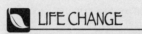

LIFE CHANGE

SECRET DISCIPLE

Someone once asked the challenging question: If you were on trial for being a Christian, would there be enough evidence to convict you? Perhaps a more challenging question might be: Are you open enough about being a Christian that anyone would be suspicious that you are one? It is hard to love God and never talk about Him. It is hard to be committed to Christ and not walk like Him. It is hard to have the joy of Jesus in your heart and not let it leak out somewhere. This secret has to get out.

sympathizer and one who was waiting for the kingdom of God. John's gospel says "Joseph was a disciple of Jesus, but secretly because he feared the Jews" (John 19:38). He was a leader of the Jews, yet afraid of them and afraid of the possible negative results of being open about his commitment to Christ. Joseph is certainly not a positive model of committed discipleship, but perhaps he redeemed himself when he risked his reputation and life in providing tenderness and respect to the body of Jesus. **He took it down** and **wrapped it in linen cloth** (23:53), stepping forward at a time when others ran away. He took the body **and placed it**

in a tomb cut in the rock, one in which no one had yet been laid (23:53). Most likely, this was a small room-like hole cut in the limestone hills outside Jerusalem. The opening into the burial chamber would be covered by a large stone.

It was Preparation Day, and the Sabbath was about to begin (23:54). Preparation Day was the day before observing Passover Day, and the lateness of the hour would not have permitted Joseph to fully prepare the body of Jesus for burial, but he did what he could. The Sabbath would begin at sundown, and the Sabbath law would not permit a Jew to carry a body to its burial place. **The women who had come with Jesus from Galilee followed Joseph and saw the tomb and how his body was laid in it. Then they went home and prepared spices and perfumes** (23:55–56). The women could not come back the next day, the Sabbath, to complete the embalming, but they got everything ready so they could do it on the first day of the week.

It is hard to look at the events of this day and see the hand of God in them. Evil men had their way with the Son of God. The One who promised life died. The life of the King was brutally ended before He could come into His kingdom. There was nothing left to do by those who believed in Him but to complete His burial, and by doing so they would bury their hopes for a redeemer. As darkness settled around the souls of disappointed and disillusioned disciples, it signaled a mission accomplished by the Lamb of God who takes away the sin of the whole world (John 1:29). The followers of Jesus would live in the shadow of death for days before seeing the light of that accomplished mission.

26

THE END OR
THE BEGINNING

Luke 24:1–53

L ife's events sometimes seem to destroy our best hopes and bring an end to our greatest aspirations. However, what we consider to be an end to our dreams may really be necessary for God to establish a new beginning. Such was the case with the disciples who had just witnessed the death of their Master and the dashing of any hope that He might be the Messiah. Their hope had been so strong, but their world quickly came crashing in with the crucifixion. Jesus was dead and buried. Three years of work had come to an end.

However, what appeared to be the end was the beginning of something they would have difficulty comprehending. As close as they had been to Jesus, there was so much they did not understand. There were so many things He had told them they were unable to connect with the whirlwind of events that enveloped them.

The final chapter of the Gospel of Luke is full of drama and runs the gamut of human emotion. It begins in sadness and mourning, only to end with joyfulness and praising. It begins with a wake and ends with worship. It begins with the end of Jesus' earthly ministry and ends with the beginning of a new mission assignment given to the disciples.

The great event that changed a devastating end into a dynamic beginning was the resurrection. Not only did it prove the divinity of Christ, it dramatically fueled the disciples for carrying on the redemptive mission of Jesus in the power of the Holy Spirit.

1. WOMEN FIND AN EMPTY TOMB (24:1–8)

Jesus died just before sundown on Friday, so the customary embalming could not be done due to the approaching Sabbath, which began at sundown Friday and lasted until sundown Saturday. **On the first day of the week**, a day and a half later, **the women took the spices they had prepared and went to the tomb** (24:1). Joseph of Arimathea had "wrapped [the body of Jesus] in linen cloth" (23:53), and the women had followed him to the burial place before going home to prepare the spices and perfumes to finish the burial customs (23:55–56).

The dead were often placed in cave-like tombs carved out of the rocks with a large stone rolled over the entrance to seal it. The women knew there was a stone covering the entrance to the tomb that was too large for them to move. The Gospel of Mark indicates they raised the question, "Who will roll the stone away from the entrance of the tomb?" (Mark 16:3). Whether or not they verbalized the question, surely they must have considered the obstacle that stood in the way of their final act of respect and adoration of their Lord—an obstacle they must have believed would be cared for one way or another. How often we do not initiate things our hearts tell us to do when our heads remind us of all of the obstacles. They acted without having all the problems solved first.

When the women arrived, **they found the stone rolled away from the tomb** (Luke 24:2). Matthew's gospel indicates that a violent earthquake moved the stone (Matt. 28:2). Luke was less concerned about how the stone was moved as he was with what the open tomb revealed. With the obstacle removed, the women entered but **they did not find the body of the Lord Jesus** (Luke 24:3). They had seen the body placed in the tomb, so why would it now be gone? Did someone move it? Did His enemies steal it to further desecrate it? **While they were wondering about this, suddenly two men in clothes that gleamed like lightning stood beside them** (24:4). The Gospel of John identifies the two men as angels, as does Matthew. Mark's gospel references the presence of "a young man dressed in a white robe" (Mark 16:5). Biblical accounts of angelic appearance sometimes identify them clearly as angels and other times as men. Isaiah saw angels as winged creatures in the heavenly realm, but it would seem that when they appeared as God's messengers on earth they usually had human forms. There was, however, a brilliance that surrounded them that caused the women to be afraid, and they **bowed down with their faces to the ground** (24:5).

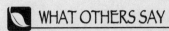

The angels asked them, **"Why do you look for the living among the dead?"** (24:5). The resurrection clearly separates Jesus from other religious leaders. Followers of other religions may make pilgrimages to the burial places of their leaders, but not Christians. Jesus is not a dead hero. He is not a great teacher and moral leader of the past. He is a living Lord whose presence can be experienced in the daily life of every believing follower. Christians do not gather each Easter to memorialize a fallen leader but to celebrate a risen Lord.

The appearance of the angels frightened the women, but the message they received turned fear into joy and tears into celebration: **"He is not here; he has risen!"** (24:6). Resurrection was not among the options they considered while they wondered what had happened to His body. The angels reminded them of what Jesus had told them back **in Galilee: "The Son of Man must be delivered into the hands of sinful men, be crucified and on the third day be raised again." Then they remembered his words** (24:6–8). Like the disciples who were secretly huddled in fear, there was no recollection of the words spoken by Jesus or connection between them and present events. There was no expectation of the resurrection. Before we are quick to point a finger at their dullness of understanding, how often have we failed to connect God's Word with our present situation?

On a couple of occasions, the disciples may have witnessed the resurrection of persons who had been declared dead, perhaps most remarkable was that of Lazarus. However, each person who was brought back to life would eventually die a natural death later. The issue of the resurrection of the dead was debated within the Jewish faith, with the Sadducees firmly denying any resurrection or life after death.

The resurrection is central to Christian faith. Paul said in 1 Corinthians 15:13–14, "If there is no resurrection of the dead, then not even Christ has been raised. And if Christ has not been raised, our preaching is useless and so is your faith." Romans 4:25 says that the resurrection completes our justification. In baptism we are buried with Christ and are united with Him in His resurrection, raised to a new life (Rom. 6:4–5). Romans 8:11 tells us that the power that raised Jesus from the dead is at work within us, giving power to our spiritual life to live above the downdraft of our sinful nature. The resurrection is our hope that death has been defeated and has no power over us. The death of Christ provided the means for our salvation, and His resurrection provided the powerful application of that salvation to our sin-affected lives. Without the resurrection, the Atonement would be incomplete.

The centrality of Jesus' resurrection to our faith is demonstrated in the day Christians have set apart for worship. Rather than observing the Sabbath on Saturday, as the Jewish community does, Christians set apart Sunday, "the first day of the week," as a day to celebrate life in Christ. It is a Sabbath day to rest from the normal labors of life as God commanded, but it is also a day to gather ourselves physically and spiritually for our mission in the world. On Sunday we focus on God and the fellowship of the saints as the beginning point for living effectively during the coming week. In Christ, we experience new beginnings, so we meet on the first day of the week to worship God, to celebrate our life in Christ, and to seek the Holy Spirit's empowerment for our work and witness.

2. TOO GOOD TO BE TRUE (24:9–12)

When the women **came back from the tomb, they told all these things to the Eleven and to all the others** (Luke 24:9). It is appropriate to acknowledge again the prominent role of women in Luke's writing. The divine announcement of the resurrection was given first to women, and they became the bearers of this good news to the others. There was no reason for them to hang around the tomb, since Jesus was not there and the reason for their being there now had no meaning. So they hurried back to the others. This kind of good news could not be kept quiet.

The disciples were dependent on each other like never before. They had each other, even if they did not have their Master. The Eleven were together. They used to be the Twelve, but Judas was now conspicuously absent. Matthew records that in remorse, Judas returned the thirty pieces of silver and went out and hanged himself (Matt. 27:5). In the book of Acts, Luke adds gruesome detail to the conclusion of Judas' life, with this footnote: "he was one of our number and shared in this ministry."

The number had dropped to eleven, but it could well have dropped to ten. Simon Peter did not betray his Lord by selling Him out to His enemies, but he had denied being one of His associates or even knowing Him. He experienced shame and remorse for his part in the dark night of the crucifixion, but the outcome for Peter was different than that of Judas. The bond between Peter and his Lord and his fellow disciples remained intact. There were eleven of them, and that included Peter.

The women of Luke 24:1 are identified in verse 10 as **Mary Magdalene, Joanna, Mary the mother of James, and the others with them**. Matthew identifies them as Mary Magdalene and the other Mary. Mark lists them as Mary Magdalene and Mary the mother of James, and Salome. John identifies Mary Magdalene without mentioning the others. Mary Magdalene is identified in all of the Gospels as one of the first to come to the tomb and the first to see the risen Lord. Throughout the Gospels she is always portrayed as a devoted follower of Christ because of what He had done for her, which, according to Mark, included casting seven demons out of her (Mark 15:9). Luke previously identified Joanna as "the wife of Cuza, the manager of Herod's household" (Luke 8:3). She was one of the women, along with Mary Magdalene, who accompanied Jesus during much of His ministry and who supported that ministry with their resources.

The message that was too good to keep was a message too good to be true. The disciples **did not believe the women, because their words seemed to them like nonsense** (Luke 24:11). Even if they believed the message, they would not have known what to do next. They were not inclined to act upon the word of silly women carrying news too good to be true.

APPEARANCES OF JESUS AFTER HIS RESURRECTION

Mary Magdalene outside the garden tomb	Mark 16:9–11
Women at the tomb	Matthew 28:8–10
Peter in Jerusalem	Luke 24:34
Two travelers on the road to Emmaus	Luke 24:13–35
Disciples behind closed doors	Luke 24:36–43
Disciples with Thomas included	John 20:26–31
Disciples after fishing	John 21:1–14
Disciples on the mountain	Matthew 28:16–20
Crowd of five hundred	1 Corinthians 15:6
James, brother of Jesus	1 Corinthians 15:7
Those who witnessed the ascension	Luke 24:44–49

Simon **Peter** was not known to be a person slow to act. If there was any possibility of truth in the claims of the women, he needed to know, so he **got up and ran to the tomb** (24:12). Our strengths often become our weaknesses, and this was the case with Peter. He was bold and action oriented, which got him into trouble at times, but you could count on him to do something when something needed to be done. Others might not grab hold of possibilities, but if there was a chance the message was true, Peter wanted to find out for sure. He ran all the way to the tomb.

Perhaps Peter was motivated to see Jesus before anyone else so he could confess his sin of denial and get things cleared up with his Lord. He could not forget the look of pain in Jesus' eyes that he had caused. As disappointed as he must have been in himself, and as guilty as he must have felt about his denial of the Lord, he is still numbered among the disciples. Peter was willing to face up to his failure. He did not run from the prospect of meeting the Lord, but he ran to find if such an unbelievable thing could be a possibility.

When Peter arrived at the tomb and looked inside, **he saw the strips of linen lying by themselves, and he went away, wondering to himself what had happened** (24:12). It is suggested by some writers that the condition of the burial clothes is one of the proofs that the body of Jesus was not stolen, as some critics have declared. Body snatchers would not have taken the time necessary to unwrap the body, but would have taken the body still wrapped in grave clothes. Seeing no evidence of what had happened, other than the abandoned grave clothes, Peter walked away, still wondering if what the women said was true.

3. A COMPANION ON THE ROAD (24:13–27)

The appearance of Jesus to the **two** travelers who **were going to a village called Emmaus, about seven miles from Jerusalem** (24:13) is recorded in detail only by Luke. It is noted in Mark's gospel only as "Jesus appeared in a different form to two of them while they were walking in the country" (Mark 16:12). Emmaus was a small town west of Jerusalem. Who were the two? Why were they headed toward Emmaus, away from the other disciples? One of the two is identified in Luke 24:18 as **Cleopas.** If "the Eleven" referred exclusively to the apostles, neither of the two could have been an apostle, since when Cleopas and his friend returned to Jerusalem, they found the Eleven gathered together (24:33). While the two walked and **discussed** the recent events, **Jesus himself came up and walked along with them** (24:15). When sincere seekers talk together about Jesus, He is sure to make His presence felt among them.

The three walked and talked, but the two **were kept from recognizing** (24:16) Jesus. Perhaps with tongue in cheek, William Barclay suggests that the setting sun was in their eyes and "so dazzled them that they did not know their Lord."[1] Most likely, it was not the light of the sun in their eyes but the darkness of their souls that kept them from recognizing Jesus. They simply presumed He was a fellow traveler headed toward Emmaus.

When asked what they were talking about before He joined them, with **faces downcast** they said, **"Are you only a visitor to Jerusalem and do not know the things that have happened there in these days?"** (24:17–18). The crucifixion occurred during Passover when Jerusalem was packed with visitors. The trek through the streets with the shouting mob would have gotten the attention of most people. The crosses were the public spectacle of the day. It was assumed that by now everyone would have known what had happened in Jerusalem.

Jesus asked for more information **about the Jesus of Nazareth** of whom they spoke, and they said **he was a prophet, powerful in word and deed before God and all the people** (24:19). They were willing to say Jesus was a prophet, but the other claims He had made for himself that they had at one time believed were now in question. They **had hoped that he was the one who was going to redeem Israel** (24:21). The death of Jesus changed everything. The hopes they had for themselves and for Israel were unrealized. The dreams they had for a messiah who would bring a new political and social order were misplaced. When you discover your hope has been misplaced, it turns lost hope into despair.

The two told their traveling companion about the women's word that Jesus was alive and that some of their companions had visited the tomb, **but him they did not see** (24:24). Empty tombs do not prove resurrections. Seeing persons alive who were once indisputably dead proves resurrections. Jesus had predicted His resurrection, and there were eyewitnesses that testified to it, but since they had not seen Jesus themselves, they chose not to believe He was alive.

Jesus said they were **foolish** and **slow of heart to believe all that the prophets** had **spoken** (24:25). To be foolish meant "wanting in thought, understanding, and consideration."[2] Being slow of heart to believe was perhaps a more serious charge. We could assume they believed some of what the prophets had spoken but not *all*. They practiced selective belief.

How often have we listened to the Word of God without understanding or believing it? How often have we been in the presence of Christ and never recognized Him? Spiritual blindness is not limited to two grieving disciples on a lonely road.

Those who waited for the Messiah to deliver them from their oppression had difficulty accepting the fact that the Messiah would come in anything other than glory and power. So Jesus had to explain to them why **the Christ** had **to suffer these things and then enter his glory** (24:26). He took them back to the Scriptures they had grown up listening to.

The Old Testament often speaks of the person and ministry of Christ. **Beginning with Moses and all the Prophets, he explained to them what was said in all the Scriptures concerning himself** (24:27). Beyond the particular Scriptures Jesus unpacked for them lies the principle that spiritual questions and life issues are answered through the Word of God and the personal presence of Jesus. The practice of Jesus was to handle temptation (4:3–12), respond to His critics (6:3–4), provide counsel (10:26–27), and set the agenda of His life (22:37) by going to the Scripture. We would do well to learn from His model.

4. THE PROOF IS IN THE TOUCHING (24:28–49)

RECOGNITION DAWNS

The three travelers **approached** Emmaus, and **Jesus acted as if he were going farther** (24:28). Even after opening the Scriptures to them, they did not recognize Him. He did not force the conversation, nor did He force himself on them. He waited to be invited. When they reached their intended destination, Jesus would have gone on had they not **urged him strongly** to **stay** (24:29) with them. God seeks all to come to salvation, but He does not force himself on anyone. He created us with the blessing and the responsibility of free will. Jesus knocks at the door of our lives and waits outside to be invited in (Rev. 3:20).

He had invited others to follow Him even though He said, "The Son of Man has no place to lay his head" (Luke 9:58). He still had no place to lay His head, but He would wait to be invited in. It was **nearly evening**, so they urged Him to stay with them as their overnight guest, which was a cultural expectation extended to traveling strangers. Their invitation is an apt description of the perspective on life when Jesus is not present: **"it is nearly evening and the day is almost over"** (24:29). They were headed west as they walked from Jerusalem to Emmaus—headed into the sunset. It suggests a picture of hopelessness. Darkness settles in upon those who do not know Jesus. **He went in to stay with them** (24:29). Jesus always responds to the invitation to spend time with us. Our agendas get full, and we may not think we have time for Him, but He always has time for us.

As they settled in for the evening, they gathered around a table, and Jesus **took bread, gave thanks, broke it and began to give it to them** (24:30). This has the sound of the sacrament of the Lord's Supper, but it was not, since Jesus said the next time He would have such a meal with them would be in His kingdom (Luke 22:15–18). Breaking bread together, such as in Acts 2:42, referred to sitting down to share a common meal. However, there must have been something about the way He took bread, gave thanks, broke it, and began to give it to them that sparked recognition. Did they notice His hands were pierced? Was there a recognizable mannerism in the way He broke the bread? Was it what He said when He gave thanks? Something in that moment revealed who this stranger was, **their eyes were opened and they recognized him, and he disappeared from their sight** (Luke 24:31).

His disappearance was as abrupt as His appearance. He had stepped into the middle of their conversation about Him and, now with renewed excitement and revelation, they returned to the discussion of their encounter with Him. In reflection, the two travelers said, **"Were not our hearts burning within us while he talked with us on the road and opened the Scriptures to us?"** (24:32). They had become people of opened eyes and burning hearts. Not a bad description of those of any generation who have encountered Jesus.

Energized by what they had experienced, the need for sleep was forgotten as **they got up and returned at once to Jerusalem** (24:33) to share their newfound joy. After we have an encounter with Christ, the direction of our lives changes, and so does our pace. How fast can you cover seven miles? Fatigue is not a factor when you are the carrier of great news. Some things are too big to be kept to ourselves but must be shared. William Barclay said, "The Christian message is never fully ours until we have shared it with someone else."[3]

When they arrived back in Jerusalem, **they found the Eleven and those with them, assembled together** (24:33). The fellowship of believers was already forming that would become the assembling together that should not be forsaken (Heb. 10:25). If you miss the meeting, you may miss out on the testimony of others and the appearance of the Lord. We know that Thomas was not present (John 20:25), therefore "the Eleven" must have become the common means of referring to the disciples, regardless of the actual number present.

The testimony of the group was one of growing certainty. **"It is true! The Lord has risen"** (Luke 24:34). The impossible had happened, and the resurrection was becoming a certified reality. Hopes destroyed were replaced with truth verified. The word of the women was authenticated by Simon Peter. The word was that the Lord had **appeared to Simon** (24:34). The Scriptures do not give the details of when or how, but somewhere there was a special private meeting between Jesus and Peter. Paul wrote that Jesus "appeared to Peter, and then to the Twelve" (1 Cor. 15:5), suggesting that Jesus knew how important it was to get to Peter as soon as possible, even before revealing himself to the whole group. There were things that needed to be cared for between the two. Peter had declared his love, his commitment to leave all to follow, and his willingness to lay down his life for Christ (John 13:37). But in the heat of the moment, he denied the Lord. Somewhere they met, and we can only imagine the content of the conversation. We can be assured that the shame and remorse Peter felt melted away in the presence of the One who is full of grace, truth, and mercy. It is

WHAT OTHERS SAY

REPENTANCE

"There are two kinds of repentance: one is that of Judas, the other that of Peter; the one is ice broken, the other ice melted."

—William Nevins

just as well that we are not given the details so we can fill them in from our own stories of failure, disappointment, and denial, only to have Jesus come to us, as unworthy as we may be. Not all confessions need to be publicized. Life transformation becomes its own evidence of forgiveness and restoration, and there is no doubt of the change that occurred in Peter. His story informs us that spiritual restoration can be a reality and that God specializes in putting broken lives back together again. Peter and Judas took different roads after their failures.

While they were still talking about this, Jesus himself stood among them (Luke 24:36). He had previously told them, "Where two or three come together in my name, there am I with them" (Matt. 18:20), and He demonstrated the reality of that promise. We should expect the presence of Christ when we are engaged in devoted conversation about Him.

The first word of Jesus to them was **"Peace be with you"** (Luke 24:36). These were appropriate words, since **they were startled and frightened, thinking they saw a ghost** (24:37). Peace on earth was the message from the angels to the shepherds. Peace was the word spoken by the angel when meeting with Elizabeth and Mary. When Jesus prepared these same disciples for His departure, He said, "Peace I leave with you; my peace I give you. I do not give to you as the world gives. Do not let your hearts be troubled and do not be afraid" (John 14:27). Peace is a precious word when spoken into the spirit of God's children when their lives are troubled.

Even though they had proclaimed the reality of the resurrection, Jesus knew their hearts and said, **"Why are you troubled, and why do doubts rise in your minds?"** (Luke 24:38). Is there room for doubt in our proclamation of faith? There certainly may be questions for which we strain for answers, but do not yet have them. Verse 41 says that even after being provided with proof, **they still did not believe it because of joy and amazement**. There is a mystery that accompanies things too good to be true. Perhaps the joy and amazement of our salvation should overwhelm us as something we accept by faith but wonder how it can be so. There is a doubt born out of skepticism, but there also is a doubt born out of wonder and amazement.

Jesus chided them for their doubts but immediately moved to eliminate them. He said to them, **"Look at my hands and my feet. It is I myself! Touch me and see"** (24:39). What does it take to prove something? Some say that seeing is believing, but proof is not always found in the seeing. Sometimes it is in the touching, so Jesus offered His physical body as evidence of His physical resurrection. "Look at my hands and feet," He said. Perhaps the invitation for them to prove He was not a ghost by touching Him also included the invitation to see the wounds on His hands and feet that would further identify Him. Christ engaged their senses to help them verify

 GREAT THEMES

AUTHORITY AND POWER OF SCRIPTURE

We believe the Scriptures to be truth. The Word of God is the source of our understanding of truth and the authority against which we test our discoveries in life. John Wesley described himself as a man of one Book—the Holy Scriptures. Wesley integrated Scripture, tradition, reason, and experience in developing his theology. This has come to be called the "Wesleyan Quadrilateral." Truth is found by engaging each of the four sources, with Scripture always providing the start and finish of the search.

truth, which encourages us that God allows our senses, our reason, and our experience to be involved in the determining of truth.

What was the resurrected body of Jesus like? He was there trying to convince His disciples that He was **flesh and bones** (24:39), while at the same time He was able to appear and disappear at will and to pass through walls (John 20:19, 26). He seems to have had a physical body capable of eating, of being recognized, and of being touched, yet there was an added spiritual dimension to His body that made Him different from what He had been. Paul, in writing about the resurrection, indicated that at our resurrection we shall be given a body like that of Jesus' resurrected body (1 Cor. 15:42–50). Further demonstrating that He was alive and "human," he accepted from them **a piece of broiled fish . . . and ate it in their presence** (Luke 24:42–43).

UNDERSTANDING, ASSURANCE, AND A PROMISE

There would seem to be a break in time between verse 43 and verse 44. We know that Jesus spent forty days with His disciples between the time of His resurrection and His ascension, meeting with them on several occasions. There must have been a sense of anticipation and expectancy that possessed them each time they assembled. Would this be another time of divine visitation? It is the kind of anticipation and expectation that should characterize all gatherings of the followers of Christ.

During one of these times, Jesus came to them and said, **"Everything must be fulfilled that is written about me in the Law of Moses, the Prophets and the Psalms"** (24:44). The printed Scripture possessed by the Jews was comprised of three parts: the Law of Moses, the Prophets and the Psalms. The *Law* consisted of the first five books of the Old Testament (Genesis, Exodus, Leviticus, Numbers, Deuteronomy), along with the major and minor prophets, the *Prophets* included Joshua, Judges, Samuel, and Kings; and the *Psalms*, or Writings, included the remainder of the Old Testament books.[4] All of the Old Testament spoke of the person and ministry of God's Anointed One, and each thing written about Jesus *must* be fulfilled. The authenticity of a prophet lay in the accuracy of his prophecy. It was essential that Jesus fully and accurately fulfill the prophetic word of the Old Testament—all of it.

Not only did Jesus explain Scripture to them, **he opened their minds so they could understand the Scriptures** (24:45). He gave them the gift of discerning minds so they could more readily understand the meaning of Scripture when they read it. It is a wonderful gift when God quickens the mind and enlightens the intellect so that understanding and application accompany the reading of His Word.

A ministry of the Holy Spirit is that of opening our minds and helping us to understand the Scriptures. As mentioned earlier, John Wesley said, "Scripture can only be understood through the same Spirit whereby it was given." The Spirit who inspired Scripture interprets it to the seeking mind. Our reading of God's Word should be preceded by asking God to help us to understand it and to discern its appropriate application to our lives.

Jesus **told them, "This is what is written: The Christ will suffer and rise from the dead on the third day, and repentance and forgiveness of sins will be preached in his name to all nations, beginning at Jerusalem** (24:46–47). The Atonement was necessary for God to forgive and justify sinful humanity. Now that the sacrifice had been paid, the way to justification was to be preached. The essentials of the gospel message are repentance and forgiveness of sins. Peter demonstrated in Acts 5:31 that repentance and the forgiveness of sins was the message of the early church. Salvation is found as a person responds to the gift of grace from God. Salvation involves repentance on the part of the persons who are seeking it, the forgiveness of sins on the part of God who is offering it. It is called synergism—God and humankind responding together to make salvation a reality. Gospel preaching is the offer of forgiveness of sins and a call to repentance.

The preaching of the gospel was to begin in Jerusalem, the center of rebellion against Jesus and the place of His crucifixion. From there it was to reach out to all nations. Salvation is offered to all people, regardless of status, nationality, or depth of their sinfulness. Luke wrote to a Greek audience, so he made the point that salvation is inclusive—offered to Gentiles as well as to Jews. Throughout his gospel, Luke emphasized the universal appeal and availability of the good news, beginning with the angel's pronouncement that it was for all people (2:10) and concluding with the preaching assignment to the disciples. The good news is open to the whole world and is for all people in every age.

The emerging church would center in Jerusalem with Peter as its recognized leader. Later, Antioch became the center of ministry to Gentiles, due largely to the missionary work of Paul, Silas, Barnabas, Mark, and Luke. Luke recorded the commission of Jesus to His disciples in greater detail in Acts: "You will be my witnesses in Jerusalem, and in all Judea and Samaria, and to the ends of the earth" (Acts 1:8). Unfortunately, some people never carry their witness beyond the comfort of their Jerusalem. And some people's witness in their Jerusalem is not accompanied by the evidence of transformed lives; therefore it is ineffective.

There may be several expectations that God has for His church, including being a place of worship, nurture, fellowship, evangelism, and service. To His disciples, Jesus said, **"You are witnesses of these things"** (Luke 24:48). We are not the Church if we are not His witnesses. He commissions us to simply tell the story of who He is and what He has accomplished in our lives.

Surely, since Jesus had opened their eyes and understanding, they could now comprehend what He had told them during His last days before His crucifixion. He had told them that it was essential that He go away, but that He would send the Holy Spirit to be with them in His absence. So they must have expected His departure was soon going to be permanent. And then it happened. Jesus told them: **"I am going to send you what my Father has promised"** (24:49). They knew that what the Father had promised could not happen without Jesus leaving them. He then instructed them, **"Stay in the city until you have been clothed with power from on high"** (24:49). It would have been understandable if in their exuberance to be witnesses to what they had experienced, they had burst out of their room and out of Jerusalem, to

LIFE CHANGE

GOING AND STAYING

Too often we want to stay when we should be going. It is equally bad for us to insist on going when we should be staying—waiting for God's timing, direction, and empowerment. Spiritual maturity is demonstrated in our ability to discern when to go and when to stay. Only as we are willing to do either can God effectively equip and use us.

act on the commission Jesus had given them. But they still lacked what only the Holy Spirit could provide them. Their superhuman task could not be accomplished with human effort alone.

GREAT THEMES
THE MISSION OF THE CHURCH

According to a legend, when Jesus returned to heaven following His death on the cross and resurrection from the tomb, the angels gathered in amazement. They gazed at the wounds in His hands and feet, and shuddered to recall His suffering. Finally Gabriel spoke. "Master, You suffered terribly down there. Do they know and appreciate the extent of Your sacrifice?"

"No," said Jesus. "Not yet. Right now only a handful of people in Palestine know."

"Then what have You done to let everyone else know?" asked Gabriel.

"I've asked Peter, James, and John, and a few others to spread the news. They will tell others who will tell others until the message spreads to the ends of the earth."

But Gabriel, knowing the nature of human beings, asked, "What is Plan B?"

"I have no Plan B," replied Christ. "There is no alternative strategy. I'm counting on them."

Twenty centuries later, He still has no other plan. He's counting on you and me.

If God wants you to wait, the time spent waiting is not wasted time. Enthusiasm, motivation, and ambition are wonderful things, but not when they create shortcuts around spiritual preparation and endowment with the Spirit's power. Power from on high is greater power than the power of personality, position, or persuasion.

5. THE ASCENSION (24:50–53)

A FINAL BLESSING

The time for His departure was at hand, and Jesus **led them out to the vicinity of Bethany** (24:50), most likely as tradition has it, to the Mount of Olives between Jerusalem and Bethany. There, **he lifted up his hands and blessed them** (24:50). If this was the traditional Jewish blessing, it involved placing His hands on their heads as well as speaking words of promise and blessing. **While he was blessing them, he left them and was taken up into heaven** (24:51). His physical presence permanently left them, and they were now without Him, yet they were not alone. They had each other, but more important, they would have the Holy Spirit that Jesus had promised them. Luke is the only Gospel writer who recorded the ascension—here and in Acts 1.

The disciples **worshiped him and returned to Jerusalem with great joy** (24:52). True worship grows out of discovering the reality of Jesus and experiencing His blessing. In Jerusalem they went to **the temple** where **they stayed continually . . . , praising God** (24:53). It is fitting that the last picture we have of the disciples is in the house of God, continuing their daily prayers and praising God in the Temple courtyard. They were in the Temple doing the work of their Father, just as Jesus had when He made His first trip to the Temple in Jerusalem.

TO BE CONTINUED . . .

Luke's gospel ends rather abruptly, perhaps indicating there was more to come. This was the end of the record of the life and ministry of Jesus on earth. Another book would be written to tell the story of the Spirit of Christ working through the life of His Church. Luke would only temporarily lay aside his pen, soon to pick it up again to continue the story in the book of Acts.

The work of Christ continues in the lives of those who believe in Him and experience the transformation that accompanies His salvation. Your story of redemption can be added to the record of countless others who have come to Jesus and then gone into their world as agents of transformation.

ENDNOTES

1. William Barclay, *The Gospel of Luke* (Philadelphia: Westminster, 1956), p. 308.

2. J. C. Ryle, *Ryle's Expository Thoughts on the Gospels*, vol. 2 (Grand Rapids, Mich.: Baker, 1977), p. 504.

3. Barclay, p. 310.

4. Ralph Earle, *The Wesleyan Bible Commentary: The Gospel of Luke* (Grand Rapids, Mich.: Eerdmans, 1964), p. 348.

SELECT BIBLIOGRAPHY

Barclay, William. *And He Had Compassion*. Valley Forge: Judson Press, 1975.

———. *The Gospel of Luke*. Philadelphia: Westminster, 1956.

Clarke, Adam. *Clarke's Commentary*. New York: Abingdon, 1977.

Earle, Ralph. *The Wesleyan Bible Commentary: The Gospel of Luke*. Eerdmans, 1964.

———. "Revelation and Inspiration," *A Contemporary Wesleyan Theology*, Grand Rapids: Zondervan, 1983.

Krabill, Donald. *Upside Down Kingdom*. Scottdale, Penn.: Herald Press, 2003.

Larson, Gary N. *The New Unger's Bible Handbook*. Chicago: Moody Press, 1966.

Life Application Bible. Wheaton: Tyndale House, 1989.

Lockyer, Herbert. *All the Books and Chapters of the Bible*. Grand Rapids, Mich.: Zondervan, 1966.

———. *All the Parables of the Bible*. Grand Rapids, Mich.: Zondervan, 1977.

Ryle, J. C. *Ryle's Expository Thoughts on the Gospels*, vol. 2. Grand Rapids, Mich.: Baker, 1977.

Ryrie, Charles. *Ryrie Study Bible*. Chicago: Moody Press, 1978.

Shoemaker, Melvin. "Good News to the Poor in Luke's Gospel." *Wesleyan Theological Journal*, no. 27 (1992).

Smith, William. *Smith's Bible Dictionary*. Peabody, Mass.: Hendrickson, reprinted 2003.

Stafford, Gilbert W. *Theology for Disciples*. Anderson: Warner Press, 1996.

Staples, Rob L. *Outward Sign and Inward Grace*. Kansas City: Beacon Hill Press, 1991.

Stowell, Joseph. *Following Christ*. Grand Rapids, Mich.: Zondervan, 1996.

Thayer, J. H. *A Greek-English Lexicon of the New Testament*. Grand Rapids, Mich.: Associated Publishers and Authors, Inc., 1981.

Unger, Merrill. *Unger's Bible Dictionary*. Chicago: Moody Press, 1986.

———. *The New Unger's Bible Handbook*. Chicago: Moody Press, 1984.

Vincent, Marvin R. *Word Studies in the New Testament*. Grand Rapids, Mich.: Eerdmans, 1973.

Young, Robert. *Young's Analytical Concordance to the Bible*. Grand Rapids, Mich.: Eerdman's, 1970.